David Michie was born in Zimbabwe and began his career in public relations in Johannesburg, South Africa. Moving to Britain in 1988, he worked at senior consultant level with major public relations agencies before becoming an independent consultant in 1996, specializing in high-level communications planning. He now advises blue-chip British and multi-national companies on corporate communications, and writes for industry and national publications. He lives and works in London.

invisible persuaders david michie

BANTAM PRESS

LONDON · NEW YORK · TORONTO · SYDNEY · AUCKLAND

**To my parents, Bill and Mona,
and to Koala, with love**

TRANSWORLD PUBLISHERS LTD
61–63 Uxbridge Road, London W5 5SA

TRANSWORLD PUBLISHERS (AUSTRALIA) PTY LTD
15–25 Helles Avenue, Moorebank, NSW 2170

TRANSWORLD PUBLISHERS (NZ) LTD
3 William Pickering Drive, Albany, Auckland

Published 1998 by Bantam Press
a division of Transworld Publishers Ltd

A catalogue record for this book is available
from the British Library
ISBN 0593 042387

Typeset in 11/14 Sabon by Falcon Oast Graphic Art, East Sussex.
Printed in Great Britain by
Mackays of Chatham Plc, Chatham, Kent.

CONTENTS

ACKNOWLEDGEMENTS

There is a very obvious difficulty in writing a book about spin doctors: you are dealing with people who are trained professionals when it comes to looking an interviewer straight in the eye and delivering a version of events which may, or may not, accord with reality. This is not to say that all spin doctors are professional liars; only that in negotiating one's way through the marshlands of media relations, great care must be exercised to stay on factual terra firma and avoid the siren calls of the swamps.

In order to do this, a writer needs his guides, and I am fortunate to have been assisted by some of the best in the business, in particular those from whom I originally learned the art of media relations of the more principled variety, my friends and former colleagues at Fishburn Hedges. Especial thanks, then, to the Fishburn Hedges team who have been so encouraging and supportive over the last few years: Dale Fishburn, Neil Hedges, Andrew Boys, John Williams, Charles Downing, Marc Moninski, Martin Winn, Philippa Dale-Thomas, Michael Slater, Simon Matthews and Rhiannedd Jones. During the process of writing this book I was helped by Ron Finlay, who cast his particularly acute eye over portions of the manuscript; by Graham McMillan, who put his phenomenal network of parliamentary contacts at my disposal; by Julia Alexander, whose analyses of goings-on in the City were highly instructive; and by Ann Rossiter, whose insight into the 1997 elections was indeed compelling. I am most grateful for their kind help, especially in light of their overcrowded diaries.

While much of the material for this book was derived from off-the-record briefings by some of the biggest players in public relations whose names, alas, must remain a closely guarded secret, I am especially grateful to those high-profile practitioners who agreed to on-the-record interviews, including Brian Basham, Quentin Bell, Roddy Dewe, Michael Regester, Max Clifford, Mark Borkowski, Charles Lewington, Paul Kafka and Jackie Elliott. Turning to the lobbying industry in particular, special thanks to Michael Burrell of Westminster Strategy, Charles Miller of Public Policy Unit, Nick DeLuca of APCO, Roger Liddle of PRIMA and former MP Dudley Fishburn, all of whom endured my lines of questioning with great forbearance. Special thanks, too, to Gordon Heald of ORB, pollster to popes, princes and politicians.

I am truly appreciative of the responsiveness with which my requests for interviews and soundbites were received, sometimes at short notice, by so many in the industry. My thanks for their suggestions and support to Andy Laurence, Ciaran Baker, Iolanda Minasi and Elizabeth Ballard at Hill & Knowlton; Adrian Wheeler, Sue Ryan and Vicky Bolger at GCI; Emma Brasier and Mary Sweeting at Countrywide Porter Novelli; Aurelia Cecil of Aurelia PR; Nigel Chism and Dick Millard at College Hill; Neil Mainland of Neil Mainland PR; and Sandra MacLeod of CARMA. For his insight into investor relations activities, my thanks to David Forster of Salomon Brothers. The experiences of Margaret Lochrie and Rachel Thomson at the Pre-School Learning Alliance were especially well articulated, and Toby MacManus of Bournemouth University was an invaluable source of information on media studies programmes in the UK. For their thoughts, support and suggestions, thanks also to those veteran head-hunters of the industry, Airdre Taylor, Ros Kindersley, Peter Childs and Lynn Beaumont. Authors John Stauber, in America, and Andy Rowell, in the UK, offered extremely helpful pointers, as did Dan Mills at the McLibel Support Campaign. Especial thanks to Tom Curtin for his constant flow of stimulating ideas and warm encouragement delivered, in that finest, time-honoured PR tradition, over many a gin and tonic.

I owe thanks also to many on the other side of the media relations divide, among those on the receiving end of the spin doctors' activities. Once again, several high-profile journalists did not wish to reveal themselves in these pages, but I am particularly grateful to those who were happy to speak openly. Thank you to Anthony Hilton, the *Evening Standard*'s City editor, one of that rare breed of journalist capable of both educating and entertaining simultaneously. Thanks also to Damien McCrystal, formerly of the *Daily Telegraph*, for his colourful insights into City diary writing; to the *Independent*'s Chris Blackhurst; to Mark Palmer and John McEntee at Express Newspapers; to Philip Hall, editor of the *News of the World*, Jane Procter, editor of *Tatler*, and Joanne Walker of *Marketing Week*. I was saved many hours of research thanks to the kind offices of Stephen Farish, group editor of *PR Week*, who gave me the benefit of his views formed from a unique industry vantage point, as well as access to his archive library; thanks also Steve Bevan, formerly of *PR Week*, and Barrie Cree at Mediacom. Chris McDowall of the PRCA made available reference material and industry data which also proved most helpful.

An author's debt of gratitude is probably greatest to those who are close to him. In my own case I have always felt exceptionally lucky to have such a wonderful circle of friends, whose support in my writing endeavours has been unswerving. To my parents, who encouraged my writing aspirations from an early age, my heartfelt thanks. To friends and family, in Britain, southern Africa and Australia, I'm delighted to reward your confidence in my abilities with a book on the shelves at last! Bearing the brunt of rejected interview requests – of which there were dozens – hard disk crashes and other operational setbacks was my wife, who successfully affected an interest in my monomaniacal rantings on the subject of spin doctors for the better part of two years; Koala, I'll be forever grateful.

D. M.
January 1998

INTRODUCTION
who makes the news?

This book is a wake-up call to media consumers everywhere. Before you read your next newspaper, watch your next news broadcast or leaf through your next magazine, ask yourself this: do you *really* know where the information you are digesting came from? Who wants you to consume it? And why?

It is one of the great ironies of our consumerist times that while we have become acutely aware of the pesticides, growth hormones and artificial additives contained in much of the food we eat, we are largely oblivious to the fact that the media output we consume has undergone similar treatment. While we understand that tinkering with the food chain has profound consequences for our physical well-being, we aren't even conscious that the information we absorb has very often been subjected to unseen manipulation. And unlike the food on offer at our local supermarket, when it comes to the mass media there is no organic alternative.

Every working day in Britain, people read an average of 28 million newspapers. Such is our appetite for the printed word that if the pages of every newspaper sold in any one week were placed end to end, the result would be a paper trail taking us to the moon and back – four times. We devour the electronic media output with even greater voracity, spending an average of three and a half hours in front of the box every night; and four out of five of us

1

have the radio turned on for almost twenty-four hours each week. In addition, many homes are now equipped with videos, cable or satellite television, fax machines and home computers wired up to the Internet – more media-gathering technology, in fact, than state-of-the-art newsrooms had at their disposal twenty years ago.

Few would dispute that we now live in the information age. As media theorist Douglas Rushkoff observes: 'Power today has little to do with how much property a person owns or commands; it is instead determined by how many minutes of prime-time television or pages of news-media attention she can access or occupy.' While the all-pervasiveness of the media continues to expand, the power of the media has long been recognized. In fact Napoleon Bonaparte is attributed with the line 'Four hostile newspapers are more feared than a thousand bayonets.' Despite the huge presence and power of the media in our lives, however, most people have only the haziest picture of how the news media actually work. Even though the British are probably the most cynical and sophisticated connoisseurs of advertising in the world, the majority are seriously deluded about the process by which news items reach their eyes and ears.

Why are they deluded? Because they entertain the giddy notion that the news they consume is generated entirely by journalists. Their visions of noisy newsrooms of reporters, jabbering down telephones and beavering away on stories, may not be far removed from reality; but quite how those journalists get hold of their stories to begin with is not a question often asked. In fact, as PR luminary Quentin Bell would tell you, 80 per cent of what appears in the business pages, and 40–50 per cent of general news, has been produced or directly influenced by PR practitioners. 'The interesting part', according to Bell, 'is that the media have double standards. They are highly dependent on us, but they won't admit to the influence of PR.'

The fact is that few people outside the PR industry know how effectively it works, and even fewer realize how much we're all influenced by it. Very little is known about how much of what we accept as news, interviews, or feature articles actually originates from the desks of PR consultants. To quote an industry maxim, 'The best PR is never noticed.' But PR cognoscenti are certainly able to pick up any of our national newspapers and quickly identify which of their colleagues placed or massaged a particular story. They know who wrote the quotes attributed to some captain of industry and can sometimes even tell which of their fellow spin doctors' pet theories are being conveyed in what is supposedly the editor's column. In business, sport or politics, on celebrities, consumer goods or any other subject you care to mention, the influence of PR is as ubiquitous as it is powerful.

Writing about PR in America, authors Jeff and Marie Blyskal say: 'The press has grown frighteningly dependent on public relations people. Outsiders – the reading and viewing public – would have a hard time discovering this on their own because the dependence on PR is part of behind-the-scenes press functioning . . . Meanwhile, like an alcoholic who can't believe he has a drinking problem, members of the press are too close to their own addiction to PR to realize there is anything wrong. In fact, the press, which has a seemingly inborn cynical, arrogant, down-the-nose view of public relations, seems sadly self-deceptive about the true press/PR relationship.'

The same dynamics are clearly recognizable on this side of the Atlantic. As one of Britain's most influential spin doctors told me candidly: 'People would be horrified by the degree to which journalists prostitute themselves. In a recent case I had final clearance of the picture, the headline and all the copy of a supposedly "un-PR-able" newspaper.' As telling as the revelation itself is the fact that the PR guru concerned agreed to meet me only on the strict understanding that he wouldn't be identified or quoted in anything I wrote. Invisibility is a prerequisite of the dark art of spin doctoring. It is a delicious irony that the true masters of media manipulation, those who are most adept at conjuring up front-page headlines out of the ether or killing off negative tales at birth, have for the most part a visceral aversion to any form of personal publicity. The prospect of having their activities exposed to the cold, clear light of day is enough to send them, like vampires of the media world, flitting for the hallowed safety of their offices in the City or West End. Why? Because, as the spin doctor I have just quoted told me: 'PR is very much an invisible art and it doesn't serve our purpose to reveal how much we manipulate journalists and the public.'

Others in the industry will put a more publicly acceptable spin on their reasons for remaining invisible. 'We don't like to get between our clients and the footlights' is the well-worn explanation provided by another leading practitioner demanding anonymity. It's undoubtedly true that no client wants to see what they regard as their share of the media glory going to a retained consultant. It was, after all, for precisely this reason that Diana, Princess of Wales, was reported to be fed up with the growing visibility of her then PR adviser Jane Atkinson – not, it should be said, that Atkinson had much option, given her relative accessibility compared to her royal client. But the 'clients and footlights' explanation really is a classic case of spin, using as it does a perfectly valid and even rather high-sounding argument by way of a full explanation rather than as only part of it.

The *real* reason why spin doctors remain invisible is the existence of a tightly knit set of interdependent vested interests. It doesn't benefit spin doctors' relationships with journalists to have the extent to which they lead the media by the nose revealed. Nor is it in any client's interests for the whole world to know that that glowing write-up in *The Times* was the work of an intensive PR exercise, rather than the free expression of a challenging and articulate reporter. And the presence of spin doctors is certainly not going to be signalled by journalists, who would then appear not as resourceful investigators but as – very frequently – the simple conduits for PR feed.

A fascinating picture would emerge if newspapers were required to print the names of the PR consultants providing them with material in each issue, in the same way that foodstuffs manufacturers have to give details of their products' contents on the packaging. Even without such a guide, the unannounced presence of public relations can be detected by scanning the various national newspapers in any one week and marvelling at the coincidence that they not only carry so many of the same stories but frequently use the same phrases when reporting those stories. The names of the true authors of the reports never, of course, appear in any by-lines.

Some journalists are quite prepared to talk about the influence of public relations on the media. While researching this book I interviewed senior writers, and in some cases editors, from as diverse a range of newspapers as *The Times*, the *Daily Telegraph*, the *Independent*, the *Daily Express*, the *News of the World* and the *Evening Standard*, all of whom testified to the growing influence of PR. There is not, then, any great conspiracy of silence about what spin doctors do. The more prosaic truth is that they are an accepted and intrinsic part of the media machinery – and that there is no incentive whatsoever to publicize their activities. So those outside the media have no idea how much they are influenced by spin doctors.

Most people, indeed, have no very clear idea what public relations is in the first place. This is hardly surprising, since even within the industry the term 'public relations' means different things to different people. Ask ten different PR practitioners to define their trade and you will get ten different answers. The industry encompasses a huge range of activities – from market research and planning to media relations, sponsorship and corporate hospitality – and operates in sectors so diverse they bear scarcely any resemblance to one another.

There are some in the PR business who consider it a supreme paradox that the industry of image management seems unable to manage its own image. There are many who would like PR to be taken more seriously as a profession. But PR is not a profession. You don't need a degree to get into public relations – you don't even need any GCSEs – although the quality of graduate recruits to the industry has risen significantly in recent years. You do not have to register with any trade organization to practise, nor are you answerable to any regulatory body – there isn't one. This last issue takes on a particularly dark significance during corporate takeover battles, when merchant bankers and stockbrokers are free to use PR people to do the dirty work they are prevented from doing themselves because of the regulatory constraints of their own professions. PR consultants being happily unfettered by such constraints, the leaking of price-sensitive information continues in the City. Inside the Square Mile or out, anyone with a stretch of dining-room table to spare and access to a telephone and fax machine can set up in PR. And so long as both car-launch bunny-girl and corporate communications guru can claim with equal justification to be 'in PR', the business of public relations will continue to bewilder those outside it.

At a populist level, many people equate PR with advertising. But the whole point about PR is that it's *not* advertising. When we, as consumers, are exposed to an advertisement, we know exactly who is advertising what, and why. When we read a piece in the newspaper about an individual or company, do we know why a journalist picked the subject? And does the article really reflect an objective view – or is it rather the case that a journalist has to get 300 words to his editor in twenty minutes and hey, that PR briefing actually reads quite well? Do we know when reading a particular piece of vitriol whether the journalist who filed it has had poison poured in his ear by a spin doctor working for a company's commercial enemy? Do we know that he's just been fishing in Iceland courtesy of a company of which he now writes in fulsome praise?

To quote Sir Tim Bell, who was himself one of the most successful ad-men of the Eighties: 'The truth is that a strong story placed in the newspaper, picked up by everybody else, will actually have more impact than an advertising campaign.' Sir Tim is by no means alone in this conviction – many marketing directors have come to share it perforce. During the recession of the early Nineties most British companies faced the unhappy prospect of having to slash their marketing budgets, and in many cases it was the large and somewhat over-ripe advertising budgets which proved the easiest to prune. Forced to abandon the joys of long and seriously alcoholic lunches in the restaurants of Charlotte Street, marketing directors turned more of their attention to other aspects of the marketing mix – and were pleased to discover the impact of a well-directed PR campaign. With the return of more clement trading conditions, PR held on to its increased share of many corporate marketing budgets, spurring a massive boom in the industry (see Chart 1).

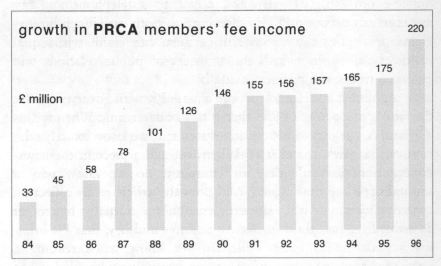

growth in **PRCA** members' fee income

£ million

Chart 1: Growth in PRCA members' fee income: a rise of over 560% since 1984. (In the same time PRCA membership rose from 110 to 136 consultancies.)
Source: PRCA

In fact, PR and advertising work very effectively together and it is no surprise that most of the world's major advertising consortia have snapped up PR subsidiaries in order to provide their clients with a seamless blend of paid-for and free media. Hill & Knowlton, the UK's third largest agency (after Shandwick and Lowe Bell Communications), is owned by WPP Group – which also owns advertising giants J. Walter Thompson and Ogilvy & Mather. Countrywide, the fourth largest agency, is owned by Omnicom, which also owns the massive BBDO advertising group. Burson Marsteller is owned by Young & Rubicam advertising agency. And so the list goes on. Moreover, not only are PR and advertising increasingly integrated, but the whole communications services industry is becoming increasingly globalized as the world continues to shrink. Having seen the internationalization of their clients, the big names in PR and advertising are now doing the same thing – striving to become the dominant players wherever in the world there is a market for their services, be it New York, London or Beijing. Small wonder, perhaps, that the distinction between advertising and PR is so blurred in the public mind.

Just to muddy the waters still further, there is that particular quirk of British PR, which is that neither of the two best-known personalities in the business actually made his name in public relations. Max Clifford and Sir Tim Bell are probably the two most famous spin doctors of all – yet it has been as a deal-broker that Clifford has achieved his unique status in the public mind, and it was as Margaret Thatcher's favourite ad-man – or 'the ampersand in Saatchi & Saatchi' – that Sir Tim first came to prominence. The names of some of Britain's other most powerful spin doctors, meanwhile, remain as unknown to the public as their activities are invisible.

spin doctors and PR consultants

We should make the distinction between those who are the true masters of the dark arts of spin doctoring and the rest of the public relations industry. Like most other businesses, public relations works according to the 80 : 20 rule, with 80 per cent of the influence retained in the hands of 20 per cent of the players. In fact, in the case of PR it is probably more like the 90 : 10 rule. Whatever the precise figure, for the vast majority of PR practitioners the power in their relationships with journalists lies very much with the journalists. These are the poor souls who spend their lives on the phone to Wapping or Canary Wharf trying desperately to persuade some hard-pressed hack to take an interest in a story which, in their heart of hearts, they know can't fly – but their client won't be told that the winning of a cleaning contract in South Wales isn't national news. These are the beleaguered middlemen who assiduously cultivate relationships with those journalists who dwell on the slopes of the media's Mount Olympus, hoping that a slap-up lunch here and an exclusive briefing there will oil the wheels of a relationship such that – Oh Happy Day! – it's their client, rather than the client of a PR rival, who is quoted next time the journalist turns his attention to a particular subject. In short, these are PR practitioners who understand all too painfully the reality that it's not who you know that counts; it's who knows you.

This is not to say that the majority of PR practitioners are without influence, only that their influence is circumscribed. Many are extremely creative in the way they hoodwink the media into giving their clients coverage for events which have no intrinsic news value. Many are highly resourceful in the way they manufacture news where it didn't exist before – such as through merchandising the results of market research surveys, for which the media has an unceasing appetite. Some, who focus on particular industries or geographical regions, have considerable clout in their constituent media. But invariably, among these worker bees of the PR world, there are also the drones, who do little but irritate journalists like Christa D'Souza, who wrote in the *Sunday Times*:

> There is that predominant sub-species of PR, mostly female, who have a lot of clients and a lot of 'projects' going on, none of which, curiously, ever seem to get written about. I call them Handbag PRs, because that is what so many of them seem to be promoting . . . handbags, very minor celebs, appalling painters, the occasional very good but misguided fashion designer, titled folk, and all those desperate little over-designed bistros that keep sprouting up all over the SW quelque-chose area. Handbag PRs are not so much sharks as bottom-feeders as in those millions of little fish that swim right on the bottom of the pond, eating whatever all the other fish leave behind.

*

This book is not about those who operate at the lower end of the PR food chain. Even the frenetic and, in large part, worthy activity of the vast majority of PR consultants is peripheral to our main focus. Because in shining a torch into the darker corners of the PR industry one inevitably happens upon the activities of those true media masters, the 10 per cent of spin doctors with 90 per cent of the power.

So what is the difference between a 24 carat doctor of spin and your average, jobbing PR man? The distinction is easily defined in that he – and they are mostly hes – takes more calls from journalists than he makes. Not for him the ceaseless hours of phone-banging, or the brainstorms or smart lunches trying desperately to come up with new ways to interest journalists in his clients. Now the boot is on the other foot. Journalists are constantly calling him for a quote about this or to arrange an interview on that. He is the object of their interest and hospitality. And why are they so keen to court his favour? Quite simply, because he controls access to the news sources on whom they utterly depend. Whether it's celebrities of stage and screen, corporate warriors, sports stars, fashion designers or political heavyweights, he who controls access has power. And it is usually the case that those who are trusted gatekeepers to the few become gatekeepers to the many.

American magazine editor Mark Dowie writes: 'Even the most energetic reporters know that they have to be somewhat deferential in the presence of a powerful publicist. No one on a national beat can afford to get on the wrong side of a Frank Mankiewicz or a Harold Burson knowing that their firms [Hill & Knowlton and Burson Marsteller] together represent a third of the most quotable sources in the country.' In the more liberal British media, reporters are less deferential to anyone; but even so, the same principle holds true. Instead of Frank Mankiewicz and Harold Burson, the most influential corporate spin doctors are Alan Parker, creator of Brunswick, Anthony Carlisle of Dewe Rogerson, Des Wilson of BAA, Sir Tim Bell of Lowe Bell, Shandwick's Lord Chadlington, Nick Miles of Financial Dynamics, Angus Maitland and Anthony Cardew. When it comes to celebrity PR, the most powerful gatekeepers to the stars include Matthew Freud, Max Clifford, Mark Borkowski and Liz Brewer. And in political PR, Peter Mandelson MP and, once again, Sir Tim Bell are the true masters of spin.

These are Britain's invisible persuaders, the men entrusted with protecting the reputations of some of the world's highest-profile individuals and organizations by managing the media, ensuring that the positive messages come across loud and clear and that any inconvenient negative stories are, at the very least, presented with the balancing arguments – if they can't be made to disappear completely. This last point is critical. Those who believe that PR is all about putting a positive spin on things know less than half the story. A large proportion of a spin doctor's energies is focused on stamping out the fires started up by clients who, without sufficient training, can behave like media pyromaniacs; and it is on occasions such as these, when a journalist has got hold of some blurted-out revelation, that the collective client muscle of the spin doctor is flexed to greatest effect. As one of my anonymous interviewees put it:

> If all you have on your client list is a whole lot of product brands and a few second-tier celebrities, you have no way of stopping a journalist writing about something. What are you going to say to him? 'Don't write about that or I'll stop sending you press releases about tomato-flavoured crisps? Don't write about that or we won't invite you to our next golf day?' No, it's the clients you represent that give the people in our business any amount of leverage. The stronger your client list, the more leverage you have.

This last point is critical in drawing a distinction between spin doctors and in-house communications chiefs – who may also be on the receiving end of more incoming journalist calls than they send outgoing press releases. The corporate affairs directors of Glaxo-Wellcome or British Telecom or Barclays Bank have tremendous power within their own organizations – but they do not have nearly the same degree of leverage with journalists as the external spin doctors they employ, who can wield impressive client lists to powerful effect.

Client lists are not born overnight, nor can a large number of clients be serviced by a lone spin doctor – which is why many of Britain's invisible persuaders head up companies which are, in themselves, vast service organizations. Sir Tim Bell's Lowe Bell Communications, for example, has over 500 clients, over 200 staff and a turnover of over £33 million per year. Anthony Carlisle's Dewe Rogerson has over 170 clients, 140 staff and an annual turnover of about £24 million. These figures refer to UK operations alone; both consultancies head up large international networks. According to the WPP Group, the total spend on PR in the UK, when one includes both in-house as well as consultancy figures, is approximately £2.3 billion a year.

The burgeoning fortunes of Britain's mightiest PR empires are symptomatic of the growth trends of the industry as a whole, which are nothing if not spectacular. In 1967 the Annual Directory of press and public relations officers listed 46 PR companies and 720 firms with in-house PR and publicity departments; the corresponding figures in Hollis's 1997 edition were 2,700 PR companies and 6,500 in-house departments. With the population of PR professionals estimated at approximately 25,000 and growing, this massive increase introduces an interesting dynamic into the operations of the media. For there are, at present, about 50,000 journalists in Britain – which makes one PR person for every two journalists. This sheer pressure of numbers cannot fail to affect the relationship between PR and the media.

Many people in Britain subscribe to the view that the media, however low they fall on occasion, do perform a 'watchdog' role. It is ironic, therefore, that it should now be the reporters themselves who are the watched – their activities studied carefully by a growing PR industry, their every article monitored and subjected to analysis, their professional and personal *penchants* and *bêtes noires* briefed back to clients. Any professional PR consultancy will have a file of journalist biographies which it keeps updated, passing the relevant individuals' details on to clients before any meeting so that conversational minefields can be avoided and the right 'hot buttons' can be subtly massaged. This is all part of the standard process of training clients to handle the media.

If PR industry trends in Britain continue to reflect those of America (PR is, after all, an American invention) then we will see the balance between watchers and watchdog tilt increasingly in favour of the PR industry. The US boasts a population of some 150,000 PR practitioners, actually outnumbering the country's 130,000 reporters. Will Britain reach a similar state of PR saturation? There are certainly strong indicators that things are heading in that direction, from the downsizing of national newsrooms and the withering of the regional press on the one hand to the continuing expansion of PR consultancies and in-house departments on the other.

What's more, the growth of the PR industry has not gone unnoticed by those whose job it is to prepare the next generation for employment. In the last decade there has been an explosion in the number of universities offering courses and degrees in media studies. Research conducted by Professor Alan Smithers and Dr Pamela Robinson at Brunel University shows that ten years ago there were 100 admissions for media studies degrees. That figure recently reached 1,500. This is not to suggest, of course, that everyone who embarks on a media studies course has a burning ambition to be the next Sir Tim Bell – Maurice Saatchi, Michael Brunson (political editor of ITN) or *Sunday Times* columnist Chrissy Iley may hold more aspirational appeal. But PR certainly attracts increasing numbers of graduate high-fliers, who might in the past have been drawn to careers in law or management consultancy. According to Toby Macmanus, head of public relations at Bournemouth University, this can't fail to have an impact on the industry:

It is all part of the professionalization of the industry. Seven years ago there was only one academic writing papers about PR – now there are twenty. I liken it to the development of the medical profession. In the mid-eighteenth century there were about forty thousand quacks going up and down the country selling coloured water. There was no evidence of efficacy and evaluation had yet to take hold. It was only when theory could be used in a predictive way that medicine took off. That is now beginning to happen in PR.

Evaluation is, in fact, one of the most persistently painful thorns in the side of PR. For while the industry's top spin doctors have little need to prove their power to anyone, 90 per cent of the industry has a much harder time of it. Unlike the big-budget advertising world where pre- and post-campaign market surveys are routine, the cost of this process is usually out of all proportion to the budget for a PR campaign. To spend £40,000 measuring the effectiveness of a £3 million advertising campaign is one thing; to spend £40,000 measuring the effectiveness of an £80,000 PR campaign is quite another. Most PR managers would opt to spend the £40,000 evaluation fee beefing up the impact of the campaign itself.

So how does the industry evaluate its performance? Measuring media coverage and conducting some form of content analysis is still the most widely used route, even though many practitioners recognize that this constitutes a measurement of means rather than ends. What's more, PR often involves activity beyond media relations for which there is no obvious unit of measurement.

Just as the PR industry as a whole has yet to deal with the fact that it does not meet fundamental defining criteria of a profession, so too it has still to face up to the challenge of evaluation. For without any kind of regulation or accepted form of measurement, the PR industry will continue to harbour bunglers and virtuosos, fools and savants, pillars of probity and masters of duplicity – and few outsiders will be able to tell the difference. Isn't any profession like that? Probably. It's just that in PR the distance between the two extremes can be quite breathtaking.

vance packard revisited: is democracy under threat?

In 1957 Vance Packard published his classic study of the American advertising industry. *The Hidden Persuaders* soon became a best-seller, revealing as it did the workings of an industry which was already gaining enormously in influence, but about which little was understood. Forty years later, a reader finds little in the book to so much as raise an eyebrow. Today, terms like 'product image' and 'brand loyalty' are so well embedded in our contemporary lexicon that they scarcely require definition; but at the time Packard's book first came out the notion that the only difference between two products might be an image manufactured by the advertising industry seemed novel and somehow perverse. Today, market research is an accepted part of commercial life; then, the idea that advertisers might conduct in-depth research among target audiences before developing advertising messages also seemed vaguely sinister. In the event, from advertising exerting an increasingly machiavellian hold over consumers, what has happened is that consumers have become increasingly sophisticated to the point where advertisements that are too crude in their appeal are simply laughed out of court. Some of today's most effective advertising parodies the advertising process itself. For instance, the early 1997 TV ad for Worthington's beer, in which comedian Harry Enfield dressed in drag talks about how good Worthington's is for her lads' hair and coats, hilariously sends up generations of dog-food advertisements.

It's never easy to extrapolate from the early stages of an industry's development to make specific predictions of future developments, and with the benefit of hindsight some of Packard's prognostications seem bizarrely off-track – at least in terms of *modus operandi*. For example, Packard contemplated the prospect of 'biocontrol', whereby consumer behaviour would be manipulated by means of electrodes implanted in their brains. In a country which can't agree to forfeit individual freedom for so much as an identity card, this Orwellian prospect remains reassuringly remote. We should not be so diverted by the ludicrous mechanics suggested here that we miss a fundamental issue Packard raises which should concern us as much today as it ever did him. For it does not require electrodes and biocontrol to prompt questions about the nature of information control in a democracy.

As this book shows in case after case, the media in general, and the press in particular, have become highly dependent on the PR industry, while the reading and viewing public have no way of discovering on their own just how much bias in any story is the product of behind-the-scenes spin doctoring. As Mark Dowie says: 'It is critical that consumers of media in democratic societies understand the origin of information and the process by which it is mediated, particularly when they are being deceived. Thus it is essential that they understand public relations.'

Is PR undemocratic? Does the influence of spin doctors represent a benign or malign force in the media? Looking ahead, is the power of the PR industry set to diminish or increase? My purpose in writing this book is to raise these questions rather than to provide easy answers, for this is a territory both unknown to the vast majority of media consumers and rarely traversed even in PR consultancies themselves, where the frenetic scramble to assemble that new business pitch or get out this urgent press release often militates against a more considered view of what is actually going on.

It is certainly the case that the PR industry's largest paymasters, big businesses, have had to move into a more transparent and accountable world. Jackie Elliot, chief executive of Manning, Selvage & Lee, says that in today's business environment PR consultants have a role as corporate conscience: 'It's up to us to stick our necks out and say to a client "You can't do that" if they want to do something which we know would not be considered acceptable by the public and media. We do this out of enlightened self-interest because we can't afford to be associated with a client whose behaviour is unethical.' No doubt this is the practice of some corporate PR consultants – the same kinds of company which would not, for example, countenance taking on a tobacco client, or conducting PR for some foreign tyrant. But there are many in the industry, as we shall see, who take an altogether different view. They say that as barristers in the courtroom of public opinion, their job is to present a case as effectively as possible, whatever a client's track record or behaviour. It's not only smaller PR shops who make this point, motivated by financial imperatives; some of the largest consultancies and most powerful spin doctors become engaged on behalf of clients in activities which would leave their more scrupulous peers distinctly queasy, and many in the public outraged – if only they knew.

The assault on the reputations of their fledgling competitors by British Gas and British Airways is a classic case of PR at work in a sinister way. For years, major tobacco companies have used every PR trick in the book in a long-running battle to avoid taking responsibility for the fact that they manufacture addictive products which cause disease and premature death. Oil producers, chemical manufacturers and fast-food giants have all pressed PR into service to construct greenwashed corporate images which, in many cases, are grotesquely out of kilter with reality. In the City, PR consultants continue to leak price-sensitive information to analysts, leading to decisions to buy and sell which can send share prices sky-rocketing or into free fall – good news for those in the know, but very bad news for the many private investors up and down the country who can't possibly compete. New Labour embraced and perfected its practice of spin to such a degree that its 1997 electoral victory was a ringing endorsement of its PR management rather than its policies – which were largely unknown. Paradoxically, the one dimension of PR most tainted by scandal, public affairs lobbying, is probably the least threatening of all.

PR can be deeply undemocratic; it can also be a force for enlightenment. Where along this spectrum any particular PR activity occurs is something for each one of us to decide – could we only see it to judge. What should not be in dispute, however, is the enormous, if unseen, power of the invisible persuaders, whose activities permeate every aspect of our daily news media consumption and whose influence on our newspapers and broadcast media is one of the most fascinating stories never told.

PART I: financial and corporate PR

CHAPTER ONE
the rise and rise of city PR

'I understand perfectly. Just an idea I thought I would run by you.'
The PR man tried to sound magnanimous as he sensed his all-too-
brief conversation with the *Times* reporter coming to a close. 'Must
do that drink sometime, when you have a moment? Of course.
Quite understand. Bless you.'

Slamming down the receiver, he cursed with feeling: 'Bitch!'

He leaned forward in his desk chair and took a last, hasty drag
of his cigarette before stabbing it out furiously in an already over-
loaded ashtray. Exhaling heavily, his gaze wandered over a
paper-strewn desk to the clock on his office wall. 8.15 p.m.

It was not a particularly late night for Tim Reynolds. He took a
special pleasure in staying on at the office in order to make more
junior colleagues feel guilty if they left before him. It was all part
of the game. Reynolds was acutely aware of being one of the last
of a dying breed – a PR man who'd slipped under the wire into the
industry without any formal qualifications to speak of. Like many
of the old-school PR types, he'd spent the first chunk of his adult
life in the army, before moving on to a stint selling advertising at
the *Daily Telegraph*. 'After three years at the *Daily Telegraph* . . .'
the CV he sent to clients read, allowing them to make the convenient misapprehension that he'd actually been a journalist. In fact,
he still found it difficult to write a press release. All of which made

21

him eye rather nervously the influx into PR of polished young things with media studies degrees.

Reynolds' own ascent in the PR world had been founded on a standard issue army technique – licking the boots of those above, and kicking the teeth of those below. It had worked a treat. Here he was, at the age of thirty-six, despite having wasted the first decade of his career, director of a high-powered PR company on a hundred and twenty grand a year, plus bonus. Of course it had meant sacrifices. Even though he conveyed a gregarious charm, he didn't really have a social life to speak of outside the constant round of journalist drinks. As for women, well, *they* rarely appeared in his life, and when they did, they didn't stick around long.

There were always problems demanding his attention – which brought him back to the offending press briefing now on his desk. He regarded it wearily. His client, Salisbury Electronics PLC, was putting pressure on him to get national media coverage for the opening of its new administration office in Leicester. The simple fact was that however momentous this development seemed to the chief executive officer of Salisbury, as far as the rest of the world was concerned it wasn't news at all. And, as his conversation with *The Times* had just testified, not all the charm in the world was going to make it news. Reynolds had tried to 'manage expectations', as the PR cliché went. But his Salisbury clients weren't having any of it. According to their flawless logic, they were paying him good money and expected press coverage. The unspoken message was clear to one with as well-developed a paranoia as most PR men, including Reynolds: get us in the papers, or you lose our account.

Racking his brains for journalists who owed him favours, Reynolds was wondering what to do next when the phone rang. It was Opal Sykes, a young journalist at one of the broadsheet newspapers with whom Reynolds had a semi-flirtatious relationship and who, he believed, secretly carried a torch for him. Working to deadline, as always, Opal was phoning for something she'd asked him a dozen times before: the salary details of Bill Smith, financial director of Chalton PLC. Reynolds' answer for the last few months had been an unequivocal 'no'. Now, as she posed the question for the umpteenth time – under pressure, once again, from her editor – Reynolds began to wonder.

Chalton had been one of his biggest-paying clients and, as such, had commanded his complete loyalty. But three months ago, much to Reynolds' irritation, Chalton had become the subject of a hostile takeover bid by a large German manufacturer. Even though Chalton had managed to winch up the price paid by the Germans, there was no question now that it was all over. There had been a period of eight weeks during which Reynolds was involved in an intense media battle on Chalton's behalf, meeting daily in the war room of its merchant bank, and on the phone constantly to the likes of Opal Sykes. It had been an enormously lucrative period – at times of corporate crisis, PR budgets were thrown out of the window – and Reynolds personally had quickly ratcheted up over a hundred grand in fees. During this time, the national media had been interested in all aspects of Chalton as never before – including the remuneration packages of its directors. And while the salary of Chalton's CEO was known and frequently published, that of its financial director Bill Smith wasn't.

Smith had repeatedly lectured Reynolds on the importance of keeping his salary out of the public domain, and, given the huge cheques he was writing Reynolds, the PR man had been only too happy to oblige. Smith was a genuinely shy man who went out of his way to shun publicity; the thought of having something as sacrosanct as his income pasted all over the media filled him with horror. What's more, he'd been in this position – finance director of a large plc that had been taken over – twice before and, having been awarded two massive redundancy payouts in less than five years, was conscious that this latest turn of events could be seen as evidence of a somewhat embarrassing trend. Also, to be practical, with the demise of Chalton he would soon be looking for another job, a process which would definitely not be helped by feverish press speculation about his salary – let alone publication of the actual details.

So, in the past, Reynolds had fought hard to move journalists off the subject of Smith's salary and potential payout – an issue which was increasingly preoccupying them. Now, though, he had a new calculation to make. That morning, the acquisition of Chalton by the Germans had been confirmed. There was no more money to be had from the once substantial Chalton coffers. Bill Smith would soon be kicking about his home in Buckinghamshire, temporarily jobless and powerless. In the meantime, Reynolds had Salisbury breathing down his neck for coverage of an utterly unnewsworthy event. And here was Opal Sykes on the phone. An elegant solution presented itself:

'Tell you what, sweet-pea. If I give you Smith's salary, will you run a piece for me on a major new development in Leicester?'

At the other end of the line the journalist grimaced. She should have known Tim Reynolds well enough to realize he'd never hand over something for nothing.

'Keep talking,' she sighed.

Next morning, trudging back up his gravel driveway towards the conservatory, Bill Smith opened his daily newspaper with horror. Together with all the business news about the German takeover of Chalton, there was a major subsidiary piece headlined 'Having his cake and eating it too', featuring a photograph of himself, and giving chapter and verse on both his salary details and the generous package he'd negotiated from the Germans – as well, of course, as raking over the last two generous payouts he'd received from previous takeovers. Putting a call through to Reynolds right away, he was told the PR man would be in a meeting all morning. As he flicked through the rest of that day's business section, he noticed a substantial piece on Salisbury PLC who were opening some office in Leicester . . .

To say that this particular mean-spirited tale is a true story – which, the names apart, it is – would be to miss the point rather. For it is a recurring true story. It is, in fact, a story about one of the stock-in-trade means by which financial PR consultants convince newspapers to publish what isn't news at the expense of broken confidences. But, aside from that, it also provides a glimpse of the relationship of <u>mutual dependency</u> that exists between spin doctors and journalists. And it shows how spin doctors are able to achieve things which their clients would never have a hope of achieving on their own. Just some of the reasons for the inexorable rise and rise of financial and corporate PR.

the shamen of the city

'If you really want to know what is going on in business and the City, don't bother reading the financial press,' writes Sarah Whitebloom, herself a City journalist on the *Guardian*. 'Ninety per cent of their stories have come hot off the fax machines of public relations firms, or have been "provided" by one of the innumerable PR men who stalk the Square Mile.

'When it comes to "spin-doctoring", political practitioners such as Peter Mandelson and Charles Lewington are amateurs compared with their financial PR counterparts. This highly paid breed has effectively sewn up the business press over the last few years, so that these days a good contact is regarded by many junior reporters as a PR man who actually pays for lunch.'

Nowhere is the grip of corporate propaganda more tightly applied than in the City, where the stakes are highest, the battles are biggest and fortunes can be made or lost on the nod of a handful of institutional investors. Nowhere is the PR industry dirtier than in pockets of the City, where the censuring of major PR firms such as Financial Dynamics and Citigate for mishandling price-sensitive information should not distract attention from the fact that their real offence was getting caught. The leaking of inside information, in fact, is regarded by some merchant bankers as the *raison d'être* of financial PR, particularly during takeover battles. As Paul Kafka, executive director of corporate communications at Fidelity Investments and former chairman of the IPR City & Financial Group, says: 'If the prospect of winning a City tussle can be improved through the judicious use of price-sensitive information and no trail is left, then the rewards for contributing to corporate success are enough to make Midas weep. In such circumstances, codes of conduct, professional standards and regulation mean nothing. The client loves it, the press love it and the PRs can add another notch to their pistol.'

For all that many outside the City remain bemused and even bored by its goings-on, financial spin doctors operate in a high-stakes, high-pressure environment where massive personal fortunes are to be made in a way which just isn't possible in any other area of PR. During takeover battles it would be unusual for a PR consultancy fee to be anything less than £100,000 for eight weeks of work and £200,000–£250,000 would not be exceptional. Even in calmer corporate times, financial PRs charge hourly rates which their industry peers couldn't possibly hope to match (£200–£350 per hour is typical, but master spin doctors go way above this), their fees paid by finance directors or chief executives who expect to pay top whack for the services of a consultant who breakfasts with City editors, lunches with corporate peers and dines with brokers and merchant bankers. As one consultant told me: 'Clients love to be on the inside track with gossip about who's screwing whom in the newsrooms, what this editor thinks about that one and the personal habits of their corporate rivals. We're an important link to the outside world.'

It's a power thing, and no other area of PR has assumed such power so quickly as financial PR. Like a fecund plant in the teeming hothouse of the City, during the past ten years financial PR has thrived, multiplying beyond all recognition. In 1986 British companies spent £37 million on financial PR. By 1996 that figure had soared to £250 million. Despite the spectacular collapse of several of the biggest names in the business during the late 1980s, and the recession of the early 1990s, City PR has grown by more than six times in a decade. And, far from slowing down, as we look towards the new millennium this rampant growth is set to accelerate.

What has fuelled this massive expansion? Some would say that financial transactions, such as flotations, mergers and acquisitions, have transformed the scale of City PR. But they would be only partly right. Undoubtedly, City PR came of age around the time of the Big Bang in the high-rolling Eighties when the Reichmans alone were paying Sir Tim Bell £500,000 a year to extol the virtues of Canary Wharf, when Brian Basham's Broad Street and Valin Pollen mushroomed into mighty communications empires, and when each successive privatization saw Dewe Rogerson awash with profits. After the inevitable fallout of the early Nineties, the era of the mega-deal is now most definitely back – but it would be wrong to attribute the burgeoning fortunes of City PR to one-off deals alone. In reality, transaction work accounts for less than a third of most City consultancies' incomes, sometimes much less. The real reason for the rise of the City spin doctor is far more sobering.

Despite successive privatizations and eighteen years of the Conservative Party's best efforts to turn us into a shareholding democracy, 80 per cent of UK stocks and shares are still controlled by a small number of institutional investors operating on behalf of insurance companies and pension funds. According to investor relations firm Frew McMaster, thirty institutions control 45 per cent of the British market. In the post-Big Bang world in which we live, 'public' companies can be bought or sold over breakfast at the nod of a handful of institutional investors. For example, the struggle of the titans in 1995–6, when Granada attempted a takeover of Forte, was resolved only when a single fund manager, Mercury Asset Management, came down on the side of Granada.

As we approach the new millennium, fund managers are now, more than ever, the gods of the City. It is at their bidding that company share prices rise or fall, that chief executives are celebrated as stars or castigated as failures. During times of corporate crisis they decide which companies will survive to fight another day, and which collapse in ignominy. So is it surprising that those who claim to be able to shape the thoughts and attitudes of fund managers take on an almost superhuman significance?

Enter the financial PR consultant, the modern-day shaman of the City with his claimed abilities to divine and influence the will of those who hold the corporate future in their hands. In place of a divinatory bag of bones he has his 'analyst and journalist audit'. Ritual incantations are performed, not around a fire with tribal elders, but in the River Room of the Savoy, or some similar establishment, where the City shaman will ensure his guests, be they analysts or editors, are plied with the right corporate messages as well as Pouilly Fumé. And yes, the notion of sacrifice is one which the City shaman rigorously upholds. No need for black cockerels, of course – but supplicants do need a hefty chequebook with which to pay for services rendered.

the invisible fixers

The massive growth in influence of City spin doctors during the last decade is remarkable in itself. But equally fascinating is the mystique surrounding their activities – a mystique which, in the finest shamanic tradition, many PR practitioners cultivate assiduously. Not only are they often at pains to conceal how they go about practising their dark arts, but – as already mentioned in the introduction – some are extremely wary of having their own identities too widely disclosed. It really is astonishing that the biggest names in financial PR are still virtually unknown outside the City. According to a survey conducted by market researchers City Insights in August 1997, just five City PR agencies handle 80 per cent of those FTSE 100 stock that have nominated advisers. These five are: Brunswick, Lowe Bell, Financial Dynamics, Dewe Rogerson and the Maitland Consultancy. Many – probably even most – chief executives of Britain's biggest PLCs remain blissfully unaware of the existence of such men as Alan Parker, Nick Miles, Anthony Carlisle and Angus Maitland; but these are some of the most important wielders of influence in the City. Corporate self-obsession blinds companies to the intricate webs of influence that connect direct competitors and potential aggressors with the media. Many captains of industry don't even know which spin doctors their corporate rivals consult – until it is too late. And – again as noted in the introduction – PR consultants themselves will be among the last to signal their presence in any given relationship because, in the words of Anthony Hilton, City editor of the *Evening Standard*: 'If you want to be effective at PR, you have to be anonymous. Being centre stage might get you clients, but your value as an invisible fixer diminishes materially.'

It is significant that of all the City PR agencies, Brunswick – probably the most successful, with a blue-chip client list the envy of all its peers – guards its invisibility most jealously of all. Not only does it refrain from all advertising and any other form of self-promotion, it won't even allow *PR Week*, the industry journal, to include it in industry league tables. It doesn't publish a company brochure. New business is acquired through referral only. Its partners turn down all requests for media interviews as a matter of course. Invisibility, it would appear, is law.

Brunswick is not alone in remaining rigorously off the record while generating acres of newspaper coverage for its clients. Many other consultancies are circumspect about discussing what they do for their clients. As one of the most powerful City spin doctors told me off the record:

> I could give you the whole, anodyne spiel about the work we do for our clients – financial calendar stuff, that sort of thing. But it's not really what they pay us for. Nine months of the year we take their retainer from them and give them back precisely sweet FA. What they're doing is taking out insurance. Because when the shit does hit the fan they know we'll fix the media for them. We'll get the right stories in the right papers and we can do more to get their shareholders on side than anyone else can.

In short, City shamen don't like to talk about the work they do because it's very definitely not in their interests to. They aren't going to ruin their cosy relationships with various City journalists by revealing the extent to which they manipulate them – whether it's by trading stories (*à la* Tim Reynolds), giving them exclusive access in return for a sympathetic piece or hinting at denial of future access to their full client list if too negative an article appears in print. Nor does it benefit a spin doctor to be associated with feeding reporters with negative results of research conducted into the activities of his client's corporate enemies. No PR person can be seen to be flouting the law by allowing price-sensitive announcements to pass into the hands of journalists before they're supposed to be made.

Also – as if all these practical business reasons for keeping a low profile weren't enough – there is another set of far more personal considerations. Invisibility is also convenient in helping conceal the rapid burgeoning of personal fortunes. Within eight years of setting up his own PR agency in the mid-1980s, Brian Basham was the proud owner of a business worth an estimated £25 million. Even though Broad Street's ultimate demise was as spectacular as its initial success – Basham ended up selling the company to Financial Dynamics – Basham is still active in City circles with his consultancy Basham & Coyle (he once told the *Daily Telegraph* that 'no one works in PR for less than £100,000') and a company that looks after old people's homes through which, he told the *Financial Times*, he turned £200,000 into £5 million in four years.

Alan Parker has been even more successful at amassing a substantial fortune in a relatively short space of time. Said to own over 90 per cent of the equity in Brunswick, the company he founded with two colleagues in 1987, he is estimated by industry insiders to be worth at least £30 million should he decide to sell. Not bad for a man barely in his forties. Described by Damien McCrystal of the *Evening Standard* in one of the few profiles ever written about him as 'the most powerful PR man in the City, and the City is the place where PR men exercise more power than anywhere else', Parker learned the PR business at the knee of none other than Brian Basham, leaving Broad Street in its final days with two colleagues and a handful of clients. The son of former British Rail boss, Sir Peter, brother of the two actors Nathaniel and Oliver and of a sister, Lucy, who runs a company called Professional Presentation which is associated with Brunswick, Alan Parker now lives with his wife and four children in West Kensington. He is chauffeured about town in a Bentley bristling with mobile phones, has a penchant for tennis, sturdy cigars and Savile Row suits, and enjoys a bit of a flutter on the horses, frequently dispatching his driver down the road to place bets on his behalf. Equally conspicuous, it is said, is his hourly rate, a subject on which Parker himself will not be drawn

As for Sir Tim, he has long been used to the finer things in life; even in his pre-Saatchi days as a media salesman for Geers Gross in 1970, he was the proud owner of a Rolls-Royce in which he used to take his wife to Paris, staying at hotels such as the sumptuous George V. Leaving Saatchi with a nest-egg estimated to be of the order of £2.5 million – according to his unofficial biographer, Mark Hollingsworth – Bell currently enjoys an annual income in excess of £350,000 and made £1.6 million on the flotation of his Chime Communications Group, in which he has a significant chunk of shares. He enjoys all the trappings of success: a lavishly furnished Regency house in Belgravia, a home in the country and a jet-set lifestyle. 'I'm not rich, I'm well off,' he once famously told the *Independent*. 'Rich people have more money than they can ever spend. Well-off people have enough to live well without borrowing.'

For an industry in which fortunes can clearly be made, and indeed lost, in short order, public relations attracts less press scrutiny than it might, and that which it does receive is usually to be found at the 'City diary' end of the reporting spectrum. This is, of course, because senior City journalists who have devoted their careers to cultivating useful sources of information are hardly going to start ferreting about in an investigative fashion if the end result can only blow their access to many of the most quotable sources in the country. Better to leave those particular stones unturned and continue to enjoy the patronage of the men who have it within their power to give them some of their biggest journalistic breaks.

Which is why compelling questions go unanswered. The dark arts of the City shaman remain veiled in mystery, and fascinating corporate and human stories go untold. So who are the key players, and what are the methods they employ to influence journalists and analysts? And what, in the first instance, is City PR all about?

champagne and chicanery inside
the square mile

Forty years ago in *The Hidden Persuaders* Vance Packard quoted a prominent PR practitioner of the day, Carl Byoir, as saying that 'public relations is whatever the individual practitioner thinks it is'. As we approach the new millennium, those words are as true as they ever were. Nevertheless, the activities of a City spin doctor can be placed somewhere on a spectrum which has a basic messenger service at one end, and at the other – infinitely more interesting – the exercise of influence on journalists, analysts and ultimately fund managers, through fair means or foul.

We will pause, briefly, at the messenger end of the spectrum, because the basic 'grunt-work', or leg-work, of PR has such an impact on practitioners' lives. It is easy to form the impression, when visiting the sumptuous offices of City PR shops, that life is lived on a rarefied plane, a veritable montage of power breakfasts with City editors at the Waldorf and lunches with clients at Quaglino's, suffused with bottles of Bolly regularly proffered by leggy Fulham gels in celebration of successive agency triumphs. And then there's the client entertainment: croquet at the Hurlingham Club, yachting at Cowes – even skiing trips to Aspen are not unheard of. Behind this veneer of charming civility, however, lies a very different existence.

Every company listed on the London Stock Exchange is required to provide trading figures to the exchange twice a year. Most use their PR consultancies to issue these, together with a chairman's statement, to the Stock Exchange in time for its 7.30 a.m. opening on results day. In addition, the PR consultancy simultaneously sends out press releases to City journalists and analysts. This seems a straightforward requirement, but the process is rarely a smooth one. Client companies are rarely in a position to provide their full- or half-year results until after a board meeting, usually the afternoon before they are announced. A good deal of toing and froing will already have occurred between a PR man and his client – usually the finance director – to get to final draft stage. But it is frequently the case that the board will decide to make changes – and it is up to the PR company to input these accurately. Even the slightest alterations can have a ripple effect across whole tables and, indeed, documents, and it is far from uncommon for companies to make wholesale changes to the chairman's statement.

Consequently, in March and September, when most companies report their full- and half-year results, lights burn all night in PR agencies throughout the City as consultants and their exhausted secretaries read and reread aloud changes to complex financial statements, in which even a minor error can have the most profound financial consequences. 'Never assume' is one of City PR's several mottoes, and 'Never assume you can't read a financial statement for a tenth time in pursuit of perfection' is one of the several reasons why, during the results season at least, City practitioners frequently work through the night, living on a diet of take-away burgers and phone-in pizza. 'Everyone hates their jobs during results season,' one ex-Brunswick employee who eventually left in despair told me, 'there are a lot of extremely pissed-off people who want out. But where else is there to go? At Brunswick you are encouraged to believe you are working for the best agency in town. You know there are plenty of others in the wings ready to take your place. When you're caught up in that never-ending treadmill there just seems no alternative.' This kind of comment is by no means unique to Brunswick. It is indicative of the industry as a whole – at a particular level.

Practitioners have to go through apprenticeships lasting anywhere from two to seven years, depending on their previous experience. But by the end of that period they are well rewarded. In the mid- to late Nineties salaries have sky-rocketed to the extent that it is now by no means unusual to find twenty-somethings earning well over £100,000 a year. These sums are not paid out to reward them for working long hours and getting the figures right: those are merely prerequisites. The main reason for their telephone-number salaries and sleek, European cars goes way beyond grunt-work and has to do with the influence they can exert on three particular groups of people: business journalists, City analysts and their clients.

spinning in the city press

> *You cannot hope*
> *To bribe or twist*
> *Thank God! the financial journalist.*
> *But seeing what*
> *Such men will do*
> *Unbribed, there's no occasion to.*

Only *Private Eye* would publish so jaundiced an assessment (with apologies to Humbert Wolfe) of financial journalism – although, as the British Gas story told in Chapter 6 shows, the willingness with which some City journalists will swallow wholesale PR feed is staggering, even to the most cynical among us. But even without the dark arts of 'negative PR', there are powerful reasons for the huge and growing influence of PR on the financial media.

'There is no question that editorial agendas are more influenced by PR today than they ever have been,' says Anthony Hilton, City editor of the *Evening Standard*. 'This is not only because companies are having to take PR more seriously. It is also because of the way that PR–journalist relationships have changed.'

To begin with, Britain's biggest PLCs have become a lot more effective at media relations. By fending off all press calls and referring them to a single point of contact – an internal or external PR person – companies are imbuing their PR controllers with more power than ever before. If company executives are trained to say nothing to journalists, that leaves only one gate through which to pass for news on anything and everything to do with the company.

Along with increased gateway control, spin doctors have also become incomparably more sophisticated at presenting information in a style that is readily digestible to journalists as well as putting the right spin on their clients. With an arsenal of powerful techniques at his disposal, today's spin doctor makes it easy for a journalist to take the corporate line without even thinking. This is not to say that City journalists today are less discerning than they used to be; but at the same time as spin doctors have become, by leaps and bounds, more effective, journalists have found themselves increasingly stripped of their traditional information-gathering resources and so are necessarily far more dependent on the spin doctors.

Damien McCrystal, ex-City diary editor with the *Daily Telegraph*, points to the most important cause of this dependency:

> Staff numbers in most City newsrooms have been slashed dramatically in cost-cutting exercises. This puts enormous pressure on the journalists that remain. If you don't produce X-hundred words a day, you're out. If you're away from your desk, people don't think you're out meeting contacts or doing research because there isn't time for much of that – they assume you're skiving. So you come to rely on a fairly small number of contacts who come to you – the PR people.

The drastic downsizing of journalist teams means that there are fewer and fewer reporters to cover more and more industry areas. Each journalist is expected to know the personalities, policies, structures and issues relating to all the major companies in each industry to which he is assigned. He is also expected to have a detailed understanding of trends affecting the whole industry – such as regulation – not to mention the thinking of analysts following the sector. But with the multiplication of sectors and constant changes in the newsrooms, many journalists have only a skin-deep knowledge of the sectors they follow. To whom does the hard-pressed reporter turn for insight? A friendly spin doctor, of course – who will not only be delighted to educate him, but will also provide the stories he needs, conveniently packaged for publication, to help set his journalistic career on an upward path.

As Sarah Whitebloom remarks:

> Senior journalists worry that in a few years' time very few reporters will actually know anything about any company, making their reports virtually worthless. But, according to PRs, this is already true. They say an increasing number of reporters would prefer to deal with them because they do not feel sufficiently confident to talk to a company director, but are happy to ask a familiar PR: 'What's the story?' If he is doing his job properly, the PR will be only too happy to provide one.

Geography provides another explanation for the increasing PR-dependency of the City press. In 'the old days', when most papers were based in Fleet Street, journalists were only ever a short walk or taxi ride away from many of the companies they wrote about. Now that the great newspaper empires are based in Wapping, Canary Wharf and Kensington, distances, allied to deadlines, mean that journalists don't get out nearly so much. Isolation from direct news sources and a more ivory-tower perspective on the world have made journalists far more dependent on external purveyors of stories – to the extent that an estimated four out of five stories appearing in the business pages have been directly influenced by a PR consultant.

Some senior editors identify yet another reason for the rise in the influence of PR: the decline of regional newspapers. It used to be that many journalists on the national press had had their training in the provinces – today's *Birmingham Post* City editor became tomorrow's senior reporter at *The Times*. Having to cover regional companies in a relatively PR-free environment sharpened the investigative skills of regional journalists, so that by the time they hit the nationals they were resourceful gatherers of information. With the decay of the regional press, however, this valuable training-ground is on the wane. New recruits to the nationals often lack the inquisitional skills of their forebears.

There are, in short, a number of very compelling reasons why the business media are becoming increasingly dependent on PR. In an environment in which journalists are so reliant on spin doctors for stories across a wide variety of companies and sectors, it is especially easy to see how City PR practitioners are able to apply a great deal of leverage on reporters in their efforts to ensure that news is reported in a way that is to their satisfaction. And their motivation to do so is strong. As Alex Sandberg, chairman of City agency College Hill, says: 'Our trade is at the sharp end. We will be beaten up by the client if he doesn't read a glowing article about his company – whatever the financial results were.'

During corporate takeovers the need to control what appears in the press is more critical than ever, and spin doctors are frequently encouraged by the merchant banks who introduce them to their embattled clients to leak information which will help their cause, both to journalists and to analysts. For example, in February 1977 the Takeover Panel described as 'reprehensible' the leak by City PR shop Citigate to the *Financial Times* and *Guardian* of confidential information about William Cook – the subject of a hostile takeover bid by Triplex Lloyd, for whom Citigate was working. The Takeover Panel's deputy director, Peter Lee, said Citigate had clearly flouted the law by intentionally passing confidential information to newspapers.

While transgressions like these don't often make the headlines, that doesn't mean that high-level leaking doesn't often happen – only that those in the industry who do it tend not to get caught. No one should be fooled into thinking that whenever an accusatory finger is pointed at a particular PR consultant, he alone is necessarily responsible for what happens. During takeover battles there are daily war meetings at the merchant banks concerned, where decisions are taken on all aspects of communication. There is frequent contact between spin doctor and broker, banker, finance director and chief executive. Spin doctors do not shoot off missiles like loose cannons on a warship without reference to all other activity – and especially not when an action which clearly breaks Stock Exchange rules is to be undertaken. Of course, blunders made out of ignorance do sometimes occur. But, in general, leaks are discussed and carried out with the greatest of care; who knows how many times the course of some major corporate activity has been turned as a direct consequence of a discreet PR leak?

City spin doctors are the more willing to carry out clandestine activity of this kind given the absence of any industry list off which they can be struck should they be found guilty of a misdemeanour. True, they are subject to the same overall Stock Exchange rules as merchant bankers and the like; but while City professions choose to set standards well above minimum legal requirements, PR practitioners do not. On the contrary, some spin doctors use the ability to leak company results to journalists in advance of their announcement as a means of leverage: I give you a scoop on Bloggs PLC in return for which you don't publish the damning story on Smith PLC, or you give one of my other clients a bit of puff. In the case of results, there can be more in it for the journalist than simply pipping his rivals to the post and getting his by-line on the front page. As one spin doctor told me, off the record: 'Let's say a journalist hears from an insider that a company's results are going to be ahead of forecasts, and let's say he hears this a day or two before the official announcement. That gives him plenty of time to buy a few grand of shares through Aunt Mabel, write an upbeat exclusive, see the share price rocket and offload his shares, turning an easy 10 per cent.'

It is this felicitous understanding that is behind the financial PR practice of the 'Friday afternoon drop'. An anonymous brown envelope arrives by courier at the City desk of a major Sunday newspaper on a Friday afternoon. Addressed to a named journalist, it contains the financial results of a company – due to be announced only on the following Tuesday. All the journalist has to do is turn to his screen to find out what analysts are forecasting for the company and he has his story – and, potentially, a very fast buck too.

The 'Friday afternoon drop' is by no means a conduit only for positive news about a company's results. Negative information is imparted this way as well, to prepare the market for worse than expected results. True, in the latter case there's no implicit financial reward in it for the journalist – which is why explicit rewards have been known to occur, announcements arriving with £50 notes thoughtfully paperclipped to their underside. In the meantime, the market for shares in the company is set over the weekend, when no one can do anything about it.

If you are the financial director of a company whose disappointing results appeared before announcement day in a Sunday paper, unless you authorized the leak yourself you will be hard pressed to prove it was your trusted PR adviser who dispatched the results; chances are he will appear to be apoplectic with fury and will have drafted a sternly worded letter to the newspaper concerned. If you are an investor who subscribes to the wrong newspaper, is out of the country, or took the family away for the weekend you may wake up on Monday morning to find yourself considerably worse off than you imagined. You are also, however, just another statistic – another one of the many casualties of unregulated financial PR.

pitching to analysts: the financial dynamics scandal

Apart from journalists, the other main focus of attention for spin doctors is that other, even more powerful, City breed: the analysts. Analysts are a super-intelligent City species whose job it is to acquire in-depth knowledge of a portfolio of companies in order to advise their clients whether to buy, sell or hold shares in those companies. According to research by Dewe Rogerson, the most successful global financial PR company to originate in the UK, 91 per cent of fund managers consider analysts' reports to be their most useful sources of information. The gods themselves read these reports, and on the basis of the documents huge volumes of shares are bought and sold. In addition, analysts are the other main source of information to which journalists turn when writing up a company – particularly during a time of heightened corporate activity such as a takeover battle. All of this means that understanding analysts and trying to influence the reports they write is one of the most critical functions of a City spin doctor.

PR practitioners' relationships with analysts are very different from those they have with journalists. At the most fundamental level, analysts rely on spin doctors hardly at all, and certainly don't regard them as their primary source of information on a company; for this they go direct to the company's finance director or CEO. The leverage provided by a large client base is of no use to a spin doctor trying to 'persuade' analysts to communicate messages that would please their clients. So how do spin doctors influence analysts? Occasionally, it has been said, by resorting to desperate measures; there are tales of analysts being threatened with physical violence by desperate PRs if they put out a 'sell' notice on a particular stock. Back-alley confrontations aside, though, the approach can only be an indirect one. The spin doctor acts as a conduit between finance director and analysts, feeding a stream of carefully massaged corporate messages one way, and perceptions and pricing information the other. It is a continuous process, in contrast to the intermittent frenzy of financial media relations which tends to occur in frantic bursts of activity twice a year. What's more, except at specific times of corporate crisis, leakiness of price-sensitive information is to be avoided at all costs – which is why, as Salomon Brothers' equities media analyst David Forster says: 'The trend has been increasingly for companies to build up their own in-house investor relations teams. One of the reasons for this is growing concern about the confidentiality of information.'

Not only are internal PR practitioners far easier for a finance director to control than external advisers, the spin they put on information is derived, in most cases, from a far deeper understanding of the company than is the case with an outside consultant who will be looking after half a dozen clients or more. In-house or out, a City spin doctor is expected to know a great deal about the main analysts following the sector or sectors in which the company operates – just as he is *au fait* with the journalists he wheels in front of his client. He will carry out soundings of the analysts' opinions and produce reports for his client, providing vital clues as to how the major institutional investors are likely to behave. On the basis of these, he will help develop analyst presentations, designed to deal with thorny negative issues and emphasize the positives. As one analyst told me: 'I suppose it's true that you're more prepared to tell a PR person what you don't like about a company than the finance director. What happens is that this all gets fed into presentations. Some of the talks you go to are quite amazing. They will cover off, point by point, all the negatives you've told their PR people, even if that means marginalizing the main focus of their business.'

After every presentation, the practitioner will ring round to find out what attending analysts thought of his client's performance. While this kind of activity is of critical importance even in the calmest of corporate climates, its significance – as indeed the significance of all investor relations work – is amplified when a company becomes involved in a takeover battle. It's at times like these that financial PR people can be extremely effective – or score deeply embarrassing own goals, as the following salutary tale demonstrates.

In 1995 Financial Dynamics was, with its 122 clients, the largest City PR consultancy in Britain. Other consultancies may have had bigger billings, but FD had the most clients. Like other City agencies, FD had benefited from a return to the economic good times and, under its chairman and chief executive, Anthony Knox and Nick Miles respectively, had established a strong reputation in the marketplace. So on 12 December 1995 City observers were astonished to discover on their Reuters screens that the City's Takeover Panel had publicly rebuked FD for its conduct in the takeover battle between the Norwegian company Kvaerner and its target, the construction group AMEC. FD, acting for AMEC, had apparently leaked price-sensitive information about AMEC's profits to an analyst – albeit one unconnected with the bid – thus committing a 'serious breach' of bid rules. The further news quickly followed that FD had been summarily dismissed by AMEC, who turned instead to rival agency Dewe Rogerson to help them fight the bid battle. Gossip swept through the PR community like wildfire – nothing so humiliating had happened to one of their number in years. There was, however, little apparent *schaden-freude*: the more commonly expressed view was rather 'there but for the grace of God go I'. This is not to say that all City spin doctors are unscrupulous – though some certainly are – but rather that the issue of what constitutes a leak is by no means as straightforward as might be supposed.

Giving guidance to analysts is, as we have already seen, something that investor relations practitioners, whether in-house or out, are asked to do at critical moments in a company's life. If corporate profits are going to be somewhat less rosy than the market believes, it is up to City spin doctors to create 'the right climate' into which to release news of the poor performance. Fund managers don't like surprises of any kind, and especially not nasty ones. So it's up to the spin doctor to 'talk up' or 'play down' expectations over a period of time. But there is a right way and a wrong way to do this, and nuance is all-important. For example:

Spin doctor:	So tell me, what are your forecasts for year end?
Analyst:	Profit of £49 million and EPS [earnings per share] of 15p.
Spin doctor:	Hmm.
Analyst:	Am I a bit wide of the mark?
Spin doctor:	Well, you'd be more in the region with a profit of £38 million and EPS of 10p. The travel division was quite badly hit by the weather problems last summer, as you may recall.

That is the wrong way: price-sensitive information has been disclosed. A better – yet only subtly different – way of making the point would be as follows:

Spin doctor:	So tell me, what are your forecasts for year end?
Analyst:	Profit of £49 million and EPS of 15p.
Spin doctor:	Hmm.
Analyst:	Am I a bit wide of the mark?
Spin doctor:	Well, as you probably know, most analysts are more in the region of a profit of £37–£39 million and EPS of 9–11p. The travel division was quite badly hit by the weather problems last summer, as you may recall.

All analysts' telephone calls are automatically tape recorded by their employers and can be hauled out and replayed at any moment to check that information has been handled in an appropriate way. Which brings us back to the unhappy tale of Financial Dynamics.

FD might well have weathered the AMEC/Takeover Panel scolding as an unfortunate error, made in the heat of a takeover battle, were it not for the fact that within weeks, in February 1996, the agency was being blasted in the headlines again. This time Anthony Knox, FD's chairman, no less, was named in media reports as having discussed price-sensitive information with analysts at merchant bank Robert Fleming about the upcoming financial results of his client Caradon – a charge FD strongly denied. Fleming had conducted an internal investigation as a result of which it had sacked two of its analysts. Far worse for FD was the confirmation that the Department of Trade and Industry was looking into the affair.

In a business all about the discreet handling of price-sensitive information, the mere suggestion that the firm was to be the subject of a DTI investigation was a damning indictment. Coming on top of the Takeover Panel's extraordinary rebuke, it made Financial Dynamics suddenly look at best ham-fisted. According to industry insiders, the flow of new business enquiries into FD – hitherto a 'must have' agency on City pitch lists – was abruptly stemmed. In a market where experienced practitioners are in short supply, those potential clients who might have been attracted by FD's impressive track record now had cause for second thoughts. And a matter of weeks later, after the DTI investigation was confirmed, FD's most recent high-profile new appointee, Jeff Randall, announced he was leaving his job with the agency, with its alleged £200,000 package, to return to a rather less well-paid position with the *Sunday Times*.

To prolong the agony, the chairman of the Takeover Panel, Sir David Calcutt, then issued a severe letter to financial PR agencies, warning them that the panel would deal 'very firmly' with unauthorized leaks, about which it was becoming increasingly concerned. No names were mentioned, but there was no doubt in anyone's mind which agency had prompted the fuss; so Financial Dynamics once again found its name dragged through the national press, practically hanged, drawn and quartered before a single DTI inspector had walked through its doors.

It should be said that, despite the DTI investigation launched in 1996, Financial Dynamics has managed to hang on to its sizeable share of the market, as the seventh largest PR agency in the UK with a fee income in 1996 of over £8.6 million.

The censure by the Takeover Panel of both Financial Dynamics and Citigate, two of the biggest PR firms in the City, and the panel's expression of its concern about PR leaking, throws into sharp relief the issue of regulation. As long as PR consultants are free to operate on a different ethical plane from other City advisers, many see no reason why any form of regulation, based on a code of conduct or accreditation, should be introduced. After all, why damage your own ability to attract business, based on a reputation that you are prepared to 'win at all costs'? As Paul Kafka says: 'While some in the Institute of Public Relations may seek to improve the ethical reputation of PR, those who are making serious money out of the status quo will probably oppose change tooth and nail, even if they pay lip service to such aspirations in public.'

There is no appetite for regulation on the part of financial spin doctors – why close off a loophole which has time and again provided an extremely convenient way of getting out information you couldn't possibly hand out yourself? Nor is there any incentive for clients to press for regulation, for precisely the same reason. And ultimately, it's what the clients say that counts, because as service providers financial PR consultants have to be utterly committed to serving their clients' best interests.

'trust me, i'm a spin doctor'

Serving a client's best interests, as we have already seen, can take any number of forms, from stamping out a negative press story to carrying out a piece of judicious leaking, to the painful but neces- sary tedium of financial calendar work. But it is in the area of corporate advice and handholding that Britain's invisible per- suaders have greatest influence – and in which, therefore, any errors of judgement become most spectacularly visible.

Scan the company brochures handed out by even a few of the big-name consultancies and you will come across a few key phrases consistently repeated: 'strategic advice', 'high-level consultancy', 'corporate counsel'. In fact they all mean the same thing. They all suggest that in times of crisis there will be a cool, calm voice of experience to which the beleaguered company head can turn. When the media wolves are baying for blood, and when a chief executive finds his company and his career on the ropes, enter the spin doctor, to soothe the troubled brow, work his magic on the headlines and snatch victory from the menacing jaws of defeat.

Sir Tim Bell is the spin doctor who, perhaps more than any other, is known for providing counsel to corporate tycoons and Conservative grandees, not to mention right-wing prime ministers and presidents across the globe. Lowe Bell Communications is now second biggest PR consultancy in Britain, with a fee income of over £21 million in 1996: a multi-tentacled operation servicing over 500 clients across a diverse range of industries, with a worldwide network of influence. Famous for his special relationship with Margaret Thatcher during her rise to power and occupation of

Number Ten, Bell has also had the ear of such political leviathans as Ronald Reagan, Jacques Chirac, Boris Yeltsin and F. W. de Klerk. A more high-level adviser would be hard to find. Such pre-eminence raises a number of questions. Is Sir Tim's advice always heeded? Is it always right? Does the same hold true for other spin doctors? And how did a boy from an unremarkable, middle-class background rise to a position of such sweeping influence?

No doubt the very ordinariness of Sir Tim's background, combined with his fervently competitive nature and stunning success at Saatchi & Saatchi – a combination that epitomized so much that Margaret Thatcher held dear – helped create their special chemistry. Bell was born in north London in October 1941. Leaving school in the summer of 1959 with four O levels and two A levels, he made no attempt to go on to university – he didn't like the kind of people who went, and saw student life with its protests and alcoholic binges as stupid and facile. Instead, he looked for work in the 'real world', and as luck would have it his first job was as a chart boy at Associated British Picture Corporation, the fore-runner to Thames Television. His task, which earned him a salary of £7 10s a month, was to reserve time slots on behalf of ad-vertisers; it wasn't long before the advertising bug had bitten. He progressed through several positions in media buying – a largely unexplored area at the time – and was one of the most highly paid executives of his kind when, in 1970, he joined two Iraqi Jewish brothers in a new agency which was to become the world's biggest name in advertising: Saatchi & Saatchi. Bell was the perfect com-plement to the creative genius of Charles and the financial and strategic skills of Maurice. The agency needed a front man, a role for which Bell, with his consummate charm, ability to translate complex arguments into simple truths and enormous charisma as a salesman, was perfectly suited. By 1973, the Saatchis had made him managing director.

Several volumes have already been written about the incredible achievements of Saatchi & Saatchi and, breathtaking though they are, this is not the place to revisit those successes, except to say that it was Bell who presided over many of them. His ability to generate extremely high levels of commitment from his staff underpinned much of what he did. As Bell's (unauthorized) biographer Mark Hollingsworth notes in his book, *The Ultimate Spin Doctor*,

> Everyone liked Tim Bell. He would walk around the office in his socks with a friendly word for everyone. He was renowned for knowing everyone's name – from the most senior to the junior staff – but on the rare occasions that he forgot who someone was, he compensated: 'Thanks, Prince,' he would say, giving a junior employee a glow after talking to the managing director . . . Bell helped colleagues with their mortgages, ensured they received decent pay rises and bonuses, organised and sometimes paid for their holidays. The Saatchi attitude was to keep employees happy.

By the time he met Margaret Thatcher, his own reputation and that of Saatchi & Saatchi had preceded him: 'I know you.' She shook his hand. 'You're the man from *Starsky and Hutch*.'

It was Bell's relationship with Thatcher which, in many respects, defined what followed in his later life. As an outsider, not one of the Conservative establishment – many of whom opposed her – Bell was in a position to give her genuinely independent advice during the run-up to the 1979 general election which swept her to power. What's more, there was something flirtatious in his regard for her, and he was one of the few in her inner circle who treated her as a woman without in any way compromising her position. Thatcher warmed to that, and gave the impression that she would forgive him any indiscretions which might have spelt an end to the careers of advisers with whom she didn't enjoy such a close rapport.

While Bell grew closer and closer to Thatcher and the cause of the Conservative Party, he grew further away from the Saatchi brothers, into whose confidence he had never been completely taken. Major corporate decisions were being made without even his knowledge, much less his consent. This, combined with unhappiness in his personal life, including a failed marriage, an unstable relationship and a drug problem, took Bell to the edge of crisis before he left Saatchi & Saatchi under a cloud of bitter recriminations in 1985. The parting of the ways, acrimonious though it was, marked a turning point for Bell. Joining rival agency Lowe-Howard-Spink just before it acquired PR firm Good Relations saw him metamorphose from ad-man into a figure with broader concerns as a corporate and political adviser, confidant and image manager: at the age of forty-five, Tim Bell became a spin doctor.

The very phrase 'spin doctor' is one that provokes a wide variety of responses from PR consultants – not all of them welcoming. Sir Tim, however, recently told the industry organ *PR Week* that: 'I would rather be called a spin doctor than a hidden persuader. Actually I rather like the term. After all, doctors are qualified professionals, and putting the right spin on things is exactly what we do.'

In the late Eighties, when Thatcherism was at its zenith, the paramount importance accorded to the free market and successive privatizations brought politics and business together in a way which hadn't been seen for years. Many of those chairing the boards of once nationalized industries owed the existence of their jobs to Margaret Thatcher. Toasted by self-made men, captains of industry and the recently enthroned overlords of privatized industries, she was the centre of the new order. Anyone who had direct access to her in turn occupied an elevated status. And everyone knew that Sir Tim was one of Mrs T's greatest admirers – and one of her inner circle. He took care to remind them of it – which was part of the reason why he very quickly acquired a client list studded with blue-chip corporate names of the Thatcher era: British Gas, Thames Water, British Rail, Hanson, Canary Wharf, to name but a few. Bell has forged relationships with the chairmen and chief executives who head up these massive operations, and it is opposite them that he plays his key role – whether one calls it strategic counsel or high-level advice. And it is to Sir Tim's spin-doctoring credit that he has succeeded in continuing to be perceived as one of the leading purveyors of corporate counsel, despite being linked with several major PR controversies during the last decade.

Perhaps the most high-profile of these came about when he was advising Lord Hanson at the time of the latter's raid on ICI in May 1991. Bell was one of a team of high-octane spin doctors representing different ingredients in the communications mix: alongside Rodney Dewe, whose brief was to look after institutional investors, and Brian Basham, Bell was looking after City PR and political lobbying. The presence of both Bell and Basham in the line-up was a cause of tension from the word go, their skills and personalities being far from complementary. A large part of the reason why Basham was invited on to the team was because during Hanson's takeover of Imperial, the massive food and tobacco conglomerate, Basham had been working on Imperial's side and had made life extremely uncomfortable for the Hanson Group. In future, in the memorable words of Hanson's partner the late Lord White, Hanson wanted Basham 'on the inside of the tent pissing out'.

On the occasion of the ICI raid, it was none other than Basham's protégé, Alan Parker, who was leading the defence of ICI – and Basham knew that Parker could be counted on to put up an extremely tough fight at the merest suggestion of a threatened takeover. Lord Hanson would chair early morning war meetings with various company executives and advisers at which Basham and Bell were both present, and sometimes barely able to contain their personal and political differences: unlike the arch-Thatcherite Bell, Basham was a lifetime Labour supporter. Of the two 'high-level counsellors', Bell would usually dominate proceedings, irritating Basham with what he regarded as long and rambling monologues that achieved little. Reduced to a key theme, Bell's sustained advice during the course of the ICI bid was that Hanson should speak only to those journalists they knew and trusted. This played well to Lord Hanson's natural suspicion of the press – but went completely against Basham's view that Lord Hanson had to get his side of the story across to whomever cared to listen.

Parker and his Brunswick team were meantime inflicting considerable media damage in ICI's war against Hanson. Instead of focusing on the bid itself, Parker was scoring hit after hit with his revelations about Hanson's avoidance of corporation tax and Sir Gordon White's lifestyle. ICI's adviser fees were running at £220,000 a week and the company enjoyed the support of a wide range of decision-makers, including several powerful newspaper editors. As the summer of 1991 wore on, Lord Hanson, who had in the past taken the support of the right-wing press for granted, became more and more frustrated at the way the reputation of his mighty empire was being besieged by a Parker-led press. Hanson found himself constantly on the defensive.

The publication of a *Mail on Sunday* piece headlined 'Is Hanson such a good gamble?' was the final straw for the peer, prompting a furious letter to Bell. No PR man – not even one lacking Bell's super-sensitive antennae – could have failed to get his client's message. The letter amounted to a damning rebuke of Bell's advice and his activities. And, as if this wasn't bad enough, Bell was to be further humiliated when, seven weeks later, the *Observer* published the letter in full:

> *Dear Tim,*
>
> *Since we reduced the direct approach (from us) to editors et al., we have had lots of advice from you, most of which seems to address how best we should keep the institutional investors correctly informed on Hanson. I think you're missing the point.*
>
> *At that time we left you to spread the Hanson gospel to the media and politics, without involving us directly. What you had to offer us was based on 'who you know' and that you would be serving us best by influencing them indirectly but constantly. We've left that to you while we've been working, as agreed, directly on the institutions.*
>
> *We're disappointed with the press recently, exemplified by this article. Libellous, in our opinion, but a clear puff from Alan Parker who shows himself to be running circles around us. Alan Parker to advise ICI on financial matters? . . . What kind of clown is he? How about exposing his expertise for a change. Come on, chaps, let's do something. He spends his client's money trying to discredit us.*

Can't you dispel all this garbage in advance? Who is Lawrence Lever [city editor of Mail on Sunday] *anyway? I've never heard of him, but by now all the media should have the true story and realise that they shouldn't be able to get away with blatant puffs like this? And your own loving relationships? Apart from Jeff Randall and Ivan Fallon and John Jay – who contact us direct – everyone else seems to have drifted against Hanson and comment is deteriorating. This letter is intended to show our unhappiness.*

It's not for us to tell you how to do your job, but it is up to me to judge the results. Let's take just one thing. Parker and Co have managed to imprint in the media's mind the 'Lord White Lifestyle' lie to the degree that even you partly believe it, judging from what I hear from you about our dispelling it. Shouldn't you be addressing this – and the minor bloodstock deal – day, night and holidays too? After all this time, Parker's still making plenty out of it.

I think we're entitled to better results. Weekly strategy meetings are a waste of time. We've put our faith in your ability to sell Hanson to your contacts. You know what a great story there is out there, but it's not getting through. You know what we need but I begin to have my doubts. Each time I raise them, back comes a message: 'May we get together to discuss . . .' You know your story sufficiently well by now to sell it for us.

You're in the communications business so I hope you don't mind this frank communication from me. I know you'll understand that we're entitled to look for some positive results and to let you know when we don't see them.
Sincerely, James

Exactly how this letter found its way into the hands of the *Observer* is one of PR's great mysteries. For some time, however, there had been a suspicion of a well-placed mole at Hanson, as newspapers always attributed inside information to a 'City source'. While Bell clearly had most to lose from publication of the letter, Lord Hanson was furious too, and pressed the Press Complaints

Commission for action against this flagrant breach of his right to privacy. But by then, not only had Hanson lost the media war, but its bid for ICI was effectively all over. Whether this was a result of a strategic error (not buying a big enough stake in ICI to begin with) or media relations failure is a moot point. But there is no doubt that a hostile press did Hanson no favours – and for that he had the twin media conductors, Parker and Bell, to thank.

If Bell felt mortified by revelations of Lord Hanson's displeasure, he disguised it well in bluster: didn't newspapers have better things to write about than other people's correspondence? And within weeks the matter was very visibly pushed to the side when he threw a huge bash at the Dorchester Hotel to celebrate his fiftieth birthday. The party was attended by the great and the good of the Thatcher era, politicians and industrialists alike. If it hadn't been apparent before, it was abundantly clear that night: a few lacerating press pieces weren't going to destroy the relationships built up over years, and Tim Bell was still very much 'one of us'.

The Tim Bell story is related in detail by Mark Hollingsworth in *The Ultimate Spin Doctor*, a fascinating and lively account of one of Britain's most powerful PR magnates. The main drawback of the book is the non-participation of its subject. Sir Tim was dead against having a biography written about him, not because he had anything to hide – most of the book's 'revelations' were already widely known – but more probably because of the penchant of spin doctors, already discussed, for remaining invisible. In Sir Tim's case, this mystique is particularly well developed, and having his early career, personal life and professional mistakes dissected and presented in black and white hardly served his interests.

For the purposes of this chapter, the Hanson/ICI tale is illustrative of the nature of the relationships that exist between Britain's top spin doctors and the tycoons they advise. Clients depend, to a very much larger degree than might be supposed, on the advice of their PR gurus: poor advice can substantively damage a company's cause, while good advice can see it fending off predatory attacks. Behind every merger and acquisition project, and in the wings of every stock market flotation, you will find a City spin doctor, whose counsel is critical in devising a strategy that will deliver the right media commentary.

Supportive column inches in City pages are about far more than corporate puff and boardroom vanity. They can be a powerful way of influencing those gods of the City, institutional shareholders and the analysts who advise them. By creating a tide of opinion against a bid, as Parker did on behalf of ICI, a hostile bidder can be stopped in its tracks – notwithstanding the merits of its takeover proposals. Spin doctors don't always get it right, of course, and in Sir Tim's case he has been big enough and colourful enough to admit to his own past errors. In any case, despite the strain on his relationship with Lord Hanson caused by the failed ICI bid and subsequent *Observer* piece, he continued as a retained adviser to the group. Twelve months later he was working with Hanson on yet another takeover bid, that of Rank Hovis McDougall. And in 1995 it was Lowe Bell which advised on the de-merger of Hanson's operations in the United States.

What the Hanson/Bell story also shows is the close relationship that exists between financial PR and corporate PR. In times of corporate crisis in particular, the boundary between the two sectors becomes blurred as the current and potential future financial value of a company is vigorously contested. But financial and corporate PR are two quite distinct dimensions to most businesses. There are many financial PR consultants who are dumbfoundingly ignorant about corporate PR – and vice versa. More sophisticated spin doctors, however, understand both fields and how they are related. Even though a crass, pinstriped City spinner may see no value in promoting a company's environmental credentials, or raising its profile outside the business pages of a newspaper, in the end corporate reputation does translate into financial value. Corporate PR may require an altogether different approach, even a different mindset, from that demanded inside the Square Mile, but it can have a significant effect on a company's standing in the market; and, as the next two chapters show, many of the most ingenious – and sinister – aspects of media manipulation are to be found in the work of corporate PR.

CHAPTER THREE
creating headlines and managing news:
the world of corporate spin

Tom Curtin, head of media relations at Thames Water, needed a miracle. Following what was, at that time in December 1989, the most deeply unpopular privatization to date, Thames' bills had started shooting up well above inflation and the new PLC was finding it hard to convince critics that the extra money was being well invested, rather than simply handed over to overpaid directors. From a media point of view, it didn't help that the vast majority of Thames' new assets were literally underground – there were no glistening displays of hi-tech wizardry to show where all the money was going.

In the continuing absence of evidence to the contrary, the media continued to play the consumer card, portraying the privatized Thames as a shambling bureaucracy taken over by money-grubbing fat cats, who presided over a chaos of crumbling assets and rat-infested sewers. It was, significantly, the rat-infested sewers which, for reasons best known to themselves, seemed particularly to preoccupy journalists. Variously described as crumbling, squalid, collapsing and vermin-infested Victorian relics, the sewers evidently gave journalists something to get their teeth into, metaphorically speaking.

Curtin, an Irishman with a ready wit and a genius for epithets, and an ex-journalist himself, knew exactly where the hacks were coming from, and possessed precisely the quirky flair required to halt them in their tracks. Curtin's background was a far cry from that of most conventional in-house PR chiefs, the majority of whom rise through long years in the ranks, or move in-house in retreat from the rigours of consultancy life. Curtin's career had been far more colourful, beginning with a stint as a cockroach exterminator in New York to fund his university studies, and including successive periods as a journalist, business publisher and even Dublin restaurateur. This broad canvas of experience lent Curtin an originality of approach that sometimes startled – as when, in response to the continuous flow of inventive tales about London's primeval sewers, Curtin invited every major business and environmental journalist on a 'Sewer Tour', offering them the chance to gain first-hand experience of London's 'crumbling sewers'. Issuing calligraphic invitation cards urging a 'return to the street of shame', Curtin outlined a proposed journey through the sewers under Fleet Street, along the lines of a rock tour. Full protective clothing, including 'Sewer Tour' T-shirts, would be provided, as well as a video and a tape recording of appropriate music. The outflows of once-favoured watering holes could be studied in detail. The news 'tag' was a new multi-million-pound sewer investment programme. Curtin even offered a £500 donation (to a charity of their choice) to any journalist who sighted a rat.

The invitations ('Back Stage Passes') provoked a flurry of disquiet in the newsrooms of the national media. A gauntlet had clearly been thrown down, but who actually wanted to spend a morning knee-deep in raw sewage? Like most people, journalists didn't realize that raw sewage is, in fact, 99 per cent water; all their previous scatological derision was becoming disturbingly unfunny. However, Curtin and his team followed up the invitations with relentless calls, wheedling and cajoling journalists into attendance. When the day of the 'Sewer Tour' finally dawned, a brave band of reporters and photographers, including BBC and ITV cameramen, did turn up, and were duly kitted out in waterproof overalls, wellington boots and lamp-bearing helmets. Descending into the cavernous depths beneath Fleet Street, led by an intrepid Thames

Water sewerage manager, to their astonishment, and against their own heartfelt prejudices, they discovered a whole new underground world. The sewers weren't by any means all narrow, black tunnels of filth; they were surprisingly large, many with impressive, vaulted brickwork in pristine condition. The network of passages was, of necessity, every bit as complex as London's street system, a below-ground replication of what went on above the surface. Reporters waded through lengthy tunnels of effluent, curiously less putrid than they had feverishly imagined in their visions of squalor and decay. And not a rat in sight.

The 'Sewer Tour' story not only appeared on national television that night and in the press the next morning; it was the talk of newsrooms for weeks afterwards. In one fell swoop Thames Water put paid to all the stories about collapsing sewers written by journalists who had never visited them. The invisible hand of PR had converted a steady flow of negative reporting into a veritable torrent of rave reviews; 'London's crumbling sewers' vanished from the national press.

This uplifting tale is illustrative of corporate PR at its best. A company is faced with an intractable perception-lag problem. Some robust, creative thinking is applied. A PR activity is implemented. Perceptions are brought up sharply in line with reality. It is rare, of course, to find such textbook cases of corporate PR efficacy. Fighting negative perceptions far more commonly involves corporate PR practitioners in wearying wars of attrition rather than short-burst Desert Storms.

But what the Sewer Tour story also shows is how the most effective corporate PR is designed to send the desired messages to a number of audiences simultaneously – a feature that distinguishes it from financial PR. As the labels suggest, financial public relations is focused sharply on a company's financial audiences, while corporate PR is concerned with opinion-forming in a far broader way, and is usually aimed at targets as diverse as customers and potential customers, key influential players in the industry, including perhaps a regulator, a company's industry peer group and possibly the public at large.

There are many major organizations which do not require any financial PR in the UK as they are not listed on the London Stock Exchange – either because they are privately or publicly owned (such as Eagle Star, the insurance giant, or the BBC respectively) or because they are listed on exchanges in Tokyo, Hong Kong, Frankfurt or New York. It is undoubtedly the case that listed companies automatically attract greater press interest than those which are not listed, by simple virtue of their size and relevance to newspaper readers. Consequently, PR practitioners working for unlisted corporates have to exercise far more creativity in coming up with story-lines which they can sell to journalists – and in stopping journalists from writing negative pieces about their client.

Creativity can, of course, be used to positive or negative effect. In this chapter we will be looking at the bright side of corporate PR, and also at how it can be marshalled to positive effect in times of corporate crisis. More unsavoury PR activities will be studied in depth in following chapters. Evil is usually far more interesting than good – but it would be utterly misleading to suggest that *all* corporate PR is driven by the imperatives of deceit and negative manipulation.

In his book *Taking the Risk out of Democracy*, Alex Carey says: 'The twentieth century has been characterised by three developments of great political importance: the growth of democracy, the growth of corporate power, and the growth of corporate propaganda as a means of protecting corporate power against democracy.' What this rather chilling assessment fails to take into account is that corporate PR can also be a powerful force working *in favour* of the public interest. At its most basic level, corporate PR is about getting across information, and as Sue Ryan, director of international PR firm GCI, says: 'If democracy is about choice, then the free flow of information is essential for people to be able to make informed choices. PR is central to that process. PR also has an important role in mediating between a company and its target audiences to ensure that the company is in touch with how its audiences think and feel – and can act accordingly.'

The downside, of course, is when a company really does only *act* according to the public interest, giving the appearance of heeding concerns and expectations rather than genuinely doing so. In such instances, PR becomes the means by which the wool is pulled over the public's eyes, the propaganda by which a company's profits and power are protected. Ozone depletion, child labour, rainforest destruction, food safety and any number of other environmental issues present many of the world's biggest businesses with a media minefield. Faced with this daunting prospect, they can either carry out the painstaking and costly exercise of de-mining, by ensuring their operations could, if things came to it, withstand the full glare of public scrutiny – or they can attempt to pick their way perilously across, constantly at risk of having an issue blow up in their faces.

strategy and tactics

Whatever the uses to which a company puts PR, one of its first requirements should be to ensure that its communications are effectively planned. While this might seem a statement of the blindingly obvious, a surprisingly large number of Britain's chief executives still regard PR as a tactical instrument, a means by which their companies react to events rather than set their own news agenda. And a surprisingly large number of PR practitioners fail to disabuse them of this notion.

The most successful spin doctors, however, understand the importance of planning, which might be expressed, in its most basic form, as a three-step process by which perceptions of a company are influenced. The three key questions are: 'Where are you now?' (i.e. in the way you as a company are perceived), 'Where do you want to be?' and 'How do you get there?' The additional question 'Are you getting there?', to be asked after a PR programme has been run, essentially about evaluation, is also a part of planning, and feeds back directly into the original issue of 'Where are you now?' – making planning a cyclical process rather than a single, linear exercise.

A number of worthy tomes have been written on the subject of communications planning, some of which give the impression that planning is an end in itself, rather than merely the means. But strategic planning is nothing if it fails to deliver effective communications vehicles, or 'platforms' as some practitioners prefer to call them. These vehicles may take any number of forms – market surveys, conferences, lobby groups or consumer guides, to name a few – but their purpose will always be to improve a company's standing with its key audiences, in order to boost the share price, sell more product, avoid regulation, massage the ego of the chairman (or his wife) – or all of these.

The difficulty with effective planning is that it requires creativity as opposed to a simple talent for exaggeration – and creativity is a resource in pretty short supply in most City and corporate PR agencies. In part this may be for reasons of temperament, the pinstriped and financially literate are unlikely candidates when it comes to setting the world on fire with any Big Ideas. It is also a product of stress. When you are working frenetically so as not to drop any of the dozen balls you are juggling, the right conditions for lateral thinking simply don't exist. But it is also true that, in the past, creativity was undervalued by financial and corporate agencies, who were wary of taking on board any of the ideas that they saw as belonging rather to the glitzy, loopy end of the PR spectrum, to be immortalized in *Absolutely Fabulous*.

However, in the increasingly competitive information marketplace, there is now no question that 'applied creativity' is the means by which the ordinary can be transformed, and by which corporate intentions can become accepted fact. Indeed, it is the application of innovative PR techniques which has powered the rise of corporate agency Fishburn Hedges.

Fishburn Hedges is probably the biggest corporate start-up success story of the Nineties. Created out of the break-up of the Valin Pollen empire by several of VP's most senior directors, Fishburn Hedges began in January 1991 with five men in a single serviced office suite at 1 Northumberland Avenue, opposite Trafalgar Square. January 1991 was not an auspicious time to be setting up any kind of business, certainly not in the recession-struck PR industry. With the economy in nose-dive, clients were certainly not in any risk-taking mood when it came to the appointment of new PR providers.

Despite a daunting business climate and the onset of the Gulf War, the complementary mix of PR experience offered by the new Fishburn Hedges team found a ready market. The band of five – Dale Fishburn, Neil Hedges, Andrew Boys, John Williams and Charles Downing – not only survived, they prospered. More staff were soon recruited, and more office space acquired. With one of the most rigorous recruitment policies in the industry, Fishburn Hedges took on only senior practitioners with the creative flair needed to ensure that press releases didn't make their way directly from fax machines into journalists' rubbish bins.

By 1995 Fishburn Hedges had grown into an operation employing forty people with a turnover approaching £3 million, making it one of the top twenty-five consultancies in the UK. It was at this point that the company came into the sights of communications giant Abbot Meade Vickers, which made a successful £15 million bid for it.

Fishburn Hedges retains its reputation as one of the more effective corporate consultancies, able to 'create' news where it doesn't exist and to get its clients positive coverage for even the most pedestrian of stories. This has been achieved by the deliberate application of consumer PR techniques to corporate purposes. A particularly striking example is that of Fishburn Hedges' client Barclays Bank, which wanted to increase its profile among students around the time that government grants were replaced by student loans. Barclays clearly wasn't the only bank eyeing up the potentially rich pickings to be had from the change, and although it was deploying student managers to branches in or near universities, so were other banks. While Barclays wanted to be seen as championing the student cause, other banks could make most of the claims about student banking that Barclays could.

Barclays needed something different, and in 1993 turned to Fishburn Hedges to help them find out what that could be. After brainstorming a number of ideas, an approach to a solution was arrived at which has subsequently become one of the most successfully applied techniques in public relations: the use of market research for PR purposes.

how to invent headlines

The idea was to undertake a market research survey to find out about student debt – at that time a fairly novel phenomenon – as well as students' attitudes to the new financial regime. The results of the survey could then be unleashed on an unsuspecting media, revealing for the first time exactly how far into debt students had been pushed by the new system, and enabling Barclays to comment on the situation – and to announce a student package of soft loans designed to alleviate the worst of students' money problems.

The results of the survey revealed greater levels of debt, and angrier students, than even Barclays had previously thought. Packaged into press releases, the findings painted a compelling picture of the financial hardships of student life – which instantly caught the imagination of the media. The switch from grants to loans had been unpopular, but here for the first time was evidence of just how deeply students had sunk into debt – in precise pounds and pence. The Barclays press releases generated enormous coverage in the national media. Juxtaposed with the survey, references to Barclays student managers achieved a newsworthiness they would never have had on their own. Through the invisible services of their PR advisers, Barclays came to be widely seen as champions of a cause. And having once attained that position, they successfully retained it.

One year after the first student debt survey in 1993, Barclays conducted another – but this time there were more questions, designed to interest educational as well as personal finance journalists. In addition, the research was structured to provide regional as well as national findings, so as to appeal to the regional media. What's more, with one set of figures already to hand, trend data could be generated which were not available in the first year. And case studies were sought to bring the statistics to life.

'The only way to maintain legitimacy in an area is through a process of continuous improvement,' says Julia Alexander, the Fishburn Hedges director who masterminded the annual student debt survey. 'That means increased standards of professionalism, creativity and presentation. While the Barclays student debt survey, now in its fifth year, has gone on journalists' calendars there is certainly no room for complacency.'

Getting on journalists' calendars itself bears witness to a continuing strand of influence. But that influence now goes much further. Having established the bank as an expert on the student market, and having a wealth of data to draw on, Barclays receives year-round calls from journalists covering the student market. Indeed, it is rare to find an in-depth story on student finances in a national newspaper that does not include a Barclays quote.

All of which proves the power of market surveys, not only as a means by which spin doctors get their clients in the papers, but as a way of identifying their clients as leaders in a particular industry sector. In fact, surveys have become so popular in recent years among corporate PR practitioners that barely a week now goes by without the release of yet another batch of research findings, packaged to create headlines. It is an educative experience to spend a few minutes scanning the broadsheet press to count the number of articles which have been written up on the basis of market research surveys created by PR people.

Does all this mean the era of the survey will soon be over? Has a once innovative idea been flogged to death? Are journalists fed up with market research? On the contrary, the media's demand for facts and figures is insatiable. Its appetite for statistics remains keen. And from the journalist's point of view, surveys will remain popular if for no other reason than that there are few stories easier to write up than those based on market research findings – the articles practically write themselves.

There are, of course, many other examples of positive platforms created by PR consultants to get their clients a favourable press. We see examples of corporate positioning and news creation daily in the news media. But what happens when corporate disaster strikes? We are not talking here about a foot-in-mouth job by a company spokesman, or some small-scale operational failure. What happens when none of the usual media rules apply? A drinks manufacturer discovers that several batches of its product are toxic – requiring the recall of every single unit from retailers up and down the country and the issue of urgent public warnings to customers. An oil cruiser runs aground, spilling millions of gallons of crude oil with devastating effect on the coastline. A jumbo jet crashes into a mountainside, killing all its passengers. Whenever a major disaster of this kind occurs there is a rather different requirement of PR. A company will suddenly find itself with literally hundreds of journalists baying for information – and if there's a scene of the disaster, they will be there. Special helplines must instantly be set up – and manned – for the tens of thousands of consumers or relatives or residents affected.

All of this is a world away from the long-term job of managing a company's financial and corporate PR; but failure to deal with a crisis effectively will undo the many years and millions of pounds invested in positive corporate PR – which is why most enlightened British companies above a certain size employ a crisis PR adviser specifically for such eventualities. When disaster strikes, chances are that somewhere in the middle of the night a telephone will ring and a strategy will be instantly demanded to deal with the crisis. And it is often the case that that telephone belongs to Michael Regester.

media pollution and crisis PR

An affable guru with a permanent suntan, smoker's voice and soothing style, Regester is a veteran of many a corporate crisis. Adviser to companies around the world, and co-author with his business partner, Judy Larkin, of *Risk Issues and Crisis Management*, a manual on how to put in place the machinery to deal with crises, Regester has been in the thick of some of the worst disasters of recent times. Crisis management was not, however, a career he was born to, but rather one thrust upon him. As an employee of the Gulf Oil Company in the late Seventies, Regester went through his baptism of fire when one of the company's carriers blew up in Bantry Bay in 1979, killing every last man on the vessel and many on the jetty. Three hundred journalists, from all over the world, rapidly congregated at the scene of the disaster within hours; relatives, environmental groups, local MPs and many others soon jammed Gulf Oil's switchboard. The company found itself ill prepared to deal with the sudden, overwhelming consequences of the disaster. For six weeks, Regester and his team averaged four hours of sleep a night as they battled to deal with the demands of the different audiences, learning as they went along.

Once the nightmare was behind him, Regester found himself invited to talk at oil industry functions about the experience, recommending the procedures which companies should put in place so that, if the unthinkable happened again, they would be better able to cope with it. When he left Gulf Oil in 1980 to set up his own PR company, he soon found his time exclusively taken up with crisis management training – and implementation.

'The calibre of a company's management comes under test in a crisis situation more than at any other time,' says Regester. 'Important decisions have to be made very quickly. And in our age of corporate responsibility, those decisions have to be *seen* to be made. It's all too easy for a company to be seen to be doing nothing or not doing something very well, even though its management may be highly focused on the problem. Perception quickly becomes reality and the damage to an organization's reputation translates directly into its share price.'

It was a perception of weak management, following its product recall crisis in 1990, that made Perrier vulnerable to takeover: the company was soon swallowed up by food giant Nestlé. Shell also suffered from perception damage arising from the question of dumping the Brent Spar rig at sea in 1995. Dr Chris Fay, chairman and chief executive of Shell UK, when cross-examined by Jeremy Paxman, responded by asking, 'Am I expected to react every day to the misinformation that the media takes in and spend all my time arguing against that misinformation while the media doesn't seem to want to take hold of the total story?'

To a chairman and chief executive, the notion of clearing one's diary for an indeterminate period of time to focus on one issue alone is patently absurd; but, reasonably or unreasonably, that's what the public expect. John Wybrew, then Shell's head of public relations (and now in charge of media relations at British Gas), later admitted that Shell had failed to understand public opinion and had underestimated the power of campaigning bodies like Greenpeace. But, significantly, he also added that political and 'emotional' factors should have been taken into account in arriving at the best practicable option: 'Businesses will now have to include in their planning not just the views and rational arguments of all concerned – whether opponents or supporters – but will also have to come to grips with an area of deep-seated emotions, sub-conscious instincts and symbolic gestures.'

The very nature of crises means that no two are ever identical. But even though the disposal of an oil platform may seem to have little, superficially, to do with a contaminated food product, there are nevertheless certain dimensions common to all crises. And at the most basic level, companies which come out particularly badly from a crisis have usually broken one of the four golden rules of crisis management. Rule number one, as we have already seen, is that the most senior management within the company must be seen to be completely committed to dealing with the problem. Secondly, coherent arguments in favour of the company's position must be distilled into simple soundbites, and repeated often. These sound-bites should encompass not only rational argument, but emotional empathy too. Thirdly, a company in a crisis must never allow an information vacuum to occur – the consequences, as we will see in a moment, will be that new, negative dimensions pop up from nowhere. And the last practical rule is that every 'at risk' com-pany should have the facilities to deal with the sudden, massive influx of telephone calls which inevitably accompanies a crisis. This isn't only about hardware and the ability to set up a 'war room' with hundreds of additional telephone lines at short notice; it is about staff training and rehearsal.

Two recent oil-spill disasters provide a fascinating insight into how a similar set of 'crisis' circumstances can be handled to very different effect. The first of these occurred when the *Braer* oil tanker smashed into the Shetland Islands in 1992. Immediately heralded by the media as another *Exxon Valdez*, after the 1989 oil-tanker spill in Alaska, within two days the disaster had brought 500 journalists to the tiny Shetland air terminal to cover the story. But gale-force winds not only made it impossible to begin oil dispersal but trapped the impatient horde of journalists in the ill-equipped terminal building.

Now, editors in newsrooms across the world wanted action. The *Braer* oil spill was a headline story. Tens of thousands of pounds of media money had been spent getting journalists on location. Stories were required. But for days the only story coming out of the daily news briefings managed by the Shetland Islands council was the same – bad weather was delaying the start of the clean-up. Reporters came under increasing pressure to come up with something – anything – that might be newsworthy. And so, in the absence of any real news, speculation and anecdote became 'reality'. Any idea for which there was even the most tenuous evidence quickly became news. It was a classic 'information vacuum', and journalists had soon filled it with stories that the Shetlands, once so popular with 'back to nature' tourists, were now splattered with carcinogenic oil. All the local salmon farms had been contaminated. Schoolchildren and sheep were being evacuated. Otters were dying in droves.

In fact, only one otter was killed – by a Norwegian camera crew's Land Rover – but this was only the start of the misinformation. It simply wasn't the case that all the islands' salmon farms were contaminated, nor was it true that the Shetlands had been grossly disfigured by the spill. But those were the stories coming out – and perceptions quickly determined reality. Within days, the salmon farms' major Japanese clients had cancelled all further orders. As for tourist revenue, well, Shetlanders could forget about that for a while. Feverish speculative headlines gripped newsrooms for days, until the *Braer* disaster was no longer fresh news – at which point the large media contingent decamped from the Shetlands as abruptly as they'd arrived and moved on to the next international story.

For Shetlanders left to cope in the wake of the spill, there was never any doubt that the media pollution had proved far more damaging than the oil pollution itself. Too late, it was realized that instead of reporters being left clutching at straws, news releases should have been issued which kept the news agenda in the hands of the local council. Journalists could have been told what measures had been taken to prepare for oil dispersal, how many helicopters had been put on standby, how much had already been done. But how many local councils, in small, remote communities in Britain, would have fared any better in managing the ferocious, all-consuming energy of the international media pack?

In marked contrast stands the *Sea Empress* disaster in Wales in February 1996. The circumstances were broadly similar – an oil-carrying vessel grounded near the coastline, with oil spilling and environmental catastrophe threatened. Here, too, poor weather conditions prevailed, and the *Sea Empress* was jammed on rocks, making salvage difficult. The hundreds of newshounds who quickly made their way down to Wales did, however, get out to the scene to see the affected coastline – but their attention was led to the clean-up operations already under way, in particular the efforts to save tens of thousands of wildfowl from a squalid death. The process by which the *Sea Empress* was to be rescued and pumped of its leaking cargo was also explained with diagrams, and cargo vessel information was provided in detail.

Nor did the Welsh Tourist Board confine itself to action being taken in the immediate here-and-now. Once the *Sea Empress* was off the rocks, the head of the board underwent an exhausting series of media interviews, getting across messages explaining how the board was doing all it could to protect the coastline, and also underlining the regenerative powers of nature. As soon as mass media attention had moved off the story, the board put into action a longer-term strategy, designed to reassure tourists, who contributed so much to the local economy that their holidays in Wales couldn't be spoiled. 'The Welsh Tourist Board acted very quickly and effectively to seize the media initiative,' says Regester. 'What's more, they showed how, even in difficult circumstances, it's possible to get positive messages across.'

It is training the client to find, and communicate, the positive messages that accounts for much of a crisis PR consultant's time. For while 'crisis PR' may be regarded by some companies as an optional extra, for 'at risk' organizations such as chemical, pharmaceutical and food manufacturers, oil companies, water utilities and hospital trusts, to name but a few, learning how to deal with disaster represents a fundamental insurance policy. Nor can this process of education remain a matter of theory alone. Once a company-specific crisis PR drill has been drawn up, usually in the form of a manual, and all the required staff have been media trained, then it's time to practise. The crisis PR consultant will, using a team of well-briefed associates, simulate a crisis. Senior management and in-house PR teams are briefed that the exercise is happening, and they are expected to respond exactly as they would to a real-life disaster. Offices are bombarded with 'hostile journalists'. Chief executives are doorstepped by cameramen thrusting microphones in their faces and demanding answers to thorny questions. Secondary crises are sometimes arranged so as to make the dry run as lifelike as possible; it has even been known for national journalists to be seconded for added authenticity. After the event, audio and video tapes are reviewed to evaluate just how well the company fared. It is very often an embarrassing process; but it is almost always a valuable learning exercise too. And, self-evidently, it is preferable to make mistakes when they can be corrected than after it is already too late.

As the demand for corporate responsibility becomes greater, with social and environmental sensitivities increasingly finely tuned, the potential for crisis of one sort or another is constantly growing. What's more, with the globalization of communications bringing crises, even in distant territories, directly into the nation's living rooms, companies need to be vigilant in every sphere of their operations – not only at home. As Andy Laurence, managing director of Hill & Knowlton Corporate, says: 'For international organizations operating in diverse political environments, a sensitive political policy will be vital in areas that could be flashpoints. The effect of getting it wrong has been all too evident in the past. Who knows, we may even see corporations developing home and foreign policy units to steer this where they have such influence on local conditions as to carry almost quasi-government status.'

But what happens when vigilance to protect against disaster and positive policy steering turn into a campaign to distort the truth? What about companies which, in the face of environmental and political sensitivities, use PR for altogether more evasive purposes? It is in this quagmire that PR becomes an instrument of perversity and deception – as Chapter 4 reveals.

why toxic sludge is good for you:
PR greenwashing

John Stauber and Sheldon Rampton had been puzzling over the issue for weeks. Co-directors of the Center for Media & Democracy in America, an organization dedicated to investigative reporting of the PR industry – happily for British PR consultants, it has no counterpart on this side of the pond – the two men had received a telephone call from their publisher. He needed, for advance advertising purposes, a title for the book they were in the middle of writing. The book was an exposé of how American PR companies manipulate the media to give their corporate clients undeservedly green credentials – a subject which evoked a plethora of possibilities. But which would grab the most attention? Which communicated most clearly? Which held the key to big sales in the bookshops?

For weeks the two men brainstormed the title and pestered their friends for suggestions. Their publisher was convinced that including the words 'public relations' in the title would 'put people right to sleep', so that cut down the options a tad. Titles such as *The Hidden Manipulators* and *The Selling of the Public Mind* went on the list of possibles, as did titles lifted from elsewhere – Arnold Schwarzenegger's 1994 film *True Lies*, and J. Edgar Hoover's classic 1950s diatribe *Masters of Deceit*.

But in the end, they drew inspiration from the 'Tom Tomorrow' cartoon shown below. Thus was born the title *Toxic Sludge is Good for You*. It was a phrase that would, with any luck, stick in people's minds – although, by going for such an extreme and cynical line, they risked the book not being taken as seriously as it deserved to be. Stauber and Rampton were not writing some joky PR spoof, but a review of serious media manipulation. Perhaps *Toxic Sludge is Good for You* would fail to get this across; after all, wasn't it the most exaggerated parody of deceptive public relations?

Apparently not. The book hadn't even hit the shelves when the two authors received a telephone call from Nancy Blatt, a public relations executive with America's Water Environment Federation.

Blatt had seen advance notice of the book's publication and was worried that it might interfere with the federation's ambitious plans to transform the image of sewage sludge.

'It's not toxic,' she said, 'and we're launching a campaign to get people to stop calling it sludge. We call it "biosolids". It can be used beneficially to fertilize farm fields, and we see nothing wrong with that. We've got a lot of work ahead to educate the public on the value of biosolids ... Why don't you change the title to *Smoking is Good for You?*'

The effectiveness of Britain's invisible persuaders at manipulating what appears in the media has, I hope, already been demonstrated. But whereas one might take the breezy view that 'all's fair in love and war' when it comes to PLC battles and financial PR, the ethics of broader, corporate PR pose far more difficult dilemmas. What happens when a company's interests don't coincide with the public interest? What happens, in fact, when a company's activities directly *conflict* with the public interest, whether in the matter of toxic sludge disposal, the manufacture of agrichemicals with deadly side-effects or the destruction of rainforests?

It is at this point that the influence of corporate spin doctors can be at its most sinister. Using the medium of apparent editorial independence to communicate their own messages, their job is to turn public opinion in favour of clients whose activities may be unethical, dangerous and quite literally poisonous. Some of the world's largest PR firms are extremely experienced in using powerful arsenals of persuasive techniques to subvert the inconvenient truth, to marginalize organizational critics, to create the appearance of mainstream support and to communicate an entirely distorted impression of their client's true motives and activities. For military dictators, cigarette manufacturers, arms dealers or chemical combines wreaking havoc on the environment, there will always be a spin doctor somewhere in the wings who, for his thirty pieces of silver, will work to bestow on his client an image of respectability.

In 1976, shortly after General Jorge Rafael Videla seized power in a *coup d'état* in Argentina, Burson Marsteller, one of the world's largest PR firms, accepted a contract from him to improve Argentina's image abroad and boost inward investment. During Videla's reign of terror, 35,000 people disappeared and hundreds were subjected to the most barbaric torture, including having rats put to feed on open wounds and being raped by police dogs. As Joyce Nelson revealed in her book *Sultans of Sleaze*, while all this was going on, leaked documents from BM showed that the multi-national PR firm was working to 'generate a sensation of confidence in Argentina . . . through projecting an aura of stability for the nation, its government and its economy'.

Washington PR firm Gray & Company took on the murderous 'Baby Doc' Duvalier in Haiti on the basis that: 'The government of Haiti, rank it wherever you will . . . has the right to try to tell its side of whatever the story is to the media . . . By definition, people who hire lobbyists and PR people have problems, they have fears, and they have needs.' This justification suggests that, in the court-room of public opinion, all clients have the right to public relations counsel. In fact, precisely this metaphor is used by Steve Ellis of Burson Marsteller in London. Says Ellis: 'I take the view that every-one has a right to a view and our job is to help clients say what they need to say. If Saddam Hussein came to me, I would take him on as a client, on the basis that as professional communicators we should at least help him get his message across. The *Sun* called him a "mad dog". By helping him communicate his message, if he is a "mad dog" that would come out.'

But the argument for the PR consultant as barrister is deeply flawed – for, unlike what goes on in a courtroom, the partisan nature of PR is not clear for all to see: the influence of public relations is utterly invisible. There is no overseeing judicial authority to decide what does, and does not, constitute fair play. What's more, PR consultants don't merely tidy up their clients' grammar when rolling them out in front of the media. They reposition them in order to promote positive attributes and suppress inconvenient truths. How ethical – let alone practical – is it, really, to attempt to win public support for a client who is unquestionably guilty of genocide and cruelty on a spectacular scale and whose idea of a good time is to go down to the central gaol in Baghdad and torture his opponents to death?

Another justification for taking on the clients who are ethically challenged – again drawing an analogy with the Bar – is known as the 'cab-rank principle'. While the PR consultant may not particularly like the look of his next client, so the notion goes, it is his duty as a professional to provide any paying client with the value of his objective advice. But PR consultants are just not like London cabbies, and don't have to pick up whoever is next in the queue. What's more, the competition for new business between consultants is fierce – in almost every case, if one PR consultant isn't happy at the prospect of servicing a client, there will be ten others ready to leap into his place with alacrity – so, all other things being equal, the client who finds it hard to secure PR representation should instantly be a source of suspicion. As Charles Miller, chairman of the Association of Professional Political Consultants, says: 'The right to justice is one thing. But there isn't any right to PR.'

All this brings us to the unsurprising conclusion that what constitutes ethical acceptability varies enormously from one PR consultancy to another. In 1996 British lobbying firm GJW accepted a contract to work for Libya. Outed in *The Times*, the company wrote a letter to the newspaper stating that it was not working on an image-building campaign for dictator Gaddafi, but rather was working for the British–Libyan Business Group. It did, however, admit to a monitoring contract with the Libyan authorities as a 'subsidiary' part of the contract. Robert Gray, writing in *PR Week*, commented: 'The impression created is that GJW would rather this particular account had not been made public . . . Its case has not been helped by the fact that at least two other lobby firms were approached by the Libyans and, for ethical reasons, turned them down.'

Other pariah governments, including those of Nigeria and Iran, have sought PR consultants in Britain in recent times. A high-level political spin doctor, who did not want to be named, described the unexpected visit to his office one day of the son of a high-ranking

Iranian leader: 'He hadn't made an appointment. He just arrived in our offices and demanded to see me. I think he'd read my name in a paper somewhere. When he came up to my office he wouldn't sit down. Instead he prowled about the place like a caged tiger and kept on repeating the same thing: "I want you to tell me how to control the people. I need to control the people." There was no doubt in my mind – the guy was quite loopy. Nuts.' Suffice it to say, the spin doctor confessed he was unable to help his Iranian guest.

Military dictatorships should not cause spin doctors too much heart-searching. Most in the PR industry would agree that representing a Gaddaffi, Rafsanjani or Saddam is a non-starter, if for no other reason than that, once revealed, it would damage their chances of winning other business. But there are many more swampy areas where the ethical terra firma is less easy to define. Lord Chadlington, chairman of Shandwick International, writing in a think-piece for *PR Week*, pointed some of these out. Should spin doctors refuse to work for a tobacco firm which is diversifying, making itself less dependent on the products to which they object? Should they work for a subsidiary of a conglomerate which has other subsidiaries working in other geographical areas to which there are ethical objections? And what happens in the case of a global PR consultancy with fifty offices around the world – should HQ in London impose its own decisions on all offices, irrespective of local cultures and mores? The ethics of PR is by no means an easy area, although, as Lord Chadlington himself concedes, 'on issues that really matter – both of principle and of practicality – we [i.e. the PR industry] have often put pragmatism before all else.'

suffer from asthma? light up a cigarette!

Pragmatism, or simple greed, has been a powerful motive force behind PR in the case of one industry in particular. Ever since the birth of PR in America, tobacco companies have pumped countless millions into advertising and PR operations throughout the world in a series of communications campaigns. First there was the battle to exhort non-smokers to smoke; then the battle to persuade smokers to switch brands. When the grim messages about lung cancer and foetal damage were first heard, the battle was to dispute them, using phoney science. And with the evidence no longer open to serious dispute, the current battle is to stop legislation preventing smokers exercising their 'democratic freedom of choice' in smoking.

It is a supreme irony that, in PR terms, the tobacco industry has come full circle. It was the 'Father of PR', Edward Bernays, who masterminded that classic in the annals of PR: a contingent of New York debutantes marching down Fifth Avenue in the 1929 Easter Parade, openly lighting and smoking cigarettes. Up till then, the only women who smoked in public were prostitutes. Now, here were America's most youthful and glamorous breaking the taboo against cigarette smoking with a 'torches of liberty' march. It was only *after* the parade that Bernays admitted he'd been paid a handsome fee to set up the march by George Washington Hill, the president of American Tobacco Company. As PR stunts go, however, it could not have been better calculated: within months, sales of Hill's Lucky Strikes had reached stratospheric levels as the ladies of America exercised their new-found 'freedom' by lighting up.

Since then, PR companies have used all manner of psychological ploys to urge people to take up the deadly habit, from reminding young women that smoking keeps them slim to suggesting to older men that smoking keeps them virile. All over the world, front groups have been set up to promote 'smokers' rights': in America, the powerful National Smokers Alliance (NSA) has an army of 3 million committed foot soldiers ready to rally to the cause of tobacco companies whenever they are under congressional threat. The origin of this massive 'grass-roots' army? Burson Marsteller, the PR company which works for tobacco giant Philip Morris and masterminded the well-funded NSA. Just as Bernays used the invocation of democratic values with his 'torches of liberty' march through New York to encourage smoking – and thereby prop up the fortunes of his client – now it has fallen to Burson Marsteller to act in the name of democracy. Current NSA literature describes anti-smokers as 'anti-Americans' and tells its members: 'If "Anti" America is pushing a discriminatory smoking ban in your work-place, speak up' and 'check the laws in your state with regard to the protection of individual rights'.

Britain's answer to the NSA is a lobby group called 'Forest' – Freedom Organization for the Right to Enjoy Smoking Tobacco. Forest's stated objectives are 'to promote equal rights for smokers and greater tolerance between smokers and non-smokers', to oppose discrimination against smokers and, significantly, 'to increase public awareness of the scientific complexities of the smoking debate, and to enable people to put the issue into its proper perspective'. One does not have to enquire too closely to understand Forest's real objectives, however. When pressed, the organization will admit it is funded by tobacco companies – its accounting records show that 90 per cent of its income is from this source – but is highly secretive about which ones: 'that's entirely our business,' snaps a Forest spokeswoman. Financing an in-dependent body which will give voice to one's own messages is a standard PR ploy, and the tobacco industry uses Forest to do just that. Forest puts out a regular magazine called *Free Choice*, which contains a bizarre editorial mix including exhortations to its members to light up on 'National Health Fascists Day' ('National No Smoking Day' to the rest of us), and breezily cynical articles about health scares with opening lines like, 'I have survived into early middle-age through the simple method of taking care to ignore all official health advice.'

More serious are the 'fact sheets' Forest produces, which contra-dict much of the received medical wisdom about smoking. Forest challenges the idea that smoking causes premature death by pro-viding mortality rates for countries with a higher incidence of cigarette smoking than Britain. What it does not do is fully explain that there are any number of variables which determine longevity, of which smoking is but one. Forest also tries to debunk the idea that passive smoking can bring on asthmatic attacks. In fact, it goes even further: 'There are still asthmatics who maintain that smoking relieves their symptoms,' declares Forest. 'Surely they should know?'

Forest has harsh words for those who advocate a ban on cigarette advertising.

> The advocates of tobacco censorship share many of the popular, but mistaken, myths about advertising in general. They act as if advertising somehow coerces people, and *makes* them do things. But all individuals have free will, and if people's actions were really determined by outside forces, they would be mindless automatons obeying the countless injunctions of the advertisers of every commercial – or indeed political or religious or health – message aimed at them. And this is clearly not the case.

This classic rhetorical ruse takes the argument against Forest to ridiculous extremes in an attempt to dispute it. No advertising agency would claim that advertisements *make* consumers do anything. But if they didn't *influence* consumer behaviour, why would British companies spend £11 billion a year on advertising?

Unfortunately for Forest, the whistle was blown on many of its arguments by none other than a tobacco company: Liggett Group, manufacturers of Chesterfields and one of the world's 'big five' cigarette manufacturers. In March 1997 the US-based Liggett became the first major manufacturer to admit that smoking is addictive and causes cancer, emphysema and other lung-based diseases. It was a landmark moment, prompting the reaction from Mike Moore, Mississippi's attorney-general, that: 'This is the beginning of the end of the conspiracy of lies and deception perpetuated by the tobacco companies on the American public.' Liggett's admission wasn't brought about by the sudden conversion of its boss, Bennet LeBow, to religion, but for far more practical reasons. In common with all the major tobacco companies in America, Liggett had been paying massive legal fees – $10 million a year in round terms – to defend itself against litigation by anti-tobacco groups. Liggett, smallest of the 'big five' tobacco firms, could least afford to keep this up. So it did a deal with the Mississippi attorney-general, agreeing to hand over to anti-tobacco litigants internal documents about the risk of smoking and further agreeing to pay 25 per cent of Liggett's profits for the next twenty-five years to settle the legal proceedings under way. In so doing, Liggett let the genie out of a bottle which the tobacco industry has kept firmly corked since health fears about smoking were first expressed. This liberated genie will make even more difficult the objectives of groups such as Forest, to perpetuate the shameful suggestions that there is no direct link between smoking and pre-mature death.

In Britain, Burson Marsteller runs the Philip Morris account out of its offices in Bloomsbury. PR giant Charles Barker manages the account of BAT; Greenwood Tighe conducts promotions on behalf of Silk Cut; the Imperial Tobacco PR account is held by Michael Joyce Consultants Ltd. While there is, of course, absolutely nothing stopping any PR agency from taking on a tobacco com-pany as its client, one can't help puzzling at the paradox presented by the discovery that these PR agencies are all members of the Public Relations Consultants Association (PRCA), a body which strives to improve the professionalism and public standing of the PR industry. Part of the PRCA charter, to which members sub-scribe, is the undertaking that 'a member firm shall conduct its professional activities with proper regard to the public interest'. Exactly how, one wonders, can the promotion of companies whose products cause disease and premature death be described as an activity undertaken with 'proper regard to the public interest'?

Steve Ellis, who heads up the Philip Morris account at Burson Marsteller, has no qualms: 'Tobacco isn't the only industry that's controversial,' he says. 'Nearly all industries have some kind of controversy attached to them – meat, water, pharmaceutical companies. The tobacco industry is perfectly legitimate. It pro-duces a product which, to my knowledge, is legally available in every country of the world. Tobacco companies operate under normal law. If a government wants to ban cigarettes then it can. Our job is to help a tobacco company say what it needs to say.'

Imperial Tobacco's PR, Jacqui Delbaere of Michael Joyce Consultants, positively bristles at the suggestion that defending a tobacco company might not be properly regarding the public interest: 'That's not a question I've been asked, and one I would want to consider. I wouldn't want to answer it now,' she tells me. I ask her when she would like to give me an answer. 'Leave it to me and I'll consider it,' she says. 'I'll get back to you at some point.' Of course, I never heard from her again, and as I put down the phone I couldn't help marvelling at her response. One of the first pieces of advice PR people give their clients in media training is always at least to *appear* to be open and willing to help.

Sue Souter of Greenwood Tighe is the most straightforward of all in responding to the public interest question. She explains to me that while her agency's work for Silk Cut had only been on a project basis, she would welcome the opportunity to work with the client again: 'We are a commercial organization and we take decisions based on the commercial value of a client to the company, not because we want to educate people. In PR agencies there are always pressures for you to take on business in order to reach new business targets – in general, the bigger the brand and the higher the profile, the bigger the budget. I personally don't smoke but I wouldn't turn down business on the basis of my own personal, ethical views.'

It would be interesting to hear the views of PR companies which have, in fact, turned down tobacco companies as clients for ethical reasons. This proves to be a difficult exercise, however, because several of the major tobacco multinationals are known to require potential PR consultants to sign a confidentiality agreement so strict that the consultants can't even mention at a later stage the fact that they were approached by the tobacco company, even if they turned down the offer to work for it. One PR company, in just such a position, rejected the huge monthly fee it would have gained from winning the business on the basis of ethics. 'We canvassed opinion at every level of the consultancy,' a spokesperson told me. 'The general consensus was that we didn't want to take the bent penny. Surprisingly, the strongest opposition came from several of the smokers who felt they didn't want to do anything that might encourage the next generation, their children, to think of taking up the habit.'

the growth of greenwashing

The ethics of tobacco-industry PR will, like the ethics of promoting smoking itself, continue to be a subject of heated debate to which there is no conclusive answer, only individual points of view. But in one sense the growing awareness of the dangers of smoking, both active and passive, is symptomatic of a much broader trend: the awakening of environmental awareness. At a popular level this awakening was a phenomenon of the mid- to late 1980s, arising from the almost simultaneous outbreak of concerns on the part of scientists, consumer groups and sociologists on a wide range of issues, all of which produced a growing realization of the damage being caused to the environment by activities we took for granted. The destruction of the ozone layer by CFCs present in aerosol sprays; global warming caused by emissions from cars; the destruction of the earth's 'green lungs' to make way for cattle ranches – these and many other horrors suddenly loomed into public consciousness.

Tapping the same vein of concern that we were no longer living in a certain world were the consumer scares – still a feature of our lives today. All of a sudden a wide variety of foods were revealed to contain preservatives, artificial flavourings and colourants, pesticides and growth hormones that, over a period of time, could harm people's health. There was evidence that the electromagnetic fields surrounding power pylons could cause cancer, that microwave ovens posed a long-term health hazard, and that every trip in an aeroplane is accompanied by a doze of radiation equivalent to having an X-ray.

What is most striking about environmental awareness is the speed with which it has moved from being the vocation of the beard-and-thong brigade into the mainstream of public life. Of course, activist groups like Greenpeace and Friends of the Earth continue to be highly effective at raising awareness of issues and marshalling public support. But the reason why they are so effective is that they appeal to an intuitive recognition in the public psyche that we cannot go on for ever wreaking havoc on the world's environment, exploiting its finite resources and using artificial – albeit cost-effective and convenient – means of production without any thought to the longer-term consequences. The implications of this recognition for big business have, of course, been extremely serious.

One leading spin doctor who didn't wish to be named told me:

> In the early days the whole green agenda became an ongoing nightmare for my biggest clients. To be frank, they were terrified of having the whistle blown. They could have been caught out on all kinds of issues. They were extremely vulnerable. The green movement had the effect of banging a lot of important heads together and what came out was a major change in approach to image. Corporate livery and packaging was changed to look more environmentally friendly. Whole marketing programmes were looked at to see how they could be made greener. We did sponsorship of environment-type events and have got involved in conferences. It's no good just having green marketing – the whole organization has to understand the importance of looking and acting green.
>
> But the basic reality hasn't changed. The company is still vulnerable, only it doesn't look or feel it. The environmental issues haven't gone away. They are like time bombs ticking away down there in the cellar. The thing is, they can't be sorted out unless whole companies are changed out of recognition. And no chief executive can expect his shareholders to accept that.

This is the dilemma faced by much of corporate Britain: the conflict between environmental consciousness and financial expediency. According to a survey sponsored by environmental consultants Entec in association with the Green Alliance in March 1997: 'The business case [for environmental improvements] seems far from proven with costs of implementation still seen as a major barrier to investing in environmental programmes.' It is for this reason that one of the most pernicious uses of public relations has arisen – greenwashing.

Greenwashing is the process whereby a company, rather than earning a green reputation, buys one. It can involve anything from simple window-dressing to undertaking a much more fundamental shift in opinions towards issues and industries. As Kenny Bruno writes in *The Greenpeace Guide to Greenwash*:

> A leader in ozone destruction takes credit for being a leader in ozone protection. A giant oil company professes to take a 'precautionary approach' to global warming. A major agrochemical manufacturer trades in a pesticide so hazardous it has been banned in many countries while implying that the company is helping to feed the hungry . . . This is greenwash, where transnational companies are preserving and expanding their markets by posing as friends of the environment and leaders in the struggle to eradicate poverty.

Of course, this is a one-sided view. The only way for a giant oil company to ensure it didn't cause any global warming would be to cease trading, and commercial suicide is not a realistic expectation of any company, however noble the calling. But at the same time, Greenpeace raises a valid point: so much corporate crowing goes on about improvements in environmental performance that consumers are being distracted from the reality of the huge environmental damage still being caused.

By the late 1980s, environmental group Friends of the Earth had become so frustrated by the scope and scale of corporate greenwashing that they set up their own 'Green Con Awards' to draw attention to companies which it considered were misleading the public on ecological issues. Past winners have included organizations such as Fisons, British Nuclear Fuels Ltd, Shell and ICI. The 1991 winner, Fisons, which was at the time a massive gardening-products-to-pharmaceuticals conglomerate, sold peat-based compost throughout Britain. Its PR machinery assured consumers that 'buying British peat-based compost in no way endangers our remaining wetlands of conservation value'. However, Friends of the Earth discovered that 90 per cent of Fisons' peat-cutting operations were on protected areas – or Sites of Special Scientific Interest.

ICI, one of Britain's largest chemical companies, has also been known to indulge in greenwashing. In April 1993 it ran misleading advertising in Malaysia claiming that one of its pesticides, Paraquat, was environmentally friendly and worked 'in perfect harmony with nature'. Its advertisements carried images of lush, rural scenes with palm trees, birds and flowers. In fact, a survey of Malaysian plantation workers conducted by the Pesticides Action Network in 1992 showed that after using Paraquat 90 per cent of workers reported skin rashes in varying degrees of severity, while others frequently reported complaints including vomiting, muscular weaknesses, sore eyes, coughing and discoloured nails. Hundreds of Malaysian plantation workers have been reported as dying of Paraquat poisoning – the pesticide is highly toxic and has no known antidote. It is freely available in Malaysia and, according to the Pesticides Trust, is responsible for a large number of suicides.

ICI's record at home leaves much to be desired, too. An exposé by the *Sunday Times* Insight team in June 1997 showed that, according to the Environmental Agency, ICI's Merseyside chemical factory is Britain's most poisonous plant, having broken environmental rulings no fewer than 472 times in two years, sometimes releasing toxic chemicals into neighbouring communities. A study conducted by the universities of Newcastle-upon-Tyne, Durham and Teesside in conjunction with the health authority and two local authorities found that levels of lung cancer among women under the age of sixty-five living close to the main industrial areas of Teesside (including ICI's Wilton plant) were four times higher than the national average during 1981–91. Past exposure to high levels of industrial pollution was viewed as the most plausible explanation for this finding. In its own glossy environmental literature, however, ICI says, 'We remain close to our goal of total compliance with local regulations and consents, wherever we operate.'

Greenwashing has so quickly become an integral part of corporate and product marketing that consumers now expect reassurance that the products and services they use are environmentally friendly. Greenwashing has become part of the advertising and PR landscape. Thus unleaded petrol, in that cheerful, green-striped pump, is heralded as 'environmentally friendly' fuel, even though it contains more of the carcinogen benzene than leaded fuel, not to mention a host of other pollutants including carbon monoxide, hydrocarbons and carbon dioxide. Cars, which are the fastest-growing cause of pollution on the planet, once equipped with catalytic converters apparently become green – some manufacturers even claim that they clean the atmosphere!

Quite apart from creating a false impression of their environmental impact, greenwashing also portrays these changes as the results of constant endeavour on the part of manufacturers to strive towards ever greater heights of environmental friendliness. The reality is rather different. For years motor vehicle companies lobbied against the introduction of unleaded fuel, catalytic converters or any increase in fuel efficiency. They also fought hard against airbags. Changes were brought about not by the companies themselves, but because they were imposed by legislation. But once they had been imposed, companies were, of course, quick to claim credit for their new, greener credentials.

The efforts by corporate Britain to lay claim to the moral high ground on environmental issues involve more than simple re-packaging, or legislative game-playing. At a far deeper level a collective, though not necessarily concerted, campaign is under way to effect a paradigm shift in the way that the public views the environmental movement. Chip Berlet, of Political Research Associates, describes this paradigm shift as 'a major negative change in the way the public perceives the political movement that is ultimately victimized'. Berlet studied the impact of American Rachel Carson's 1962 ecological bombshell *Silent Spring*, a book which in many ways might be regarded as the start of the modern environmental movement, and which blew the lid off the dangers of using a number of agrichemicals, most notably the pesticide DDT, which had been in widespread use since the end of the Second World War. When it was published, the book sent shock waves through the American public, government and agrichemical industry. A momentum of concern about DDT built up over a period of years to the point where it broke out in protests, rallies and marches. The agrichemical industry reacted by doubling its PR budget, distributing thousands of book reviews trashing *Silent Spring* and taking every opportunity to bring about a paradigm shift. As Berlet says:

> Those who oppose pesticides and believe DDT is unsafe reject science; are affiliated with 'environmental hypochondria'; circulate 'apocalyptic, tabloid charges'; have 'no evidence' for their 'hysterical predictions'; use 'gross manipulation' to fool the media; are 'unscrupulous, Luddite fund-raisers'; suffer 'knee-jerk, chemophobic rejection of pesticides' and create 'vast and needless costs' for consumers. But those who support DDT are 'pro-science and pro-logic'; have support from the 'real scientific community – the community of controlled studies, double blind experiments and peer review'; and 'help US consumers and farmers save money'.

In the end, the deadly effects of DDT became undeniable and the pesticide was banned in America, as indeed it was in Britain in 1964 (although use of DDT globally is currently at an all-time high). By the time these bans were imposed, however, agrichemical manufacturers had attempted to buy a perceptual paradigm shift through the concerted use of public relations.

In order to effect such a shift, according to American spin doctor Ronald Duchin, activists have to be defeated using a three-step divide-and-conquer strategy. Activists, he says, fall into four distinct categories: 'radicals', 'opportunists', 'idealists' and 'realists'. Any corporation looking to silence its critics has to isolate the radicals, cultivate and educate the idealists into becoming realists, and then co-opt the realists into agreeing with it.

The process by which realists become supporters and idealists are 'educated' involves a number of tried and tested tactics. Quite apart from co-opting the language of the environmental movement by marketing themselves and their products as greener than green, companies will frequently set up trade organizations that have eco-friendly names. What better name for a tobacco lobby than Forest? Oil companies wishing to reassure the public that they are committed to cracking the problem of global warming meantime have the pick of three grand, eco-sounding coalitions to choose from – the Global Climate Coalition, the Climate Council and the International Climate Change Partnership – each of them appearing to represent the vested interests of their sponsors. Internationally there are many others, ranging from the Coalition of Responsible Environmentalists to the Soil & Water Conservation Society.

Some organizations will go one step further and create green business networks, or GBNs, which give the appearance of committing members to voluntary codes of conduct in an attempt to escape mandatory regulation. Says Andrew Rowell, author of the book *Green Backlash*: 'By advocating policing itself, with schemes of voluntary oversight, industry aims to pre-empt regulations . . . The most important GBN is the Business Council for Sustainable Development (BCSD), which was formed by the largest global public relations company Burson Marsteller and worked to such devastating effect at the [Rio] Earth Summit.'

Finding friendly well-intentioned scientists and paying them to conduct research, the results of which are guaranteed to please, is another means by which corporations the world over seek to validate their green credentials, one designed to appeal to both 'realists' and 'idealists'. Sometimes scientists will be members of the front groups set up by a company's PR consultancy, their purpose to provide basic campaign fodder – studies and statistics – which support its position. Third-party endorsement is the first desideratum of all good PR, and white-coated figures bearing clipboards of figures are so much more believable than sharp-suited corporate executives. Similarly, university lecturers are much used to provide an aura of academic gravitas. And renting a peer of the realm, while quaintly anachronistic, especially in the context of the environmental debate, is also a ploy used by corporate ventriloquists. It is no coincidence that scientists, academics and several peers of the realm feature in the membership of Forest's supporters and advisory councils – as did a number of MPs, including Teresa Gorman and Dr Sir Rhodes Boyson. This is not to say that high-profile supporters of Forest are dupes or charlatans – simply that they carry far more public influence, on the subject of smoking, than would the press officer of a cigarette manufacturer. How convenient for Forest's main sponsors!

The isolation of radicals is, of course, a well-worn technique in campaigns against them. Environmentalists are fairly easy to demonize as socialists, fascists or fanatics of some other kind. And presenting the most unattractive face of a valid campaign is a trap into which environmental lobbyists fall time after time. It is easy to detest the ragged, hairy and probably extremely smelly protesters who tie themselves to trees and tunnel underground in vain attempts to stop motorways or runways being built across the countryside. They are, all too clearly, unlike you and me, and probably can't drive cars and don't use aircraft anyway. However, in dismissing these extremist factions, many of whose members disdain organizations like Greenpeace and Friends of the Earth as being too 'middle of the road', it is easy to make the mistake of dismissing from mind whatever it is they are protesting about – which is precisely what their opponents hope for most. The more extreme their green critics, the easier they are to present as ludicrous even though their arguments, more effectively presented, might well strike a public chord.

the 'green backlash'

Corporate Britain has been extremely successful at dealing with the environmental movement by using the various techniques described above. In these politically correct times, when companies have to display greater transparency and accountability in all that they do, against a background of increased awareness and legislation on environmental issues, a very real public paradigm shift has nevertheless been effected. Not only is there a sense that environmental issues are being responsibly managed, but, more than this, there is an increasingly prevalent view that the eco-scares of the late Eighties were a product of exaggerated doom-mongering. The sky has not yet fallen in, so what was all the fuss about?

Andrew Rowell points to 1995 as a critical year for the green lobby: 'In the spring of 1995, ironically the European Year of Conservation, the green backlash hit Britain. "Greenlash" or "ecobacklash" as some journalists called it, and the views of the "contrarians", was suddenly the new Zeitgeist. "It's now very fashionable to be very questioning about green issues," said Michael Grubb of the Royal Institute for International Affairs.'

While the origins of the green backlash were broadly based, media commentary was focused on three books debunking the green movement which were published in quick succession in 1995. Dr Wilfred Beckerman, Emeritus Fellow of Balliol College, Oxford, in his work *Small is Stupid: Blowing the Whistle on the Greens*, attacked 'semi-hysterical eco-doomsters' and their 'pseudo-scientific scare stories'. Matt Ridley, in *Down to Earth: A Contrarian View of Environmental Problems*, labelled environmentalists 'Gestapo' and their arguments as old socialism dressed in new clothes. But probably the most substantial volume weighing in against the greens was Richard North's book *Life on a Modern Planet: A Manifesto for Progress*. Apart from pointing out that some of the gloomiest predictions made by environmental activists had failed to be realized, North also questioned the extent of global warming, as well as criticisms of genetic engineering and biotechnology. North received funding for his book from none other than ICI, which, along with other players in the global chemical industry, has been gearing up its attack on Greenpeace and other environmental organizations.

As the contents of these three books were duly picked over by the media, Greenpeace meanwhile embarrassed itself over the Brent Spar debacle. Greenpeace's high-profile campaign in April

1995 to prevent Shell dumping the decommissioned oil rig in the North Sea had used extremely successful media relations tactics, including taking up occupation of the rig in the full glare of national television cameras with meticulous timing, ensuring the news would break on peak viewer broadcasts. The organization was very effective at mobilizing public sentiment against the idea of dumping the rig at sea and, despite Shell's protestations that that was the most environmentally sensitive option from a scientific perspective, on 20 June 1995 the oil company was forced to do a U-turn on its plans. Journalists, particularly in television, had a field day following the Brent Spar saga; but no sooner had it apparently reached a conclusion when some of the figures which Greenpeace had used to support its arguments were shown to be wrong. Greenpeace had the sense to apologize to Shell when the truth emerged, thus denying their opponents the chance to portray the organization as secretive and manipulative, but even so, Shell was handed the PR advantage on a plate. Now it was able to argue as it had all along, but with greater conviction, that the PR battle had been one of science versus emotion. Shell could take the moral high ground and present itself as the voice of reasoned sanity in the face of emotional extremism. As Shell's Christopher Fay said: 'The real issue is . . . do you want to take a balanced view to the environment, or do you want to succumb to a separate and single issue, which says that perhaps the sea is clean but we don't actually mind if people die, or the land is dirty or whatever, but this single issue is fundamental. I am sorry, but I think society, if we are going to have sustainability, has really got to take a balanced view on the environment.'

Now the media turned on Greenpeace, claiming the organization had used them. Greenpeace was accused by the *Daily Telegraph* of 'environmental jihad', and by the *Financial Times* of 'eco-terrorism'; Tim Eggar, the energy minister, was furious with Greenpeace for its 'scare-mongering'. Also weighing in against Greenpeace were a number of right-wing think-tanks which had long been opponents of the environmental lobby in general. The Adam Smith Institute strongly opposes the green movement and had published an *Environmental Alphabet* whose author, Russell

Lewis, former general director of the Institute of Economic Affairs, another free-market think-tank, wrote that the environmental scares being perpetuated by the likes of Greenpeace were 'on a par with pixies, sea monsters and weather gods'. Advocating a free market as the solution to environmental problems, Lewis went so far as arguing for the relegalization of DDT! The IEA, meanwhile, had launched its own publication, *Global Warming: Apocalypse or Hot Air?*, in which environmentalists were labelled 'eco-doomsters' and the whole process of global warming was questioned.

The varied assaults of journalists, anti-green scientists and right-wing think-tanks, combined with Greenpeace's high-profile shooting itself in the foot and the success with which the major corporate perpetrators of environmental damage have green-washed their activities, leave the green movement in a difficult position today. Andrew Rowell tries to be upbeat: 'The green backlash, though, has to be seen in a positive light, because if the environmental movement absorbs the right lessons it will start the next millennium in a much better shape than it finished this one. The backlash must force the movement to re-evaluate itself and realize that it has not run out of ideas, it has not run its course, but it is still in danger of running out of time.'

One of the ways in which Rowell says the green movement has to beat the backlash is by starting to put forward solutions and positive alternatives for the future. This, of course, is fundamental to the maturation of the green lobby if it is to be regarded in the future as a movement with a positive contribution to make, rather than as bands of carping activists who criticize loudly from the sidelines in the happy knowledge that they don't have the responsibility of having to deliver practical solutions to real dilemmas.

Where does all this leave the PR industry in the green debate? It would be naïve to expect anything but more of the same. Many public relations people, whether in-house or on the consultancy side, will continue to create and implement strategies for their corporate clients proclaiming their environmentally friendly conduct – which has often been brought about through legislation rather than free choice. On occasion they will continue to use front groups, dubious research, hired scientists – albeit who write in good fath – co-opted environmentalists and any other credible apologists that come to hand to reinforce corporate green credentials. And they will, as a matter of course, do their very best to steer media and public attention well clear of fundamental environmental issues such as ozone depletion, global warming, food toxins and radiation, which threaten the very existence of their clients.

PR executives will do this not because they are wicked or stupid. They will do it because PR is how they make their living, and 'green' messages constitute only one part of any particular company's overall communications agenda. It is terribly easy, in the frenetic round that is the lot of most PR consultants, to lose sight of the implications of what one is doing. There are deadlines to beat, journalists to meet and one's constant preoccupation is whether the client is happy. Even if one does stand back from day-to-day toil and come to the conclusion that the activities one is carrying out really are ethically questionable, there is one simple imperative for carrying on: money.

Money is at the heart of the green backlash. Corporate power, which derives from financial power, is the real threat to the environment. As John Stauber comments: 'All the environmental organizations together will never have a budget for public relations equal to that of even a single major manufacturer of pesticides. The polluter will always be able to outspend and outgun the environmentalists, and can bring virtually an unlimited amount of propaganda and lobbypower to an issue, simply by writing a larger cheque or reaching out to other businesses similarly threatened by reform.'

Huge multinationals with massive war chests don't only have the resources to conduct continuous proactive public relations programmes. They have the wherewithal to sue their corporate critics into silence. In fact, in many cases the mere threat of legal action is enough to stop environmental opponents from speaking out. But this isn't always the case, as we will see in the next chapter.

CHAPTER FIVE

don't beef about mcdonald's

One of the biggest PR disasters in recent times, where a major multinational company tried to suppress its green critics and got it badly wrong, was the 'McLibel' case. Two London-based environmental activists dared to accuse massive fast-food merchant McDonald's of a number of environmental crimes; when the corporate giant tried to sue them to silence, its efforts rebounded in spectacular style.

McDonald's is the largest food retailer in the world, with 21,000 stores in over 100 countries generating annual sales of over $30 billion. It is the world's largest single buyer of potatoes, beef and chicken and has taken over from the US Army as the West's largest staff trainer – one in ten Americans gets their first job under the golden arches. For some years McDonald's has used a two-pronged strategy to project a caring and environmentally sensitive image. On the one hand it has at its disposal a colossal worldwide marketing budget, estimated to be in the area of $2 billion annually, part of which is used to ensure that any messages about how the company sources its meat, poultry and other products show it in the greenest possible light. On the other hand, it cracks down hard on anyone who suggests that its corporate propaganda is in any way at variance with the facts. In Britain it has been helped enormously by the country's libel laws. Given that the laws and court procedures are extremely complex, that the legal costs of a libel case are huge, that the outcome of a libel case is as much of a gamble as a game of Russian roulette, and that there is no legal aid available for those fighting a libel case, it is usually enough for a corporate giant simply to threaten a libel suit for its critics to be abruptly silenced. The message is simple: apologize or risk losing the shirt off your back.

McDonald's has, in the words of the *Guardian*, 'a notoriously, unhealthy litigious appetite' and in the UK has, through its legal strong-arm tactics, silenced a wide variety of critics ranging from national media outlets such as Channel 4, the BBC, the *Guardian* and the *Independent*, to other organizations such as the Scottish TUC, the MSF union and the Vegetarian Society.

Where McDonald's went wrong in trying to silence the two environmentalist protesters was that it failed to take into account the fact that they were both deeply committed activists who, financially, had nothing to lose. To return to Duchin's model of dealing with 'radicals', instead of being content merely to isolate them – as indeed it did, when three of their colleagues apologized to McDonald's and effectively backed down – it continued with a heavy-handed persecution approach. The result was instantly to transform the two from common or garden green activists into heroes of the environmental movement, to inject huge impetus into an anti-McDonald's campaign throughout Britain and to create a David *v.* Goliath courtroom confrontation which attracted massive media interest.

To make matters even worse, the case the media quickly dubbed the McLibel Trial, which began on 28 June 1994, became the longest libel case in British history in March 1995, then the longest civil case in December 1995, and finally the longest trial of any kind in English history on 2 November 1996. As the two activists were required to prove the basis of their various accusations, the company's most embarrassing dirty laundry was aired in the national media – some of it was produced, more embarrassingly still, by McDonald's expert witnesses under cross-examination. Closing speeches were completed in December 1996 and the verdict of the judge was given in June 1997. The result of the trial was summed up in the headlines next day: 'McDonald's wins libel epic but loses PR battle' announced the *FT*. 'McDonald's wins pyrrhic victory' declared the *Guardian*, while the *Daily Telegraph* described the verdict as 'McLibel victory with little relish'.

Mr Justice Bell ruled that McDonald's had been libelled by many of the allegations in a leaflet distributed by the two defendants and awarded the company £60,000 damages. The false allegations included the company's supposed responsibility for destruction of the rainforest and starvation in the Third World, and the risk of heart disease from eating its food. But the judge also ruled that the leaflet was truthful in accusing McDonald's of paying low wages to its workers, of being responsible for cruelty to some animals and of exploiting children in its advertising campaigns – three not insignificant charges. Paul Preston, president of McDonald's UK, addressing a press conference after the High Court ruling, acclaimed victory in the libel trial which had cost his company an estimated £10 million in legal fees. But in reality it was hard for him to defend one of the most extended, self-inflicted PR disasters of recent corporate times.

'what's wrong with mcdonald's?'

The McLibel trial had its genesis in the early Seventies when London Greenpeace was established. Describing itself as 'a small, independent collective, active in environmental and social struggles', London Greenpeace was the first Greenpeace to be set up in Europe and is unrelated to its more famous namesake, Greenpeace International, which was to follow in 1976. In the mid-Eighties a number of the environmental concerns which came on to the public and media agendas pointed a finger at America's fast-food giants. The deforestation of vast tracts of South American countries for the establishment of cattle ranches to provide beef for the First World's seemingly insatiable appetite for burgers became a major issue, as did the rearing of battery hens in the cruellest of circumstances. There were broader concerns, too: for example, the relentless promotion of 'junk food' to children; the problem of disposing of massive quantities of non-biodegradable packaging; and a growing unease about the way in which America's fast-food corporations were quiet openly using their enormous financial muscle to achieve global dominance, introducing and promoting the junk-food habit in countries previously untouched by this unedifying dimension of Western culture.

The small band of activists who ran London Greenpeace decided to campaign against the junk-food giants, and, as the biggest giant of all, McDonald's was first in the firing line. Drawing together criticisms on a number of different fronts, London Greenpeace produced and distributed a poorly printed double-sided A5 leaflet entitled 'What's Wrong with McDonald's?' The areas covered in the fact-sheet, which became the issues in dispute at the trial, and on the majority of which McDonald's won their pyrrhic victory, were:

- the connection between multinational companies like McDonald's, cash crops and starvation in the Third World;
- the responsibility of corporations such as McDonald's for damage to the environment, including destruction of rainforests;
- the wasteful and harmful effects of the mountains of packaging generated and used by McDonald's and other companies;
- the promotion and sale by McDonald's of food with a low-fibre, high fat, saturated-fat, sodium and sugar content, and the links between a diet of this type and the major degenerative diseases in Western society, including heart disease and cancer;
- the exploitation by McDonald's of children through its use of advertisements and gimmicks to sell unhealthy products;
- the barbaric ways in which animals are reared and slaughtered to supply products for McDonald's;
- the poor conditions under which workers in the catering industry are forced to work, and the low wages paid by McDonald's;
- the hostility of McDonald's towards trade unions.

Once McDonald's got wind of the leaflet, its well-oiled legal machine was swung into action – but quickly hit a technical obstacle, in that London Greenpeace had no legal status. First McDonald's had to find someone to sue. But who, within London Greenpeace, was to be held accountable? With slick efficiency McDonald's hired two detective agencies to arrange for agents to infiltrate London Greenpeace so that the prime movers could be identified. If the notion of a $30 billion a year business hiring corporate spies to penetrate an unstructured and unresourced group of about ten green activists seems slightly paranoid, more bathos still was to be found in the events that followed. According to the 26 January 1997 issue of the *Observer*, one McDonald's spy, working undercover, had an affair with one of London Greenpeace's leading figures, Mr Charlie Brooke. The scene resembles the plot of a James Bond story: while Ms X and vegan Charlie Brooke were murmuring sweet nothings into each other's ears, Ms X's detective colleagues were breaking into London Greenpeace's offices, rifling through their files and 'borrowing' letters in their quest to identify the ringleaders. Afterwards, Brooke was said to have felt terribly used.

When it became clear who was behind the anti-McDonald's leaflet, writs soon appeared on the doorsteps of five individuals connected with London Greenpeace. According to the McLibel Support Campaign: 'McDonald's appeared to think that, given the time, expense and legal difficulties involved in defending a libel action, the five would apologize. The five defendants were advised that since there is no legal aid to fight libel cases, their chances of successfully fighting the case, or even getting as far as the trial itself, were virtually nil. Faced with this, three of the defendants reluctantly decided to apologize and so avoid any costs.'

Not so Helen Steel and Dave Morris, however. For both of them, committed activists and veterans of CND, the anti-poll-tax campaign, the Wapping picket and the miners' strike, there was no question of caving in to McDonald's. If anything, this was their defining moment in a career of protest, the opportunity to make life extremely uncomfortable for one of the biggest international corporate giants, in the full glare of the world's media. Dave Morris, forty-two, an ex-postman and single parent with a seven-year-old son, and Helen Steel, thirty-one, a former gardener who worked part-time in a bar, were clearly two individuals deeply committed to their cause who had absolutely nothing to lose financially and a huge media advantage to gain. McDonald's had picked the wrong people to mess with.

In pursuing a litigious course with such inflexibility, McDonald's embarked on an embarrassing corporate PR marathon which it couldn't possibly win, whatever the legal outcome, and which, once started, couldn't be called off without a serious loss of face. Its pursuit of two radical environmentalists also suggests a cultural difference in the way that criticism is managed in America and Britain. The highly litigious American culture encourages companies and individuals to sue the pants off any person or organization from whom a financial or moral advantage may be extracted – stories about US lawyers following ambulances to hospital in pursuit of potential clients are legion. The British approach is self-evidently different, especially with regard to those who exist on the fringes of society. Because of our culture of eccentricity, nutters of all varieties are tolerated – Speakers' Corner in Hyde Park being a shining example. As PR veteran Simon Brocklebank-Fowler told the *Financial Times*: 'Litigation is seen in the US as part of the everyday corporate armoury. In Europe we have not got there yet. Litigation is used less often than in the US, particularly against people. It is a last resort.'

Sarah Webb, a libel specialist with Russell Jones & Walker, pointed out another flaw in the McDonald's decision to sue the two activists: 'Even if they were completely successful, in these circumstances there will always be residual sympathy for the little guys. It is very unusual for a company to sue individuals. It is a risky strategy.'

It was true that McDonald's had a problem to deal with: two career protesters were handing out leaflets which contained untrue and potentially damaging allegations about its organization. What's more, employee morale within McDonald's was being hit.

The company had to be seen to be doing something about the terriers nipping at its ankles. But was its legal response not an utterly disproportionate means of dealing with the problem? The spectacle of a company whose turnover exceeds the GDP of most countries in Africa taking on two individuals whose combined income was less than £12,000 a year certainly provided entertaining theatre, but it hardly seemed good sense. John Vidal, the *Guardian*'s environment editor and author of *McLibel*, a book which studies the case in fascinating detail, writes: 'Was not a company with unimaginable wealth, and well able to command the best legal expertise, bound to have real advantage? Did McDonald's deliberately take advantage of the British libel laws? How can a company which spends $2,000 million a year advertising itself be damaged by a few people handing out a few thousand leaflets?'

If the McDonald's spies had been more effective they would have reported back that the anti-McDonald's campaign was turning out to be a predictably short-lived affair. Dan Mills of the McLibel Support Campaign remarks: 'It was particularly ironic that at the time the writs were served, London Greenpeace had used up its print run of "What's Wrong with McDonald's" leaflets and wasn't planning to distribute any more. The anti-McDonald's campaign had pretty much run out of steam by then and the group was looking at other campaigns.'

Instead of letting the small-scale campaign die its natural death, McDonald's virtually rolled out an international media platform for the lobby group, ensuring that the contents of the hitherto little-known leaflet were reported not only in Britain's national press, but in media throughout the world. And once reported, the accusations struck a chord with the public. Adam Woolf, former public relations manager at Greenpeace International, once said that a key reason for his organization's success was that 'People trust us. Not just because we are politically and financially independent. But because in an increasingly cynical world, they believe in what we do and trust what we say.' Similarly, Steel and Morris were more likely to be believed by the public on issues to do with rainforests, animal welfare and the dumping of poly-styrene than was a fast-food giant with such clearly vested interests. If 'clearing its name' was a motivation for taking on the two activists, McDonald's should have realized that even if it won the legal battle, it would lose the media war; once the green genie is let out of the bottle, there is no getting it back in.

What's more, the libel action injected a huge impetus into London Greenpeace to continue the McDonald's campaign. Activists of all kinds thrive under persecution and London Greenpeace was no exception. Transmuting itself into the McLibel Support Campaign, apart from drumming up funds to help Steel and Morris fight their legal battle, the group undertook renewed leafleting activity on a scale which dwarfed all its previous efforts. Over 2 million copies of the 'What's Wrong with McDonald's' leaflet were handed out to the public during the course of the trial, making it one of the most distributed protest leaflets in history. John Vidal's *McLibel* appeared in bookstores throughout the world. Protests and campaigns against McDonald's spread to twenty-three countries outside Britain. A site was set up on the Internet called McSpotlight, making available thousands of files of information about McDonald's activities and providing 'campaigning tools'. McSpotlight has been accessed over 12 million times since its launch in February 1996.

Why did the McLibel trial last so long? Quite simply, because McDonald's insisted that every criticism in the leaflet put out by London Greenpeace was libellous. On the eve of the trial the American giant issued press releases and 300,000 of its own leaflets across the country calling its critics liars – at which point Steel and Morris slapped a counter-claim for libel against McDonald's, an action which ran concurrently with McDonald's own libel action. In the counter-claim, the burden of proof rested on McDonald's to prove that the London Greenpeace fact-sheet was untrue.

McDonald's successfully argued that the controversial issue of a link between diet and cancer was 'too complex' to allow for its assessment by a jury, so the trial was heard by Mr Justice Bell alone. Appointing eminent libel QC Richard Rampton to fight its corner, McDonald's prepared a succession of expert witnesses while Steel and Morris, representing themselves, were quickly immersed not only in court procedures and legal jargon, but in a welter of scientific and technical detail. Nevertheless, just as in the David and Goliath story, the pair's carefully targeted questions struck hit after embarrassing hit – all of which were related through the world's media.

The expert on cancer fielded by McDonald's, Dr Sydney Arnott, was asked by Steel and Morris about his opinion of the statement 'A diet high in fat, sugar, animal products and salt and low in fibre, vitamins and minerals is linked with cancer of the breast and bowel and heart disease.' His reply was: 'If it is being directed to the public then I would say it is a very reasonable thing to say.' The court was then told that this statement was an extract from the London Greenpeace leaflet. On the subject of the recycling of polystyrene containers, the chief purchasing officer of McDonald's, Ed Oakley, was forced to admit that, contrary to the information on 'McFact' cards championing a recycling scheme in Nottingham, the containers, which it asked customers to put into a separate bin, were not recycled but simply dumped.

As it turned out, in his final judgment Mr Justice Bell ruled that on the issues of poor diet and recycling the McLibel duo's accusations had been wrong. But there were other issues where their leaflet was accurate. One of these concerned the way McDonald's keeps animals. The judge said it was 'true in substance and in fact' to say that McDonald's 'is culpably responsible for cruel practices in the rearing and slaughter of some of the animals used to produce its food'. During the trial there had been a statement by Dr Neville Gregory, another McDonald's expert witness, who told the court that McDonald's egg suppliers keep chickens in battery cages, five chickens to a cage giving each bird a floor space less than the size of an A4 sheet of paper with no freedom of movement and no access to fresh air or sunshine – conditions which Ed Oakley of McDonald's described as 'pretty comfortable'!

There were other examples of McDonald's caring and

environmentally sensitive image unravelling under cross-examination in the courtroom, all of them reported to a far broader audience by a watchful media. While McDonald's avoided any public admission that the trial had turned into an international fiasco, a confidential internal memo from McDonald's Australia revealed the extent to which the corporation found itself in a dilemma in other parts of the world. 'We could worsen the controversy by adding our opinion,' read the memo, which said that in seeking to minimize further negative publicity, McDonald's Australia would try to 'contain it as a UK issue . . . We want to keep it at arm's length – not become guilty by association.'

So bad was the negative media coverage that around the time of the first anniversary of the trial in June 1995 McDonald's tried to settle out of court. They twice flew members of their US board of directors to London to meet Steel and Morris to try to find a way to end the case. But each side required the other to climb down, and since neither was prepared to give an inch, the talks quickly and inevitably ended in failure.

According to *Channel 4 News*, 'Observers believe [the McLibel trial] will go down in history as the most expensive and disastrous public relations exercise ever mounted by a multinational company.' Certainly it is a signal lesson on how not to deal with environmental activists, and perhaps, too, an example of how tactics which work well in corporate America do not translate well into the quirkier, less conservative British market. McDonald's is not the kind of company which has ever ranked as a top-of-the-list 'green company' in public perception, but its environmental credentials were undoubtedly eroded badly by the trial.

Outside the Courts of Justice in the Strand following the verdict, Morris and Steel were unrepentant, taking advantage of the massed ranks of TV and newspaper journalists from around the world to hand out more of the libellous leaflets in an act of defiance, and to hold up a briefcase to which was attached a placard urging 'Now read the leaflets and JUDGE FOR YOURSELF.' The courtroom of public opinion was far more important than any court of law, they declared: they would take their case to the European Court of Human Rights to challenge the UK's libel laws.

McDonald's said it would pursue the two for damages awards, but not to the point of driving them into bankruptcy – to which Helen Steel's sharp retort was: 'McDonald's don't deserve it and, in any event, we don't have a penny.' Meanwhile, up and down Britain, as the verdict was announced protesters took advantage of the newsworthiness of the occasion by picketing dozens of McDonald's outlets and handing out thousands more of the libellous leaflets.

'Pyrrhic' seems a barely adequate term to describe McDonald's 'victory'. Vidal observes: 'It is unimaginable that any company will be so arrogant or so stupid to go through the same experience again.' Libel and PR certainly combine to explosive effect and, as the McLibel case amply demonstrates, even the wealthiest and most powerful multinationals would be well advised to steer clear of this particular minefield in the interests of good PR, if it can possibly be avoided. As lawyer Tim Hardy told the *FT*: 'Faced with a similar dilemma, I advise my clients to spend their money on a Porsche as they will get far more satisfaction from it than they ever will out of a libel action.'

CHAPTER SIX
accentuating the negative:
PR's dark underworld

The cab trip from his office at the Palace of Westminster to the Covent Garden restaurant would take less than twenty minutes. Donning an overcoat and making his way outside into the grey, late November drizzle, Chris Blackhurst flagged down a taxi and gave the address before settling back into his seat. As the cab began its way up Whitehall in the midday traffic, Blackhurst mulled over his forthcoming lunch date.

A senior journalist at the *Independent*, he headed up the newspaper's Westminster office, but also enjoyed a privileged open brief to pursue any business stories he thought deserved investigation; and, as former deputy editor of the *Sunday Times* Insight team, investigative journalism was what he did best. Over the years he had developed a keen nose for a cover-up – not to mention a reputation for ruthlessness among his peers, by whom he was well known for his competitive pursuit of news leads. Most of all, Blackhurst hadn't reached such elevated heights in national newspaper journalism without a well-developed instinct for distinguishing sources he could rely on from those he couldn't. Right now, he had mixed feelings about his imminent meeting with Angus Maitland.

The stereotyped image of the City PR man – sharp-suited, silver-

tongued and brimming with alcohol-induced bonhomie – represented everything that Angus Maitland did not. Yet by the time of
his lunch date with Blackhurst in November 1995, Maitland had
come to occupy an extraordinary status in the world of City PR. In
his late forties, he was slightly built with a neatly trimmed crop of
reassuringly grey hair. A soft, Scottish accent affirming his origins,
he was always dapper in dress while eschewing the loud pinstripes
and braces of the City.

But, as Blackhurst knew, Maitland's low-key personal style
belied a wealth of high-level media contacts, a rapier-sharp mind
and an unswerving commitment to clients, making him the trusted
confidant of some of Britain's most powerful business leaders. He
ran his own eponymously named consultancy and, like Sir Tim
Bell, specialized in high-level handholding. In fact, he and Bell
shared several clients, including British Gas and the BBC, both of
which, despite the benefit of two such eminent advisers, had
walked into barrages of media fire for almost the same reason.
Cedric Brown, British Gas's chief executive, had been roundly
reviled for taking a massive 75 per cent pay rise on an already
substantial salary, just days before making thousands of British
Gas workers redundant. Whatever the rights and wrongs of the
pay rise, the announcement couldn't have been more crassly
handled. There had been little Maitland or Bell could do to prevent
their client's reputation being permanently tarnished. Avarice in a
slightly different guise came into view again with the 'Armani-gate'
revelations that John Birt, the director-general of the BBC and
another of Maitland's clients, had for six years collected his salary
gross from the BBC, avoiding PAYE tax by being paid as a supplier
– namely John Birt Productions. While the media fallout had been
a lot less damaging to Birt than it had been to Brown, the cause of
the controversial director-general had not been helped by the exposure of this stratagem.

On his way to lunch with Maitland that chill November day,
Blackhurst remembered some of the PR man's past victories and
defeats. Keenly aware that his lunch host was spear-carrier to some
of Britain's most powerful corporate warriors, Blackhurst also

recalled some of the personal mythology which had grown up around Angus Maitland.

Maitland's career in PR had begun more than twenty years earlier when, as a new graduate, he left his home town of Glasgow to join Charles Barker, one of London's largest and best-established City PR agencies. Joining the industry when it was in a state of relative infancy, its emphasis still strongly on stiff gin and tonics and long lunches at the Savoy, Maitland was quick to demonstrate intellectual capabilities which considerably raised the game: in particular, his skills at researching client issues and providing strategic solutions were highly innovative. He progressed quickly through the ranks.

Two of his more seasoned colleagues at Charles Barker were Reg Valin and Richard Pollen, PR men destined to create the most spectacularly successful operation in the history of corporate communications. Sharing a conviction that Britain's biggest businesses would respond well to a new breed of PR, one which was more 'consultancy' and less 'agency', the two sought to introduce a more rigorous, professional approach. In 1979 they left Charles Barker to create Valin Pollen. Not surprisingly, one of the first of their former colleagues they asked to join them was Angus Maitland.

As VP quickly grew and flourished in the corporate hothouse of the Eighties, Maitland grew and flourished with it, becoming chief executive of a multi-tentacled media shop offering not only public relations but advertising, design services and market research. At VP's sumptuous offices in Victoria he became something of a legendary figure, famous for a punishing work regime which would frequently begin not much after half past seven in the morning, after a one-hour commute from Tunbridge Wells, and seldom end less than twelve hours later. This seemed more than a Presbyterian work ethic; he was a man driven – but by what, not even his closest associates could ever fathom. A man of few words, his conversation rarely strayed into his private life and he never so much as hinted at the interior world of personal thoughts and feelings. Curiously, on the rare occasions when he didn't discuss work, conversation with his colleagues would turn to the most banal of subjects – almost as though he was warding off the possibility of deeper friendship. In terms of both personality and style, therefore, he could not have been more different from the exuberant and emotionally generous Sir Tim. Most telling of all, perhaps, was his choice of recreation – long-distance running. VP staff would frequently be greeted by the sight of their chief executive in track suit and running shoes, pounding his way out of their Grosvenor Gardens offices as he sought a little light relief from the rigours of consultancy management with a spot of distance training.

VP fast established itself as the largest operation of its kind in Britain – and in the euphoric late Eighties it was inevitable that the board of VP should turn their eyes to the even larger and more lucrative US marketplace. The decision to acquire a New York-based consultancy, while strategically sound, was utterly miscalculated in practice. VP shelled out £40 million for the Don Carter Organization in New York – only to find they'd vastly over-paid. Then followed a frantic period of damage limitation during which Maitland was making return flights by Concorde to New York sometimes twice a week, desperately trying to salvage what he could from the deal.

But, as events unravelled, the collapse of VP became inevitable. Different parts of the VP empire broke off to continue as success-ful, independent operations. VP imploded, its founders having to face up to the galling reality that the multi-million-pound fortunes they'd once had on paper would never now be realized. It was at this point that Maitland moved to Burson Marsteller, the UK's fifth largest consultancy, where he sat out the recession as vice-chairman before setting up his own consultancy in April 1994.

By the time of his lunch appointment with Chris Blackhurst Maitland had been running his own business for just over eighteen months. Clients had rewarded his commitment and his extensive business knowledge by following him first from VP and then from Burson Marsteller. His turnover by late 1995, he reported at the time, was an impressive £2 million a year. In credentials documents he described himself as a high-level strategic adviser, and there is no question that senior journalists valued the access he could provide to some of Britain's highest-profile businessmen, including the likes of Ian Vallance, chairman of British Telecom, Richard Giordano, chairman of British Gas, and Hugh Stevenson, chairman of giant fund manager Mercury Asset Management, not to mention senior executives at BOC, Enterprise Oil, Olivetti, Sainsbury and Unilever.

But not all journalists had reported positive experiences of Angus Maitland. The relentless battles he fought on behalf of his clients, to generate positive media coverage of their activities and limit the damage caused by negative news, inevitably put him at odds with some of the movers and shakers of the fourth estate. One journalist in particular whose feathers he had ruffled was none other than Chris Blackhurst himself.

Blackhurst had been investigating the pay and tax arrangements of John Birt during the 'Armani-gate' affair. According to the journalist's dictum that 'news is what a company doesn't want you to find out – all else is advertising', Birt's pay arrangement was news indeed. And revealing Birt's imaginative method of tax avoidance was a challenge to which Blackhurst applied himself with vigour, researching and writing a major piece for publication in the *Independent on Sunday*.

While Maitland may have been aware that something on the BBC was being prepared, it was only the day before the exposé appeared that he caught wind of its most damaging contents. In such circumstances the knee-jerk reaction of any PR man is to try to have publication of an article delayed, usually on the grounds of technical inaccuracies, and once delayed have its contents ameliorated as far as possible. If that can't be achieved, the next best course of action is to try to dilute the effect of the worst allegations, or at least appeal to a journalist's sense of fair play by presenting whatever balancing arguments may exist. In swinging into action, Maitland's error, as far as Blackhurst was concerned, was that he'd gone above Blackhurst's head. Arriving at his office on Monday morning, Blackhurst was furious to learn that, unbeknown to him, Maitland had been on the phone several times to his superiors over the weekend, attempting to use his considerable influence to reduce the impact of the Birt exposé. As it happened, the article had been run unchanged, but this only slightly mollified Blackhurst's pique.

Spats between journalists and PR men are an occupational hazard in the media game, divergent agendas frequently bringing the two sides into direct conflict. Because of their mutual dependence, however, hostilities are rarely allowed to fester. In fact, if one side can convince the other that it has overstepped the mark, this can provide useful leverage in the continuous trading of favours. However annoyed he might have been by what he saw as Maitland's meddling, Blackhurst still had to deal with the PR man. In particular, some weeks subsequent to the Birt affair, he'd telephoned Maitland regarding another of his clients, Mercury Asset Management. It had been during this conversation that Maitland had proposed they discuss matters of mutual interest over lunch. Blackhurst had accepted the invitation.

Christopher's, a trendy restaurant on Wellington Street, midway between the Waldorf and the columned grandeur of the Opera House, is popular among London's media types as a place to 'do lunch'. By 1 p.m. on any weekday, whole Camparis of ad-men – as the collective noun goes – can be found wining and dining their clients in an atmosphere of upbeat exuberance. With its gothic-style circular staircase in stone and wrought iron, its velvet curtains, gilt-framed paintings and operatic background music, there is a theatrical quality to Christopher's in keeping with its Covent Garden location – not to mention the professions of its patrons, many of whom are drawn from the communications agencies which proliferate around London's West End. As Blackhurst emerged from his cab and climbed the steps into Christopher's, however, it was less the sumptuous decor than his imminent conversation with Angus Maitland that was on his mind.

Most journalists go to similar meetings with PR men hoping to bag a story, either immediately or in the not-too-distant future. If the PR man can provide access to a major corporate figure, so much the better. But, after the Birt episode, could Blackhurst really rely on Maitland? Was Maitland pursuing a different agenda – and if so, what was it?

Blackhurst was to be disappointed, at least initially, by the pedestrian passage of conversation over lunch. Sitting across the table from him, the slightly built Scotsman briefed Blackhurst on several of his major clients, including Mercury Asset Management – the subject of Blackhurst's original enquiry – in typical, low-key style, providing background but no fireworks. However, Blackhurst couldn't help wondering about the large brown envelope which Maitland had brought with him, and which was positioned conspicuously on the corner of the white tablecloth throughout lunch. The envelope bore his own initials and was clearly intended to be passed on to him. What it contained, however, remained a mystery – until conversation turned to British Gas. Here again, Maitland *said* nothing which had Blackhurst scrambling to hold the front page; but the spin doctor seemed to suggest that what was contained in the plain brown envelope would be of rather more than passing interest. 'I found him a very tricksy character,' says Blackhurst. 'The way he went about things wasn't at all straightforward. It wasn't a question of being briefed on something and then getting back-up information. Instead, at the end of lunch he just handed me the envelope in a nodding and winking style.'

If Maitland's intention had been to arouse Blackhurst's curiosity, he certainly succeeded. Blackhurst had opened the envelope and perused its contents before he'd even got back to his Westminster office. When he saw what he'd been given, the reason for Maitland's 'nodding and winking style' became instantly clear. Because instead of finding a background briefing paper on British Gas's operations, Blackhurst discovered a far grander story. According to anonymous notes contained in the brown envelope, Claire Spottiswoode, the gas regulator, had supposedly surrounded herself with a clique of advisers who shared an ideological hostility towards British Gas, one of whom wanted to see British Gas broken up for reasons of personal animosity.

Blackhurst was astounded – though the cause of his surprise had far less to do with the apparently sinister goings-on in the office of the regulator than with the fact that Angus Maitland was trying to propagate a conspiracy-type theory in what appeared to him to be the most conspiratorial of ways. Relations between British Gas and its regulator were notoriously difficult, and the idea of separating Transco, British Gas's pipeline and storage company, from the rest of the operation had been on the agenda for some time. What struck Blackhurst, however, was the fact that instead of British Gas openly presenting him with a carefully marshalled set of arguments in support of its case, its PR man had chosen to slip him a set of anonymous briefing papers, revealing the backgrounds of Spottiswoode's most senior advisers, who were clearly viewed as corporate enemies, constructing a tale of long knives and perverse motivations which, in his view, reflected paranoia rather more clearly than the regulator's *modus operandi*. Just what exactly was Maitland hoping to achieve, wondered Blackhurst? To hound the regulator out of office? To conceal the weaknesses of British Gas's own arguments? To divert media attention from his client's own appalling public opinion ratings? Whatever the case, of one thing Blackhurst was certain: he'd landed himself the lead to an explosive story – though not necessarily the one that Maitland had intended to give him.

race for the exclusive

Events moved swiftly after the lunch at Christopher's. Back at his desk, as he read through the anonymous briefing notes again, Blackhurst couldn't help wondering if he was their only recipient. It seemed unlikely that Maitland had handed them over to him alone. And if Maitland had passed them to other reporters, how had they reacted?

As a senior journalist, Blackhurst had contacts within a wide number of newspapers. In particular, as ex-deputy editor of the *Sunday Times* Insight team he had former colleagues at Wapping with whom he was able to swap notes, albeit in a guarded fashion. Conducting a tentative sounding-out exercise, it didn't take him long to establish not only that Maitland had passed on similar material to other journalists, but that another newspaper was already researching an exposé of British Gas's 'negative PR' activities. Working on what they intended as a lead scoop of the autumn, the other newspaper team had run into difficulties with Ofgas. According to Blackhurst, the regulator had left them in no doubt about her displeasure over BG's 'negative PR' but, at the same time, she was not prepared to make any allegations on the record.

Hurriedly setting up a meeting with senior colleagues, Blackhurst and the *Independent*'s editorial team now had a tough decision to make. The clock was running on an exposé which clearly had front-page news potential – but there were no prizes for coming second. Should they claim the scoop for themselves and run the story ahead of their rival, at the cost, perhaps, of being able to collect less evidence than would perhaps be ideal? Or should they continue researching a potentially much bigger story but risk being pipped to the post? In the past, the *Independent* had been accused of sitting on stories – accusations that rankled with its senior editors. Blackhurst already had enough evidence to prove that something underhand was going on, even if he didn't have the whole story. Given the time and cost imperatives of national newspapers in general and the *Independent* in particular, the decision did not take long to make.

On Monday 4 December 1995, the *Independent* carried a front-page exclusive accusing British Gas of running a dirty tricks campaign against the industry regulator – the first time that any such allegations had been made publicly. Blackhurst's article contained a succinct resumé of Maitland's anonymous briefing notes. Apart from the overall suggestion that Claire Spottiswoode was involved in an ideologically driven clique to break up British Gas, the notes also highlighted the roles played by some of her advisers. One of Spottiswoode's three 'co-conspirators', Professor Colin Robinson of Surrey University, was alleged to have a hatred of British Gas stemming back to the 1960s, when he worked for Esso. Part of his job then had been to negotiate contracts with British Gas and, according to the unattributed document, 'the experience traumatized him and ... his attacks on BG have a personal character'. Robinson was married to Dr Eileen Marshall, none other than Claire Spottiswoode's deputy at Ofgas. The other member of the gang of three, Professor Michael Beesley, was an adviser to Ofgas and, so the briefing paper said, the Office of Fair Trading was not happy with his involvement, which had 'raised eyebrows'.

Blackhurst had, of course, contacted the individuals highlighted in Maitland's notes and reported their reactions. Claire Spottiswoode, according to a spokesman, was said to be 'concerned that this sort of thing is going on'. Professor Robinson described the claims against him as 'ludicrous'. And the Office of Fair Trading pointed out that 'It is none of our business who is appointed as a consultant to Ofgas.'

As for Maitland himself, whom Blackhurst had telephoned for comment before running the article, he strongly disputed that he was involved in a campaign against Ofgas. In handing over the papers he had not been acting on behalf of British Gas. And he had not given similar documents to other journalists. 'I carry all sorts of stuff in my case,' he told Blackhurst. The Ofgas papers 'were papers I happened to have with me'. In PR terms, he seemed to imply, he was only doing what any seasoned practitioner would have done in the circumstances – providing useful briefing material to a journalist interested in his client's affairs.

Unfortunately, the *Independent* didn't see it that way. The leader on the day Blackhurst's exclusive appeared pointed out that had 'Cedric Brown or the company's public affairs director, Peter Sanguinetti, called a press conference and said these things openly, then there would have been little fuss . . . Allegations in an anonymous briefing paper are slightly different. The whole business reeks of cloak-and-dagger and shenanigans.' The editor also asked if it was legitimate for a large company to pay a PR consultant to badmouth the opposition anonymously. 'The test to be applied is a simple one: would the ordinary person in the street believe that would be an acceptable or fair way to go about things? If the popular morality of Hollywood films is anything to go by, the answer would be no, we do not think this is the right way to behave.'

maitland goes on a war footing

The altogether unexpected and deeply unwelcome publicity in a major national newspaper had British Gas and Maitland faced with serious choices. Richard Giordano, British Gas's chairman, Cedric Brown, his chief executive, Peter Sanguinetti, head of public affairs, and Angus Maitland had jointly weathered the storms of hostile media attention for several years already. But this most recent assault was also the most potentially devastating to date.

So, on the morning the Blackhurst article appeared in print, Maitland ascended to his eleventh-floor eyrie in Orion House, Upper St Martin's Lane, even earlier than his usual 7.30 a.m. start, to preside over a massive damage-limitation exercise. First, there were all his clients and associates to contact, to be reassured that the *Independent*'s attack was without substance or foundation. Then there were the City editors, with most of whom he had long-standing relationships, whose support was required to stop an unsavoury story from leaking across the pages of the national press. There were the meetings with his lawyers, and with British Gas, and British Gas's lawyers, debating strategy and scenario-setting. Then followed a period of watchful expectancy.

Blackhurst seemed to have taken the bit between his teeth, and who knew where he might be headed next? Early every morning, Maitland and his consultants scanned the national press with a sense of foreboding. It just didn't seem possible that a story as potentially big as this could remain cooped up in only one of the four broadsheets. And as for the tabloids – the very thought caused shudders. Prepared for the worst, and wondering from which quarter the next salvo would be fired, Maitland waited; but events took a course he could only have hoped for in his most optimistic moments.

Nothing happened. Blackhurst seemed to lose interest in the story, and returned to covering events at Westminster. Other national papers were strangely mute. Or perhaps not so strangely. Some had very good reasons not to rattle the bars of Angus Maitland's cage – their own City editors were right there in the cage with him. Others might have debated the cost–benefit ratio and decided it didn't tilt in their favour. Maitland provided access to many of Britain's largest PLCs. Alienate him and you risked falling out of the information loop, and certainly being denied access to future exclusives.

And Maitland had laid his advance defences well. Overall, there was a remarkable similarity between the initial press response to the British Gas story and that which occurred when British Airways' dirty tricks first came into public view. None of the serious newspapers questioned BA's contention that Richard Branson had been running an extended publicity campaign against the company. Peter Sanguinetti, corporate affairs director at British Gas, through his thirty-three-strong department and high-level advisers like Angus Maitland, had been assiduous in cultivating the same editorial support which had shielded British Airways from Virgin's allegations until a High Court settlement blew apart BA's defences. And even though British Gas has been considerably less successful at winning the battle for hearts and minds – could you ever imagine the strapline 'the world's favourite gas company'? – to this day it has been remarkably successful at concealing its own dark secrets.

For events appear to contradict the idea that Blackhurst's lunch at Christopher's had been a one-off episode. Over a period of many months before that day, briefing paper after briefing paper had been delivered to senior journalists on leading national newspapers. At least one of Britain's most influential City editors had become so faithful to Angus Maitland's version of reality that he'd loyally reproduce facts and arguments in briefing documents sent to him, lambasting British Gas's nascent competitors and railing at flaws in government policy. Clandestine activity bearing a secret codename had been set up to attack British Gas's corporate enemies at their most vulnerable moment. And at the heart of this campaign was Angus Maitland, one of the most invisible persuaders in the business. A man whose name was, and probably still is, virtually unknown outside the City; and who continues to hover, unseen, at the elbows of some of Britain's most influential chief executives to this day.

dirty tricks – clean hands

When Virgin Atlantic sued British Airways for running a dirty tricks campaign against it, the world's favourite airline ended up paying Richard Branson £610,000 in damages and an estimated £4 million in fees – the largest libel settlement in British legal history. During the course of legal proceedings, PR veteran Brian Basham achieved the dubious distinction of being the only named individual held personally responsible in the High Court by British Airways for any of its wide-ranging and nefarious activities. At a single stroke, he became the most celebrated Mephistopheles of the PR underworld.

The collective sins of the PR industry cannot, however, be heaped on any one man's shoulders, and in BA's case by no means on Basham's alone. Among the massed battalions of Britain's invisible persuaders there are others who have indulged in negative PR, arguably with greater success – in the sense that they haven't been caught. But what, exactly, is meant by 'dirty tricks' and 'negative PR'?

The two terms are used in the PR industry, interchangeably, to mean the anonymous placing of negative stories in the media by a company about its corporate enemies. On the surface of things, there may seem to be little, if anything, wrong with activity of this kind. Isn't it part of the normal marketing process to highlight one's company's own strengths – and contrast these with one's competitors' weaknesses? Does it really matter how journalists get their source material, so long as they bring to it a robust independence of view?

What arguments like these don't sufficiently take into account is the issue of journalist endorsement. Nowhere is this endorsement more compelling – or destructive – than when used as a tool for 'negative PR'. For, in contrast to the commercial honesty of advertising, when we, the consumers, have no doubt who is advertising and to what end, when we read a newspaper or watch a TV report we take the information we receive on trust. Cynical as we may be about journalists, for the most part even the most jaundiced among us tend to give credence to what we read in the paper. If that news-paper happens to be one of the broadsheets, as opposed to the tabloids, our confidence in editorial objectivity is greater still. And if we are reading a business story in a broadsheet newspaper, under the City editor's by-line and carrying a suitably flattering photo-graph of him, well, it's as good as gospel!

Such confidence is, of course, greatly misplaced. Because of the relationships between spin doctors and journalists, the encum-brance of editorial independence is frequently discarded on the rocky shores of expediency or looming deadlines. Out go the high-sounding journalistic ideals of 'comforting the afflicted and afflicting the comfortable' and what gets published instead is straightforward PR feed. What's more, the chances are that the PR feed emanates from one of the most comfortable among us, such as a corporate Goliath with deep enough pockets to retain a high-level PR consultant for the express purpose of getting across well-honed messages about itself – and its corporate enemies.

Of course it is sometimes the case that journalists accept, whole-sale, the ideas and arguments put to them by spin doctors because they really do agree with them. The point should also be made that journalists are more frequently the pawns in a corporate game, rather than willing accomplices in negative PR campaigns. Nevertheless, what they write can be deadly.

In the short term, a key reason why negative PR is so effective is the difficulty of refuting a harmful allegation and remaining com-pletely untainted. As we will see when we look at both the British Gas and the British Airways dirty tricks campaigns, the most successful negative stories are never extravagant fantasies, but are credible cocktails of half-truths and distortions – which are far more difficult to combat; some of the mud inevitably sticks.

And even if a company is able to ride out the immediate storm, it is more than likely, in the long term, that negative stories will return to haunt it. This is because the original stories – however comprehensively refuted – will have found their way into the press-cutting files of every newsroom, to be hauled out and reheated whenever the company is covered again. Like an insidious virus, once stories are in the system, they are well-nigh impossible to expunge. Repeated frequently enough, they turn into fact. Indeed, they can become defining moments in a company's or individual's life even though they might represent only a fraction of a percentage of that company's or individual's total activity.

Say the name 'Gerald Ratner' to most people, and 'prawn sandwiches' – or an even shorter phrase – will spring to mind; the businessman famously told a business gathering that his chain store could sell products for less than a prawn sandwich 'because they're crap', thereby destroying his career in a single line. Even though Gerald Ratner's business achievements are extraordinary by any standards, they are not, unfortunately for him, what he will now always be famous for. True, the prawn sandwich line was Ratner's own, and not the product of an anonymous PR leak. But it is a sobering illustration of how a negative association, once made, can quickly become the single image by which a company or individual is widely known.

Given the enormous and undisputed power of negative PR, some communications desperadoes may be tempted to consider it as an option. What about the legality of it? As it happens, unless you are caught saying something slanderous, 'negative PR' is perfectly legal. In handing over documents questioning the gas regulator's motivation, Angus Maitland broke no law, and indeed it should be emphasized that none of Maitland's or Basham's activities revealed in this chapter was in any way illegal. But the ethics of negative PR are seldom black and white. It may be *true*, for example, that millions of people all over the world find cigarette smoking a relaxing and enjoyable pastime. But would it be *right* to teach that fact to children – to circulate such one-sided nonsense among an impressionable audience that doesn't know any better?

For those still prepared to contemplate embarking on a campaign of negative PR, there is another very practical consideration – what happens if you get caught? Living, as we do, in an era that has seen the publication of the Cadbury and Greenbury reports on corporate transparency and accountability we – the public – have come to demand good corporate governance. Given that negative

PR thrives in the very opposite environment, one of obfuscation and anonymity, a company which is caught trying to wreak havoc on a competitor's corporate image inflicts even greater harm on its own. As Quentin Bell puts it succinctly, 'I would never dream of getting involved in negative PR. You always get caught.'

Bell is by no means alone in this contention. Mention the phrase 'negative PR' to most PR consultants and a nervous look will come into their eyes. So why is it that some PR practitioners not only in the UK but also in America risk all for a client who wants to bend the rules? Is it simple arrogance in thinking they can get away with it? Or is it more a question of getting sucked into the boardroom debates of their clients to such an extent that they start to lose the very objectivity for which they were originally hired?

british gas falls from grace

It is hard to credit that as recently as 1992 British Gas enjoyed a reputation among consumers second only to Marks & Spencer. That July, the *Evening Standard* reported that 'An independent survey, commissioned ironically by the water industry watchdog, reveals that British Gas is rated more highly by consumers than any of the other privatised utilities'. Having reduced prices by around 25 per cent in real terms since privatization, BG was regarded by consumers as a benign giant, and even its industrial users were impressed by its apparent efforts to support the introduction of competition into the market.

All that had changed by November 1994, when Cedric Brown was awarded his whopping 75 per cent pay increase. His new pay package now totalled £475,000. The public outcry which followed was inevitable; and yet, in what was seen as a gesture of colossal corporate arrogance, within days British Gas was announcing massive cuts to its workforce – 25,000 jobs were to go over the next eighteen months. Nothing could have been more calculated to convey the image of corporate fat-cat-ism, the ethos of 'I'm all right Jack'. Brown's overnight 75 per cent pay rise became a symbol of all that was most repugnant about utility bosses' greed. As the national media railed against them, Brown and his fellow directors were clearly unprepared for the ferocity of the backlash. Strangely oblivious to the world in which other, lesser mortals lived, it took them too long to realize that they'd strongly alienated the vast majority of their customers, many of whom also happened to be shareholders – 'Sids' wooed at the time of privatization.

British Gas was strenuous in its contention that Brown's pay award was completely justified. It marshalled all kinds of arguments to support its decision, citing the modesty of Brown's executive share options, his contribution to company efficiencies leading to falling gas bills, and of course that old chestnut – top pay for top people. Whether Brown's pay rise was well earned is not a question that need concern us here. How that pay rise was announced is – and it was, by British Gas's own admission, handled disastrously. Its timing was particularly insensitive given that most of the country was still in the grip of the feelbad factor. Against a backdrop of job insecurity, single-digit pay rises, negative equity and national malaise, this was not the time for one of the country's highest-profile corporate leaders to be accepting a massive pay increase while turfing thousands of his workers on to the streets. It was not really surprising that the media reacted the way it did, with public opinion finding its ultimate expression in the now-famous *Sun* photograph of a pig with its snout firmly in the trough.

The pay row made British Gas all the more vulnerable when it came to dealing with an issue which had much more far-reaching consequences for the organization: the introduction of competition for domestic customers. When BG was privatized, it had a 25-year monopoly of the market for individual users consuming up to 25,000 therms a year. This included all the domestic market, most of the commercial market and even some of the industrial market. Nice business to be in. Like the other great privatization successes, British Airways and British Telecom, for as long as Mrs Thatcher was in power, the simple fact that British Gas had made the successful transfer from public to private ownership – and especially its part in making Britain a 'shareholding democracy' – was almost enough to protect it from having its near-monopoly of the market-place called into question. After Mrs Thatcher's departure, however, in the dark days of the early Nineties, the once-lauded heroes of privatization began to look decidedly overfed. The public mood shifted in support of greater competition, and in response the government passed the Competition and Service Utility Act 1992, then the Gas Act 1995, opening the way to competition among domestic customers.

The response of British Gas to having its monopoly taken from it was, like British Airways just a few years earlier, one of steaming indignation. When the government refused BA's pleas to keep Heathrow closed to Virgin and other, American, carriers, BA chairman Lord King gave a furious interview to the City section of the *Observer*, edited by Melvyn Marckus, his son-in-law: 'If I had been told by the government that this would happen at the time of privatization, I would have felt compelled to refer to it in BA's prospectus,' he thundered. A few years later it was the turn of John Jay, City editor of the *Sunday Times*, to document British Gas's outpouring of angst: 'Perhaps the government should now act honestly – in the knowledge that it has not only moved the goal-posts since privatisation but has relocated the pitch – and assist in the renegotiation of the contracts.'

While the two reactions are virtually interchangeable, the difference was that while Lord King went on record with his bitter denunciation of government policy, criticisms of the Gas Act came – apparently – from the pen of one of the most influential City editors in the country. As it happened, Angus Maitland provided Jay with one of his briefing notes, which Jay had seen fit to repeat, including several closely patterned phrases. No doubt Jay agreed with Maitland's arguments. And what a felicitous state of affairs for British Gas! Carrying the headline 'Next sell-offs in peril if Sid is made to suffer', Jay's article conveyed a warning to the government which could not have been clearer.

Not only were the reactions of British Airways and British Gas identical when presented with the horror of having to fight for market share in a competitive world, the pattern of events that accompanied the reactions in each case was, in PR terms at least, uncannily similar. One might say that 'only the names changed' – but even that would not be true, given that the dramatis personae of the national press contained several journalists who featured in both performances, happy to reproduce PR feeds directly, complete with spin. And while the invisible persuaders hired by the two organizations couldn't have been more different in terms of temperament – Basham, the flamboyant south Londoner, worlds apart from the low-key Maitland – the strategy employed by both was identical: it began with the intensive research of corporate enemies, followed by the handing over of selected findings to senior City journalists.

king's unhealthy interest in heaven

In Basham's case, the beginning of his activities on behalf of British Airways coincided with the start-up of his new consultancy, Warwick Corporate. It was not a pleasant time for Basham, who only a few years before had been an undisputed champion of City PR, one of the toughest hard-ballers on the block. Basham's was a classic Eighties tale of ferociously hard work and material success crowned by overgearing. Having left school with only a handful of O levels, Basham, a butcher's son from Catford, south London, had started out on adult life as a newspaper messenger before finding his way into journalism. It was only a short step to the far richer pastures of public relations, and once there it didn't take the street-smart Basham long to work out that the only way he was going to make a fortune in PR was as the boss of his own business; so in 1977 he set up Broad Street. A workaholic who inspired strong feelings of loyalty among many of his staff, Basham never allowed the absence of a formal education in any way to dent a supreme self-confidence – the quality which, more than any other, defines the successful spin doctor. Only a few years after setting up Broad Street, he was advising the likes of the Fayeds, Robert

Maxwell and Ernest Saunders – all of whom, at the time, were untouched by the controversy which was later to beset them.

Eight years after launching Broad Street, Basham was the proud owner of a business worth an estimated £25 million. And, as might be expected, moving in the high-flying circles that he did, he'd acquired a taste for some of the more glittering symbols of success. According to an article in the *Daily Mail* in March 1991, at the height of his career he bought two houses in southern Spain and two in Regents Park, a Sunseeker speedboat, a £70,000 mobile home, various limousines, a vintage American convertible and a Harley Davidson motorcycle. One particularly bizarre purchase was that of a dark blue London taxi, which he had converted to include a turbo engine, three clocks inside showing the time in London, New York and Tokyo, a TV, video, two fax machines and three phones. The whole package, back in the mid-Eighties, cost £30,000 – but Basham quickly decided the taxi was too noisy and had it sent back. But when the high-rolling Eighties ground into the recession-struck Nineties, Basham was badly hit. Realizing that Broad Street, once a mighty force in financial PR, was now a sinking ship, he decided to sell it to Financial Dynamics and float a new, more stable vessel called Warwick Corporate.

The £46,000 report investigating Virgin, which Basham carried out on behalf of BA, was – according to respected investigative journalist Martyn Gregory, who produced two ITV documentaries on BA's activities – the start of Basham's efforts to dig up as much dirt on Branson as possible with a view then to circulating the material through the nation's newsrooms. Basham understandably has a different explanation: 'It was Richard Branson who started things.' Branson, according to Basham, sparked off a media battle with BA and BA were foolish to rise to the bait. Against Basham's advice, BA wanted to spread 'scuttlebut' about Branson. 'I said no. What evidence do you have? There isn't any.' Basham says he suggested BA employ a firm of management consultants to conduct a competitor analysis – but BA didn't want to spend the money. So in early 1991 Basham offered to produce the report himself – 'a sterling piece of work of which I'm exceedingly proud'. The inspired codename he dreamed up for this exercise was 'Operation Barbara' – because, he decided, when you thought of Virgin, you thought not of Richard Branson but of Barbara Cartland!

BA's then Chairman, Lord King, as Basham soon discovered, nurtured a loathing of Branson, whose relaxed business style and casual indifference to the establishment represented a negation of everything to which King himself aspired. An ex-factory-floor worker who'd left school without any qualifications, King had made his life an epic tale not so much in social climbing as social mountaineering. Married, for the second time, to the Honourable Isabel Monckton, King kept photographs of himself with various members of the royal family on his desk at BA. With homes in Scotland and Leicestershire and a flat in Mayfair, and a penchant for all the trappings of success – most especially Havana cigars – King clearly identified with the establishment – a figure to whom 'Grinning Pullover', as Richard Branson was known to some at BA, was the very antithesis.

In particular, King had a dark fascination with Branson's gay London night club, Heaven, and a rumour he'd heard that rubbish collectors from Westminster Council refused to collect black bags from outside the club because they might contain AIDS-infected hypodermic needles. David Burnside, then in charge of BA's PR, had briefed Basham to investigate this rumour, as part of Operation Barbara, and in his final report Basham dutifully presented a version of the allegation, along with what he saw as other weaknesses in BA's enemy. Basham maintains that his report was a fair one, and even that it served as a caution to BA. Says Basham: 'My report starts with the words "There are certain misconceptions about Virgin . . ." It was a report to BA saying "you're wrong".'

Nevertheless, the report on Virgin, which contained statements that Branson believed to be highly damaging, was not for BA's eyes only. Basham gave a copy of the 'Operation Barbara' report to Frank Kane, a reporter on the *Sunday Telegraph*. Basham had cultivated Kane's boss of the time, John Jay, as a prime contact during his twenty years in financial PR, and over the period when he had been representing the Fayed brothers during their campaign for Harrods, the *Sunday Telegraph* had been one of the most enthusiastic supporters of the so-called phoney pharaoh's most lavish fantasies (for more on this see Chapter 13). Having provided Jay and Kane with a copy of his 'Operation Barbara' report, it came as no surprise to Basham when the two journalists concurred that Virgin was vulnerable and the Government was unwise to support Branson to the detriment of British Airways.

A major, 1,500-word article in the *Sunday Telegraph* under Frank Kane's by-line followed, using facts and figures about Virgin which had come directly from BA. Headlined 'Virgin heading for stormy skies', it warned how easily Virgin could slip into the same early graves as Laker, British Caledonian and Air Europe. Half-truths were cleverly combined with dark speculation to paint an overall picture that could not have been more damaging to Virgin's cause.

Of course, there was no clue to the part played by BA or their invisible persuader in all of this. 'Operation Barbara' had scored a first direct hit, and BA had good cause to be delighted with the result. Soon enough the story would be circulated through the press files of the national newsrooms. Versions of it would find their way on to the pages of other newspapers. It had been a classic exercise in negative PR – and a bolt out of the blue for Richard Branson.

british gas and the austrian theory

Angus Maitland took to the dark arts of negative PR on British Gas's behalf in an altered business climate – and at a very different stage in his career from Basham's. The Cadbury and Greenbury reports of 1992 and 1995 reflected a trend towards a more evolved sense of corporate governance in keeping with the Nineties backlash against the 'greed is good' culture of the Eighties. In this new climate, the treatment by one of Britain's largest companies of its competitors was one of those issues, like the treatment of its staff, the environment and directors' salaries, to which rather more stringent requirements now applied.

Like Basham, Maitland had launched his own consultancy in 1994, although his client list by far outstripped anything Basham had achieved at the launch of Warwick Corporate. Located in Orion House, the one and only skyscraper on the edge of Covent Garden, Maitland's new consultancy provided a panoramic vista through the eleventh-floor windows of many of central London's most historic landmarks, from Nelson's Column and Trafalgar Square to Big Ben and the Houses of Parliament. In this rarefied environment no expense was spared in the wining and dining of the high-level contacts whom Maitland had spent his career cultivating assiduously.

It was at lunches in the Maitland boardroom that plans were discussed to rescue British Gas from the company's all-time low in public opinion ratings. It has been said by some industry insiders that while Maitland's intimate involvement with British Gas, a company for which he'd consulted for several years, gave him an unparalleled grasp of the complex issues facing the industry, at the same time he'd become so close to the company's senior management that he had 'gone native' – a view which may possibly explain why he ended up engaged in the dangerous pursuit of negative PR. Certainly, as an ex-researcher, Maitland understood better than anyone the value of scrutinizing the workings of British Gas's corporate enemies to identify how and where the greatest damage could be inflicted.

One of the theories Maitland helped propagate was the one which was later to bring him, briefly, to the *Independent*'s attention. The 'Austrian' theory was that the supposedly tight-knit circle around Claire Spottiswoode all owed their ideological allegiances to the ideas of Friedrich August von Hayek, leading light of the 'Austrian School' of economics in the interwar period. Sinister as the notion may be of some remote Austrian academic wielding his invisible influence over national policy-makers, Hayek's theories were hardly of the variety to raise eyebrows. He proposed that the best form of government is minimalist, intervening only where services or goods cannot be supplied by competing producers. Individuals should make choices themselves rather than rely on the state. Why is it that a blue dress and stout handbag spring to mind?

According to the Austrian theory, the free-market think-tank the Institute of Economic Affairs was a Hayek stronghold. Michael Beesley, formerly professor of economics at the London Business School and adviser to Claire Spottiswoode, is a managing trustee of the IEA. The husband of Spottiswoode's deputy, Professor Colin Robinson, was editorial director of the IEA. And IEA tentacles penetrated other regulatory regimes too. Stephen Littlechild, director-general of Offer, the electricity regulator, was one of Beesley's star pupils. Ian Byatt, director-general of Ofwat (water) and Sir Bryan Carsberg, former head of Oftel (telecommunications), were both longstanding Beesley acquaintances.

'So what?' the average person might be forgiven for asking. Don't kindred spirits congregate in all industries? And if some may be more strident in their views than others, does that make them all fanatics? Angus Maitland may well have realized that evidence of conspiracy was pretty thin. But presented to a friendly journalist, with smoke and mirrors and a roll of drums, the Austrian theory might take on a more sinister dimension. And he had one such journalist very much in mind.

Melvyn Marckus, who in his *Observer* days had been so faithful to the cause of British Airways, was by 1994 City editor of *The Times* – one of the half-dozen most influential posts in financial journalism. Maitland had invested a great deal of time promoting the cause of British Gas to Marckus, who was probably the company's best ally in the press. Marckus was therefore a natural target for the Austrian theory, on which Maitland had first begun to brief him as early as March 1994. But it was the following February when Marckus wrote a prominent article, the contents of which bore an astonishingly strong resemblance to the anonymous briefing papers Maitland was later to pass on to the *Independent* and to a feature which appeared in *Utility Week* on 3 February 1995.

Marckus's piece, a 1,000-word article with the sweeping

headline 'The great privatised energy utility farce', went further than British Gas could possibly have hoped for. 'Should your daughter prove insistent about going on the stage,' it began, 'perhaps you should encourage her to join a GenCo, or a REC, or British Gas. Limited talent? No problem. Urge her in the direction of a regulatory troupe such as Offer or Ofgas, particularly if she has a smattering of Austrian.' In a venomously satirical article, Marckus listed the relationships which British Gas's spin doctor had so carefully noted in briefing documents. He went on to describe one of Michael Beesley's works as displaying 'a schizoid obsession with subdividing everything'; he labelled Professor Colin Robinson 'Blue Robbo' and depicted him as a figure who 'has stalked the great British Gas whale with an Ahab-like obsession for almost three decades'; and he couldn't resist the reference to Robinson's wife joining Claire Spottiswoode at Ofgas. A beguiling mix of fact and exaggeration, Marckus's article hammered the regulator's credibility with glee. British Gas's most senior directors must have been delighted to have doubts about their corporate enemy so loudly trumpeted in *The Times* – and by its City editor, no less.

BA's dirty tricks escalate

The dirty tricks campaigns waged on behalf of BA and BG had enjoyed similar success. Not only were Basham's major placing with the *Sunday Telegraph* and Marckus's piece in *The Times* victories in themselves; in the future, whenever any other journalist wrote on these subjects, out would come the press cuttings and, once again, allegations and innuendo would be repeated until they were accepted as fact. (Maitland, according to Chris Blackhurst of the *Independent*, later said that the Austrian theory was 'common knowledge' – a supreme irony, Blackhurst considered, given that it was he, Maitland, who had made it so!)

Despite these successes, however, neither of the invisible persuaders was allowed to rest on his laurels. Colin Marshall, chief executive of BA, complained to Basham that Jay's article had not been hard-hitting enough, while Maitland, faced with the prospect of a critical amendment to the Gas Act scheduled to go through Parliament later that year, planned to deliver results for his client, not only in relation to Ofgas, but against BG's new domestic competitors, most notably United Gas.

In BA's case, further damaging pieces were placed in both the *Sunday Telegraph* and the *Guardian*. Over the weeks, as the body of evidence against Virgin mounted up in the press, and Basham continued briefing journalists, the Virgin press office, led by the youthful Will Whitehorn, began receiving call after call from national papers, repeating a long list of identical, negative allegations. As Whitehorn commented: 'I know that when a number of newspapers phone with an almost identical story that there is a concerted campaign. It doesn't just "happen". It was concerted and somebody was organizing it. I knew in my heart where it was coming from, but I had no evidence.'

At the same time that BA was briefing the national press, Lord King, still at the height of his powers, was meeting movers and shakers in the City, only too happy to point out Virgin's corporate weaknesses in an attempt to scare away any further investment in BA's hated competitor. Together, the PR initiatives and King's activities had their calculated effect: serious doubts about Virgin began to take root at the precise time that Branson was trying to persuade Salomon Brothers, the merchant bank, to help raise money to expand his airline. Deals once talked about with certainty began to waver. Virgin's credibility was starting to come unstuck.

Branson never for a moment doubted the source of the negative stories – but, like Whitehorn, he had no evidence. Most journalists wouldn't dream of revealing their sources. But Branson and Whitehorn needed to take urgent and drastic action to stem the flow of highly damaging allegations that were circulating about Virgin. Searching for a way to stop a rumour mill which seemed to be spinning out of control, Branson's break came from an unexpected quarter.

Chris Hutchins was a journalist working for the now defunct *Today* newspaper. Hutchins had distinguished himself, certainly as far as Branson was concerned, by having written an article several years earlier announcing that Branson had been knighted by the Queen. Of course, it was only a fanciful tale written by a journalist who hadn't bothered with even a cursory checking of facts.

But when Hutchins called Branson, he urged him to take what he said seriously. He had been contacted, he said, by Brian Basham whose wife, Eileen, had worked for him at the paper. According to Hutchins, Basham had told him that he had heard a good story about 'Branson and drugs'. Even though what Hutchins was telling him merely echoed Branson's suspicions, the confirmation that the world's favourite airline was putting out negative stories about him nevertheless came as a deep shock.

'Up until that point,' he says, 'I had never come across that sort of trashing PR. I had naïvely thought that PR men were supposed to promote their own company and its products, not smear the opposition.'

When Branson told his young PR adviser of his unnerving conversation with Hutchins, Whitehorn felt positively ill. He had worked for a rival of Basham's Broad Street company in the mid-Eighties, and knew all about Basham's legendary hard-ball reputation. The two men discussed, at some length, what they ought to do next. And the more they talked, the clearer their only viable course of action became. They realized they had no choice but to ask Hutchins to meet with Basham to hear the so-called 'drug story' – and secretly to tape record the meeting. Without such evidence, no one would ever believe that the highly regarded national carrier was waging a media war against them.

As it happened, the tape recording of Hutchins' meeting with Basham turned out to be far from straightforward. To Branson's astonishment, the reporter asked him if he could borrow a tape recorder with a small microphone – apparently there weren't any available at *Today*. Will Whitehorn duly scoured the electronics shops of Tottenham Court Road for a suitable machine, which he then handed over to Hutchins only hours before his meeting, showing him how to operate it.

Arriving at Basham's home for the meeting, Hutchins was nervous and perspiring. He'd already pressed the 'Record' button before approaching Basham's front door; Eileen answered the door and spent some time talking about the gossip column they'd both worked on. Then when Basham finally did turn up, late, more time was spent on small talk. Hutchins was worried about running out of tape before they'd got to the main point of the meeting. He was also anxious about the noise of the tape turning in his pocket, which he could hear distinctly . . . would Basham pick up on it too? Would the recorder make a loud clicking noise when it turned itself off? And what if, through his inexperience with the recorder, none of this conversation was being picked up?

It was, in fact, the last of these concerns which turned out to be the problem. The afternoon following Hutchins' meeting, the journalist and the Virgin boss sat on either side of Branson's table at his Holland Park home, the tape recorder between them. Reaching out, Branson pressed the 'Play' button. So much depended on what they were about to hear. The stream of hostile calls from journalists parroting identical accusations. The vicious pieces in the press. If the tape recording proved they had a common source, and that source was Brian Basham, then Branson would at last have the evidence he needed to take on BA.

But as the next few minutes passed, Branson's initial anticipation gradually changed, first to frustration, then to hopelessness. He glanced up at Hutchins' eyes across the table with a look of despair; all that was coming out of the recorder were a series of inaudible squeaks and stray phrases of conversation. No matter how many replays they attempted, bending down over the machine, straining to listen, they just weren't getting anywhere. Picking up the phone, Branson called round Will Whitehorn from his nearby Campden Hill Road office to try listening to the tape, while he turned his attention instead to a written report on Virgin which Basham had given Hutchins.

Whitehorn, who had found the last few months fighting the tide of journalistic hostility intensely stressful, was every bit as determined as his boss to pin down Basham and his paymasters at BA. Arriving at Branson's home, he quickly realized they weren't getting anywhere with the tiny tape recorder – but perhaps Virgin's Town House Studios could help. Shortly afterwards, he was sitting in a studio listening to the contents of the tape, this time over huge speakers, while studio engineers attempted sound enhancement, labouring over a glistening array of technical equipment as they attempted to cut back on interference.

Given the poor quality of the recording, there seemed, at first, little that the sound engineers could do. But as they persisted, they gradually improved the crackling, distorted tape until Basham's briefing of Hutchins could be heard more and more clearly. Whitehorn sat forward in his studio chair as the two men's voices emerged quite audibly. It was becoming possible, now, to distinguish what was going on. But had Basham admitted to anything, on tape, that made it clear what he and BA were up to?

Some of Basham's briefing focused on Heaven and the 'AIDS-infested needles' story which had been of such consuming interest to Lord King and for which Basham appeared to have evidence. Disturbing though it was to hear their rival's PR man discussing the most vulnerable aspects of Virgin's operations, Whitehorn was more interested in something else . . . which finally came at the end of the interview. Having spent the last hour briefing the journalist with exclusively negative stories about Virgin and Branson, Basham then told him he didn't want to be in any way involved with what he'd just passed on. BA, he declared without a hint of self-consciousness, was not running a campaign against Virgin. But, having said all that – 'If you blow Branson out, it doesn't bother me as long as neither BA nor I is associated with it.'

The tape, together with the report Basham had given Hutchins, was all the evidence Virgin needed. That evening, when Whitehorn shared the enhanced tape with Branson in the quiet of the Virgin boss's home, the two men listened to it over and over and the awful truth began to sink in. Any sense of triumph at catching out BA was by far overshadowed by the realization that their worst suspicions had been confirmed. How on earth were they to take on the full, perverse might of the world's favourite airline?

BG's threatened break-up: project bunter

By the spring of 1995 senior management at British Gas's Rivermill House headquarters on Vauxhall Bridge Road had cause for deep concern. The Gas Act was about to pass through Parliament, and independent gas companies were clamouring for an amendment forcing British Gas to separate from Transco, its highly lucrative pipeline and storage company. Independent gas companies had to buy from Transco, and there was understandable suspicion that as long as Transco remained part of British Gas, competitors who had to deal with it wouldn't get a fair crack of the whip.

The potential effect of the threatened break-up on an organization already punch-drunk from the onslaught of competition and suffering its lowest public opinion ratings ever was such as to prompt BG to call in all five of its retained public relations and lobbying firms and set about firefighting on all fronts. Lashing out at what it saw as the vulnerabilities of its commercial enemies was a key part of the overall strategy. Angus Maitland took on the particular mission of setting up United Gas as a target for the national press while MPs sought to introduce the critical amendment to the Gas Act that would expose British Gas to the full rigours of competition. The top-secret assignment was code-named 'Project Bunter'.

Like the Austrian theory before it (and, indeed, Brian Basham's own 'Operation Barbara'), 'Project Bunter' depended to a far greater degree on Maitland's consummate skills as a spin doctor than on any great body of evidence suggesting wrongdoing on the part of United Gas. So what were the dark shenanigans in which United Gas was supposed to have engaged?

United Gas, the operating arm of UtiliCorp UK, was jointly owned by a US utility company and the company's UK management. It was involved in six joint ventures with regional electricity

133

and gas companies throughout Britain. Where things got complicated was that ten gas companies had been created by the directors of United Gas, registered at a residential address in Fulham – an unusual arrangement, no doubt, but not so unusual when one knew that the address was the home of United's companies formations solicitor, Malcolm Fontayne. Given the additional information that the ten entities were owned by United Gas directors personally, rather than by United Gas itself, a domestic address is less peculiar still. The directors of United gave the companies made-up names such as 'Dogstar', 'Encurium' and 'Zealtry' – which also seemed peculiar on the surface of things, until one understood that these were never intended to be used as brand names to be launched on an unsuspecting public.

But what was supposedly the really serious allegation was that the directors of United Gas had personally set up the companies to make multiple applications for gas which BG had been forced to 'release' to help new entrants into the competitive gas market. This would, indeed, have been a tale worth the telling – were it not for the fact that the Office of Fair Trading both knew and approved of what the United Gas directors were doing.

The anonymous briefing documents Angus Maitland was soon to use for 'Project Bunter' did not, of course, mention whose address was being used or why the names of the ten companies didn't matter one jot; nor, most importantly of all, did they highlight that the ten gas companies had acted with the full knowledge of the authorities. Instead, additional information about large payouts made to the ten companies' directors, and the changing of their financial year-ends, hinted darkly at yet another dimension to the conspiracy.

Rifle loaded and target within his sights, Maitland knew that what was now critical to the success of 'Project Bunter' was timing. A suitably damning article about United Gas needed to appear in the national press at the moment when it could inflict most damage. To this end he needed a journalist he could be sure of: one he could brief and trust to keep the project under wraps until the critical amendment came up in the House of Commons – at which point all hell could be unleashed on United Gas, damaging its credibility and raising serious doubts about the trustworthiness of independent gas companies in general. To this end, who better to approach than Melvyn Marckus?

Marckus, who perhaps appropriately is now a PR consultant himself, makes no bones about his relationship with Maitland: 'Every journalist has his contacts. Maitland, Parker and Cardew were people I was happy to relate to. I don't believe they'd lie to me. If I asked for help they would give it. They helped me by sending over material and so forth.' The 'material and so forth' made its way to the *Times* City desk in a flurry between late March and mid-April 1995. Marckus assured Maitland that he wouldn't write a piece on United Gas until after the Easter parliamentary recess, when the amendment would come up for debate. Maitland also manoeuvred behind the scenes, trying to get the damaging story about United Gas on to the front page.

On 18 April 1995, while a Select Committee debated the amendment to the Gas Act which British Gas most feared, Marckus's article appeared. It was a substantial piece and unmissable, carrying a photograph of No. 25 Hestercombe Avenue, Fulham, and an organogram, courtesy of Maitland, showing the complex ownership of United Gas and its directors' interests. Marckus faithfully repeated the contents of Maitland's briefing notes, the combined effect of which was to leave one in no doubt that the directors of United Gas were engaged in some extremely suspect financial transactions – that's if they weren't downright dishonest.

Marckus's piece had major impact and was widely read by the MPs most actively engaged in the Gas Act debate. But just to make doubly sure the message was heard, Marckus hammered home the same subject with another 1,000-word article four days later, headlined 'Beware a backdoor break-up of British Gas'. This time, he not only repeated Maitland's 'Project Bunter' briefing documents, but threw in a dose of the Austrian theory for good measure – a two-for-one super-duper! To the clandestine cross-ownerships and shadowy wheeler-dealing at a semi-detached house in Fulham was added the mention of 'Blue Robbo', part of the husband and wife team 'involved in the long-running plot to force British Gas to divest itself of some 90 per cent of its UK asset base'.

Even though he'd depended heavily on the good services of the invisible persuader at Orion House for his information, Marckus wasn't slow to pat himself on the back for an investigative job well done. 'What might have been of interest to an inquisitive soul such as myself . . .' he reflects at one point, as if he'd spent many hours slaving away at Companies House trying to unearth evidence of wrongdoing. But Marckus was at his most breathtakingly brazen in repeating Labour MP Martin O'Neill's tribute to his supposed investigative skills: 'Modesty does not prevent me', he writes, 'from quoting Martin O'Neill, Labour MP for Clackmannan. "*The Times* showed the complex – almost Byzantine – character of the activities of Utilicorp and United Gas in which several companies are concerned. Transparency is being pursued and one could wish that those seeking it would organise comparable transparency in their own arrangements, so that Mr Melvyn Marckus's investigative skills were not required to establish clarity."'

In case British Gas needed any further persuading that 'Project Bunter' had hit home, Marckus went on to quote Judith Church, Labour MP for Dagenham, who had clearly absorbed, and was now repeating, the question they so urgently wanted to place in the public mind: 'United Gas seems happy to ignore the legislation, to hide information from the public and to preach "pay virtue" in public while enjoying fat-cat practice in private. Does the Minister . . . think that these are fit and proper persons who can be trusted by the public to supply their gas?'

Angus Maitland's paymasters at British Gas must have been well pleased. To have prompted doubts about their competitors to be aired in the House was a major victory. In an industry where the government had the ultimate say on trading conditions, it was only a short step from questioning the activities of new domestic competitors to questioning the whole process whereby competition in the domestic market was being introduced. Judith Church's questions would be noted and repeated outside the Chamber, by politicians, civil servants and those who worked in the office of the regulator. They would also have an impact further afield. Merchant bank analysts who followed the workings of the gas industry would take note – and when the City's support was sought by one of the new gas competitors, the accusations levelled in *The Times* and made explicit in the House of Commons would certainly be remembered.

However, Angus Maitland, driven as always, wasn't going to stop there. He continued to approach other leading journalists with the United Gas story. Interestingly, one of these was Frank Kane, who, in his former position at the *Sunday Telegraph* had, Richard Branson believed, inflicted so much damage. Now at the *Sunday Times*, Kane received copies of the Austrian theory and 'Project Bunter' documents, but declined to do anything with them.

Maitland was left to approach others at the *Sunday Times* instead, and in the end set about persuading Andrew Lorenz, a senior business writer on the newspaper, to write a feature about the gas market on the basis of a non-attributable briefing by a senior British Gas executive. A major feature in the *Sunday Times*, following Marckus's pieces in its sister title, could certainly set the cat among the pigeons – and this time Maitland planned to go even further. He proposed to lay blame for British Gas's commercial nadir at the feet of the government and Ofgas. There was certainly a lot to play for, but Maitland, more than anyone, knew the risks involved. Mindful of these, and prior to the meeting that would officially never happen between journalist or client, Maitland cautioned the British Gas executive that because of implicit and possible explicit criticism of the government and Ofgas, the article had to be non-attributable.

As it happened, British Gas's off-the-record briefing, a well accepted practice in corporate PR, produced only a balanced and sensible piece of journalism from Lorenz, who showed no sign of accepting British Gas arguments hook, line and sinker. Besides, the Lorenz article which appeared on 21 January 1996 was over-shadowed by events of early December, when the *Independent* ran Blackhurst's piece accusing Maitland of dirty tricks. It was an alarming experience, both for Maitland and for British Gas, to find themselves unexpectedly catapulted on to the front page of a national newspaper – all the more so because, after months of circulating the Austrian theory and Project Bunter papers with no ill effect, they had been taken completely unawares by the *Independent*. Now the prospect of becoming embroiled in press accusations of another BA-style 'dirty tricks' scandal was just too horrifying to contemplate. But, as we have seen – and for reasons probably not unconnected with Maitland's status as a PR guru – the bomb failed to explode.

BA's end game

In the case of BA's dirty tricks, there had been factors besides the issue of 'negative PR' which were to blow up in the airline's face. Quite apart from the highly damaging headlines being planted in the national press and the rumours that had been circulating round the City, BA staff had been 'switch selling': a team of some seventeen people located in BA's marketing department carried out a systematic campaign of accessing Virgin computer records; others phoned up their passengers offering free upgrades if they flew BA. BA had also employed private detectives at a cost of hundreds of thousands of pounds to investigate what King and Burnside suspected was a sophisticated intelligence operation being run against them by Branson and Goldman Sachs – of course, no such operation existed.

The scale and depth of BA's anti-Virgin activities were such that as revelation after revelation was made, Branson himself could scarcely believe what he was discovering. He tried repeated approaches to senior executives within BA, including King himself, hoping to deal with the issue without having to resort to lawyers – hitherto Branson had not been litigious. Sir Freddie Laker, who had also famously suffered at the hands of BA in the past, repeatedly urged Branson to 'sue the bastards' – a course of action Branson resisted. Until, that is, Branson learned that the *Sunday Telegraph* was planning an article accusing him of spying on BA – an incredible hypocrisy given BA's own massive, and utterly fruitless, 'counter-espionage' operation. It was at this point that Branson snapped. Writing to Sir Colin Marshall, BA's chief executive, he demanded a withdrawal of the BA allegations and a public apology. When he didn't get either, he called in his lawyers.

Branson sued BA for libel and was prepared to go all the way to the High Court to get things out in the open. BA decided to counter-sue, having talked themselves into a state of such profound paranoia that they were convinced their own private detective operation would unearth evidence of Virgin's crimes and mis-demeanours. But BA's most senior executives were having to face the appalling truth that, despite massive private detective bills and millions in legal fees to Linklaters and Paines, they still didn't have a shred of evidence against Virgin. On the contrary, the whistle was about to be blown on their own treatment of Richard Branson and his company.

At this point it is instructive to chart the sudden change in the relationship between BA and the invisible persuader who had been so active on their behalf. As part of the preparations for the counter-suit against Virgin, Basham found himself having to sign a statement that denied BA had ever instructed him to encourage journalists to write negatively about Virgin. Persuaded that BA would stand by him in court, Basham signed.

Basham now feels his confidence in BA was completely mis-placed. By the time he signed the statement, it was becoming apparent not only to BA but to BA's lawyers that it was BA, not Virgin Atlantic, which had been indulging in a dirty tricks cam-paign. What now exercised the minds of BA's most senior executives and their lawyers was just how to distance themselves from the impending opprobrium of a failed lawsuit. The strategy on which they decided shouldn't have come as any surprise. Offering Virgin their record out-of-court settlement in December 1992, they also agreed to read out an apology to Virgin in open court early the following year. And whom did they hold respons-ible for the whole catalogue of conspiracy? Why, Brian Basham of course! The switch-selling operation run in the US and the UK, the private eyes employed in Britain, the strategy and implementation of all PR activities – BA could bring itself to name only Brian Basham as responsible. Part of their statement admitted that Richard Branson had 'grounds for serious concern about the activities of a number of British Airways employees and of Mr Basham'. The BA statement also admitted that Basham had attempted to place 'hostile and discreditable stories' in the press. 'Mine was the sole name in that apology,' Basham told me later. 'It made it look to the world at large as though I'd orchestrated the whole campaign – which is quite flattering, to think I had the power to organize a campaign around the world. But it was entirely untrue.'

So he became the fall-guy. Despite BA's assurances, not only had BA not stood by him, it had made him, very publicly, their sacrificial lamb. BA's QC, Christopher Clarke, was even instructed to tell the court that the directors of BA were not party to any concerted campaign against Branson or Virgin Atlantic. Brian Basham therefore had the singular distinction of being the only named individual held personally responsible for BA's dirty tricks campaign. To add further insult to very great injury, soon afterwards BA replaced him with his old PR rival, Sir Tim Bell.

Basham's legal trials in connection with the dirty tricks affair were by no means over, however. Feeling deeply betrayed by BA, when he was approached for an interview by investigative journalist Martyn Gregory, he agreed to help with a TV documentary. The result was a *World in Action* programme in April 1993, 'BA's Virgin Soldiers', in which Basham appeared, and which detailed BA's switch-selling and related activities. Having touched a nerve with his ground-breaking documentary, Gregory went on to write a book entitled *Dirty Tricks: BA's Secret War Against Virgin Atlantic*. Satisfied with his appearance in *World in Action*, Basham readily agreed to help with the book, seeing it as an opportunity to set the record straight. He wanted to get across the point that, from the beginning, he had cautioned BA against focusing too much media attention – positive or negative – on Branson. Why? Because that would accord their business rival more authority than if they simply ignored him. But BA didn't listen. 'The architect of Branson's success is Lord King,' says Basham. 'He lifted him in public perception and made him into a serious figure by giving him a wall to bounce his ball against.' Even more significantly, Basham wanted to get across the message that, contrary to the carefully crafted apology read out in court, BA's most senior executives had not only been fully aware of the dirty tricks activities, it was they who had commissioned them – a point which BA would dispute.

When Gregory's book was finally published in 1994 and Basham got to read its contents, however, he decided that the journalist had, in his view, misrepresented his own role in the affair and portrayed him as an eager pedlar of anti-Virgin lies. What angered Basham most were allegations in the book that he had lied to the City about Virgin – 'I can't operate with the reputation of being a liar.'

So Basham took Gregory and his publisher, Little, Brown, to court in November 1996. He won his case, although Little, Brown swiftly lodged an appeal to be heard in 1998. A court injunction prevented further publication of Gregory's book *Dirty Tricks* and ordered Little, Brown to pay £20,000 damages, in addition to an estimated £400,000 legal bill. Basham was triumphant. The verdict, he told court reporters, vindicated the fight to clear his name, which he'd spent the last three years trying to do. After a celebratory evening, the next day Basham didn't get out of bed till five in the afternoon – not on account of a monster hangover, but because from the moment he woke up the phone didn't stop ringing with former clients, friends and well-wishers phoning through their congratulations.

For Martyn Gregory, the verdict represented a blow – and not only to his own work: 'It's a very, very sad day for investigative journalism,' he told an *Evening Standard* reporter, 'and the British establishment has once again gathered around one of its own.'

Stepping back from the two courtroom dramas, one is left with a rather compelling question which has never been vigorously pursued by anyone: to put it crudely, if BA said that it was Basham who carried out the dirty tricks, and if Basham has subsequently cleared his name, then who really was responsible? Basham, for one, has no doubts at all. It was Colin Marshall with whom he is most unhappy.

> Colin Marshall is an impeccably good manager. He was a control freak who had been through two major reviews of costs in British Airways where he'd examined the role of every single individual in British Airways. Now, don't tell me that he'd overlooked seventeen people sitting in a room on a cost base – didn't know anything about them. Robert Ayling became marketing director and went through the whole marketing department in which these people were sitting and don't tell me he didn't know anything about it either. But they both said they didn't know that it was happening.

Sir Colin Marshall currently shows no signs of moving on from BA, where he is currently non-executive chairman. Nor does his chief executive, Robert Ayling. If Basham is right, they would appear to be corporate Houdinis of the first order, having escaped severe damage to their careers by making him their scapegoat. As for Basham himself, he is now back in the PR saddle at his City firm Basham & Coyle, whose future is being keenly watched by an industry in which Basham is one of the most colourful players.

BA continues to be extremely visible on the PR front, having hired Alan Parker's Brunswick, in addition to the services of Sir Tim, to promote its cause. The airline's highest-profile PR event of 1997 was all set to be its controversial new livery, unveiled in mid-June with much fanfare and a major advertising campaign, the orchestration for which was arranged by Dave Stewart of Eurythmics fame. 'Driving the change programme', gushed a BA press release, 'is a new corporate mission – to be the undisputed leader in world travel. The aim is to present British Airways as an airline of the world, born and based in Britain with a community of people passionately committed to serving the communities of the world.'

This passionate commitment to serving, however, became somewhat open to question not much more than a month later when BA cancelled or delayed half its flights: BA managers had failed to reach agreement with the cabin crew union BASSA, which called its members out on a three-day strike. All over the world passengers who'd found their flights cancelled were left scrambling for tickets on other carriers, furious that the usually reliable airline had badly let them down. The moral of the story? Corporate drum-beating can often echo back in the most embarrassing way in light of subsequent events; and the more insistent the drum-beat, the greater the mortification of those involved.

british gas – the final chapter

Will the same pattern of events be repeated in the case of BG's undercover war against United Gas and the regulator? Will BG's senior managers attempt to heap all the blame for the dirty tricks campaign against United on an easily dispensed-with external adviser? Going by past record, BG has displayed alacrity in producing scapegoats rather than solutions which may trouble Angus Maitland in his darkest midnight hours. The portly and Havana-clutching form of Cedric Brown, resplendent in the back seat of his chauffeur-driven Jaguar, may seem an unlikely sacrificial lamb, but when his early retirement was announced on 6 February 1996 it was interpreted by some as an attempt by the chairman, Richard Giordano, and his fellow directors, to propitiate a public whose resentment had escalated as customer complaints doubled and assaults in the media continued.

Yet even the announcement of Brown's early retirement, held at Westminster's Queen Elizabeth Centre, was a signal lesson on how *not* to hold a press conference. Giordano delivered a lengthy lecture on how British Gas was to be carved up and how Brown's job was, effectively, to disappear. Brown then stood up and ad-mitted that he hadn't had a pleasant fifteen months, but said that he wanted to look to the future rather than the past. When journalists tried to get answers to the questions British Gas should really have anticipated – Was Brown being made the fall-guy? How much had the salary row weakened his position? – Giordano cut them dead, saying they could 'cross-examine' Brown afterwards.

But, alas, there was to be no afterwards. In his caustic piece next morning in the *Daily Telegraph*, under the headline 'Fur flies as newshounds corner the fat cat,' Robert Hardman described how Brown was effectively trapped by a baying media pack in an office at the Queen Elizabeth Centre until the police arrived to rescue him. Hardman drily observed: 'He must be counting the days to April when he can clear his desk. Then . . . Mr Giordano . . . will surely become the fattest specimen in the entire corporate cattery.'

Quite how British Gas will respond to fresh evidence of its negative PR is anybody's guess, but the unlikeliest scenario of all is that the company will pay up the millions United Gas says it has lost as a result of 'negative PR', publicly apologize to the regulator, and quietly get on with the task of running its business. In image terms at least, British Gas is a company with its back to the wall – and so it may well feel it has little to lose by fighting. After all, neither BG nor its adviser, Angus Maitland, has done anything that breaks the law.

A *Presswatch Quarterly* review, reported in *PR Week* during March 1996, showed that British Gas came last out of 1,135 of Britain's biggest companies ranked in terms of negative press coverage. With a score of minus 2,077 points (compared to the winner, Prudential, on plus 738), British Gas found itself alongside other privatized companies like British Rail and BT as one of the organizations journalists most love to hate. And all this despite having a handful of external PR advisers and an in-house PR department that is generous by any standards. No doubt it was desperation during its all-time low in public opinion, and the threat of a corporate carve-up, which led to BG's descent into the murky underworld of dirty tricks.

United Gas has gone on record as saying it is prepared to issue writs for the millions of pounds it has lost as a result of the suspected smear campaign. While the City editor of *The Times* was firing off a volley of negative 'investigative' reports about the company, United Gas's press office received a stream of hostile calls from journalists repeating the same accusations. Roger Turner, when he was managing director of United Gas, said he would love to know who is behind the campaign. With the publication of this book, the suspicions he may already have formed will doubtless be confirmed. For there is little doubt that, reading the briefing papers circulated about his own company by Angus Maitland, he would come to much the same conclusion as Richard Branson did when reading Basham's 'Operation Barbara' report: 'The "report" would be a joke if it were not half-plausible in its presentation. It reflects the style of a private-placing document and appears to be a strange mixture of fact and inaccuracy which combine to create a most damaging impression.'

British Gas's efforts to prevent the opening up of competition in the domestic gas market did, of course, fail. During 1988 the whole of Britain becomes an open market for domestic gas suppliers. Not really strange, then, that in the autumn of 1997 British Gas embarked on a major advertising campaign telling the nation that, as of the next year, their gas bills were set to fall. For the many customers who had no idea that for the first time they were about to have a choice of supplier, it must have seemed that British Gas was making a very magnanimous gesture. Forty-eight-sheet posters also announced that British Gas would soon be in the business of providing customers with electricity. Falling bills, new product offerings...the effects of competition are, indeed, a wonder to behold.

PART II: celebrity PR

CHAPTER SEVEN

what's in a name? the power and the glory
of celebrity PR

The announcement of one's engagement to be married is usually a private affair. Close friends and family are called together, if no longer to the drawing room, then perhaps to the dining room, a wine bar or around the summer barbecue, according to taste. Toasts are offered, cheeks kissed and shoulders pummelled. A few bottles of fizz don't generally go amiss. As a rule, the notion of flying across the Atlantic, hiring a sprawling country pile, inviting the world's media and a hundred international celebrities doesn't instantly spring to mind as the most likely way to make the announcement. Unless, of course, your name is Ivana Trump, in which case such an arrangement would seem to be *de rigueur*.

Ivana's engagement to American tycoon Riccardo Mazzuchelli, announced amid the stately opulence of Syon House, was, of course, in all the papers, not just in Britain but around the world. With guests like Shirley Bassey – who thoughtfully broke into a pre-arranged 'impromptu' solo for the blushing couple – Adnan Khashoggi, Britt Ekland and Richard Branson, the engagement bash was not only a media relations extravaganza but a triumph of social engineering. Behind all the celebrity high jinks and appearance of spontaneous *bon vivant*, it was as stage-managed as any royal visit. The key difference was that, instead of being planned by a team of men from the Home Office, the whole thing was masterminded by the immeasurably more influential Liz Brewer.

It was Liz who worked out that Shirley Bassey would be in London around the time of the engagement party and who suggested she be invited – a superstar serenade would attract media exposure over and above the immodest acreage of newspaper column inches and hours of TV air time already guaranteed. It was from Liz's little black book that the names of Ivana's countless celebrity 'friends' were extracted. 'People have the impression, and it's deliberate, that I'm a slightly dizzy social butterfly,' says this PR lady to the stars. 'They never see behind the scenes. There's always somebody pulling the strings or pushing the buttons. Nothing ever happens by accident. Someone, somewhere behind the scenes is making things happen.'

The world of celebrity PR is a lot more precarious than that of corporate work, depending, as it so often does, on the whim of a single individual. But it can be a lot more lucrative. The endorsement by a celebrity of a product, company, cause or event can be worth many millions – and just a modest percentage of this kind of fee can make a celebrity PR person very well-heeled indeed.

However, the interaction between celebrities and the media is about far more than money. As the power of the media has grown in leaps and bounds during the last three decades, with it has grown the power of celebrities to influence public opinion in the media, itself a reflection of the burgeoning number of newspapers, magazines, films, television and radio stations. What's more, such is the self-referential nature of the media that the star of one medium in one country quickly becomes a celebrity in others, right around the world. If the Beatles claimed, with some justification, to be more famous than Jesus in the 1960s, how famous does that make, for example, the Spice Girls today?

Celebrity has never been so readily achieved as today. It can be created by a single event on the other side of the world, magnified and made such a part of our consciousness that to us it is as real as – and probably a good deal more interesting than – what goes on down the street. When a wife cuts off her husband's penis, when a woman falls pregnant with eight babies, when two brothers kill their millionaire parents, their names become more familiar to us than those of nearby neighbours. And while it used to be the case that celebrities from the worlds of film, sport, fashion, politics and crime all inhabited separate media worlds, that 'Balkanization' of celebrity, to use author Neal Gabler's expression, is no more: 'They've become one world. Now you're either on the side of the glass looking in, or you're on the side of the glass being looked at.'

In name-crazy America, such is the earnestness with which celebrities are followed that the *New York Observer* publishes an annual 'Gossipocracy' of the 'top 500 people', neatly tabulated and cross-referenced. While the names heading up the list confirm that origins of celebrity are of little relevance, at the same time the newspaper divides celebrities into three categories: Franchise Celebrities, like Arnold Schwarzenegger and Michael Caine, who trade on the power of their name; Conceptual Celebrities, like Liz Taylor and the Duchess of York, who are famous for the events in their lives rather than their careers; and Hybrid Celebrities like Bill and Hillary Clinton, whose names and careers jointly contribute to their status.

While most celebrities still derive their status, at least initially, from success in a particular field, their media skills determine the future of their celebrity; the media may not bring them into existence, but certainly has the power to destroy them. Effectively used, the media also enables them to earn vast fortunes through activities completely unrelated to what made them famous in the first place, or to lend endorsement to causes and charities about which they feel strongly. And, as every celebrity knows, managing the media so as to become richer and even more famous is the job of PR.

bad journalism = good PR

Even celebrity wannabes know this. John McEntee, editor of the *Express*'s gossip column, recalls how he heard that Joan Collins' daughter was getting married in Paris. He phoned her over a period of some weeks before finding her home, at which point she told him: 'You'll have to speak to my publicist.' Says McEntee of those whose claims to celebrity are only tenuous or by association, 'Every jumped-up celebrity has a PR person now.' Understandable as it is that McEntee and journalists like him should feel frustrated that every contact, even with celebrities who are less than super-novas, should be manipulated by the ubiquitous tentacles of PR, there is a very simple and compelling reason for this: the media need celebrities more than celebrities need the media. It's a celebrity's market.

In the case of Joan Collins' daughter, her wedding celebration appeared in glossy technicolor on the pages of *Hello!* magazine, netting her a no doubt tidy sum. Had photographs of the wedding been splashed about everywhere, striking an exclusive deal of that kind simply wouldn't have been possible – and what control would there have been on editorial content? As it happened, the wedding was reported in only the rosiest of hues, plus there was the media dowry. Bad journalism, probably, but good PR.

Like other parts of the industry, the growth of celebrity PR since the early 1980s has been exponential, largely because of the massive expansion of media devoted to every facet of the entertainment industry. When, in the early Eighties, the *Sun* launched its 'Bizarre' column, providing half a page of news *every day* on the rock music and entertainment industry, celebrity spin doctors realized that something fundamental was changing. Daily access to half a page of editorial in a mass-market newspaper opened up an unprecedented opportunity – and one which has grown since then to the point we have reached today, when it is news which gets covered in half a page in the *Sun* and the entertainment industry which pretty much fills the rest of the paper. Not only are Britain's two biggest-selling daily tabloids (the *Sun* and the *Daily Mirror*) completely dominated by celebrity news, but the *Mail*, the *Express* and the *Star* are also strongly celebrity-orientated.

And that's just the tabloids. There are also the rainforests of columns and supplements devoted to celebrity news and features carried in weekend papers of all kinds and stand-alone magazines.

Then there are the endless hours of interviews, phone-ins and talk shows on celebrities pumped out by Britain's burgeoning national, regional and local radio stations. And, of course, the most powerful medium of all: television, with its exploding number of terrestrial and satellite channels, in which the appetite for celebrity programming is relentless and insatiable.

Clearly it is not just America that is name-crazy. Whatever it is that most of us find so bewitching about celebrity – The desire to live our lives vicariously through others, perhaps? Simple escapism? The flush of *schadenfreude* accompanying the news that some arrogant but successful bastard has finally had his comeuppance? – whatever it is that propels us to vacuum up every last little shred of news about celebrities, it is up to journalists to feed our obsession. And the huge and growing band of reporters from the constantly expanding number of media outlets all find themselves, eventually, having to negotiate their passage through the same narrow gateways which provide access to celebrity news, interviews and off-the-record briefings. It is, of course, the control of these gateways which gives celebrity spin doctors their extraordinary power.

Quentin Bell estimates that half the stories about celebrities that appear in the media come directly from the desks of spin doctors. Max Clifford, that *bête noire* of the PR industry, estimates the figure to be closer to 75 per cent. But it's not only PR people who talk up their large and growing influence. Philip Hall, editor of the *News of the World*, the biggest-selling newspaper in Britain and almost completely devoted to entertainment, says: 'Celebrity spin doctors have become a lot more influential over the last decade because people have wisened up. Celebrities are now more familiar with the workings of newspapers and magazines. They realize there is money to be made by giving them interviews – but they need professional advice on how to manage these relationships.'

That 'professional advice' will, frequently, focus on how to extract maximum financial gain from a media appearance. Payment might originate directly from a media owner seeking an interview or exclusive access to a story. More frequently it will be produced from the deep pocket of a company, such as Pepsi, Cadbury, BT, Delta and Pizza Hut to mention but a few, which understands the value of celebrity endorsement. Mark Palmer, executive editor of the *Express*, comments: 'In the tabloids we're very much in the buy-up era, where stories are up for auction. Invariably there's a middleman broking the deal.'

deal broking and editorial abdication

Money isn't all that changes hands, however, when a deal is struck between celebrity spin doctor and newspaper editor. There is also the issue of editorial control. Quite frequently a spin doctor will demand final clearance of the text of any article that appears to ensure that the final product doesn't show up his client in a poor light. As much as editors howl and protest about their cherished independence of view, the fact is that celebrities sell newspapers and if a celebrity story has to be de-barbed by a spin doctor, then so be it. I mentioned in the introduction a PR person who boasted to me of doing a deal with 'a newspaper that was supposedly un-PR-able'. This top celebrity spin doctor knew exactly where the power lay and was quite prepared to use it: 'They have this lofty reputation for having no truck with PR people and doing no deals. But they wanted the story badly. In the end they gave me final clearance of copy, photographs and headline. If they heard me say this, I'd be blown out.'

Exactly how deals are struck and structured is a process we will look at in detail later in this section. First, we should pause to consider that other key *raison d'être* of the celebrity spin doctor: keeping negative stories about his clients out of the papers. The assumption that spin doctors spend their lives setting up interviews for their clients to promote the latest movie, book or fitness video is a mistaken one. True, commercial deals can be immensely time-consuming to set up, especially when the world's most titanic and irascible egos have to be accommodated. But more often than not it is spin doctors who are taking calls from journalists, having to field a huge variety of questions from the most lethal to the most inane. And the difference between the two is not always straightforward:

'Does your actor client ever drive down Sunset Boulevard?'

'Of course he does. He works in Hollywood.'

'Frequently?'

'Just about every day.'

And so actor client becomes a confirmed, regular kerb-crawler.

Knowing where a journalist is coming from, and being able to sidestep the landmines, is one aspect of damage limitation. Knowing one's client well enough to be able to talk one's way around a rumour, whether it is true or not, is another. Just as in corporate PR, forewarned is forearmed, and celebrity spin doctors make it their business to know their clients' every weakness and predilection with a view to developing believable messages to disguise the often unpalatable truth.

Spin doctors of all persuasions generally try to develop good working relationshps with journalists in the hope that an established bond of friendship can be called upon when a favour is needed. This is as true of celebrity PRs as of any other breed. But not running a negative story about a celebrity takes a lot of persuasion, and the wining-and-dining route can actually backfire. As Mark Palmer recalls:

> I was rung up the other day by someone who's supposed to be one of the best PRs in the business. I'd got wind of a story about a minor royal. This guy phoned me up and said, 'As a friend, the story is completely bollocks.' He'd given me a dinner three weeks before, and the moment he said that to me I wondered if he'd known then that the story was coming up, and decided to invest some time and money in me. It all left a very unsavoury taste in my mouth. I decided to run the story anyway. Then he phoned me up and wanted a retraction. I said 'forget it'. It was an example of being used and it had the reverse effect.

Everyone versed in the arts of power, from Machiavelli onwards, knows that fear is generally a more powerful motivator than love. If a spin doctor has to rely on Quaglino's, Le Caprice or The Ivy for his influence, then he doesn't have much. If, on the other hand, his clients are A-list celebs, then he has considerably more negotiating power. As one interviewee told me off the record: 'It's the clients you represent that gives 90 per cent of the people in our business any amount of leverage. The better your client list, the more leverage you have.'

who's who in celebrity PR

It is for this reason that celebrity public relations tends to be concentrated in the hands of just a few spin doctors, who are among the most powerful invisible persuaders in the whole PR industry. The most famous celebrity spin doctor in Britain is probably Max Clifford. In his time he has represented some of the biggest names in the entertainment industry, from Bob Dylan, Jimi Hendrix and the Bee Gees to Marlon Brando, Frank Sinatra and O. J. Simpson. In recent years, however, Clifford has become far more notorious – and spectacularly successful – as trader in kiss-and-tell stories, an activity which constitutes deal broking, rather than PR.

Clifford occupies a unique and intriguing place in the world of media relations, so much so that an entire chapter of this book (Chapter 9) is devoted to him. If we set him to one side for the moment, however, on the basis that public relations is no longer what he is famous for, there is no contest for the crown of 'King of Celebrity PR' in Britain. That has to go to Matthew Freud, whose client list is as glittering as the Milky Way on a very clear night. Among those he represents are Arnold Schwarzenegger, Sylvester Stallone and Bruce Willis (Planet Hollywood restaurants); Marco Pierre White and Damien Hirst (Quo Vadis – restaurant again); Hugh Grant, Pamela Anderson, Bob Geldof, Paula Yates and Chris Evans, to name but a few. His agency, Freud Communications, also handles the consumer accounts of VW, Volvo, Pepsi, Britvic,

Tango, Pizza Hut, Holsten, Miller, Sol and Jiffi condoms, as well as helping drum up publicity for the Terrence Higgins Trust and Comic Relief.

Like the most powerful financial PR agency in Britain, Brunswick, Freud is zealous about protecting his invisibility. Like Brunswick, Freud Communications has no corporate brochure, does not advertise and does not give media interviews. The reasons for this extreme reticence go beyond the preservation of mystique, although Matthew Freud's pedigree as the great-grandson of Sigmund and great-nephew of Edward Bernays – the founding father of PR – lends itself to intriguing analysis. Freud is reticent because he quite simply doesn't particularly want anyone to know what he gets up to.

Once again, one can't help marvelling at the paradox of it. Here is the creator of what was arguably the biggest event ever in the history of PR, the relaunch of Pepsi in a blue can, an event which created such massive media coverage that nobody in the world with a pulse could have missed it; but ask him to say a few words into a microphone or put his own face in front of the camera, and the response is a swift and categorical 'no'.

Far more relaxed about self-promotion is another of Britain's major celebrity spin doctors, Mark Borkowski. An *aficionado* of the most wildly extravagant bow ties, with the air of a mad inventor about him, Borkowski operates his company Impropaganda out of north London offices which look like a teenager's bedroom fantasy. In the boardroom, in place of a serious stretch of polished mahogany is a covered billiard table, cues lined up against the wall in a state of constant readiness. The walls are bedecked with posters of some of the acts Borkowski has promoted: Iron Maiden, *Heathcliff*, Joachim Cortez, KIDS, Archaos, Peking Opera and that beloved rock icon of the Seventies who one feels sure is going to turn up some day on *Antiques Roadshow*, Gary Glitter. Ali Baba pots sprout palm fronds and black leather sofas are scattered about a room which positively bristles with speakers from a powerful sound system. Borkowski, clearly, is a man who lives his dreams.

'People come to me for hype,' he says. 'We have the image of being mischief-makers, but it's not really like that. It's just that we're creative and prepared to think laterally. What we're all about, really, is taking a positive risk. But it isn't always easy to sell to clients. They will come saying, "I want you to make me the biggest touring thing in the world," and you'll put together some ideas for them, and they'll say "that's too dangerous". Give me dangerous PR any day.' Borkowski's 'dangerous PR' has included taking acts from chainsaw circus Archaos out on to the streets, performers flashcubed by journalists as they leap over traffic. Similar treatment was applied to Michael Flaherty, another of Borkowski's clients, after he left *Riverdance*.

If movie stars and restaurants are the twin poles about which Matthew Freud gyrates, then rock stars and circuses are Borkowski's. Other celebrity spin doctors also have found their own particular niches. Regine Moylett is the other big rock spin doctor in Britain, representing the likes of U2, Van Morrison and Neneh Cherry. As for the stars of large and small screens, Laurie Bellew looks after John Cleese and Michael Caine, Neil Reading's clients include Victoria Wood and Jack Dee. In the theatre world, the famously laid-back Peter Thompson handles PR for Cameron Mackintosh and Andrew Lloyd Webber.

And no review of 'Who's Who in Celebrity PR' would be complete without reference to Liz Brewer, who occupies a distinctive territory in which media relations is a focus, but by no means the most important one, of her activities. While other PRs usually promote their celebrity clients with a specific, commercial end in mind – more bums on the seats of cinemas, theatres or restaurants, more books or CDs sold – Liz Brewer's clients come to her for an entrée into the world of the Beautiful People, otherwise known as café society. In the words of Lady Colin Campbell, the royal biographer: 'If you are not a social star through birth or marriage, and you have the money, then you hire someone like Liz to do it for you . . . People in café society exist only as long as they are visible. The purpose of café society is not the purpose of true social life, which is friendship: its purpose is theatre, it's recognition. It's a very narcissistic world. Other people see you, hopefully, through the eyes you wish them to.'

Interestingly, the quest for recognition of the kind Liz Brewer provides was summed up perfectly by none other than Sir Tim Bell when he spoke to the *Independent* in 1994: 'As a kid I always hoped to be the sort of person who could walk into restaurants and be well known. I love famous people and there's nothing quite as exciting as sitting in a restaurant where all the people around you are fantastically well known and they all know you.'

Brewer, who was the subject of a BBC documentary in 1995 entitled *The Fame Game*, trades primarily not on her media contacts – although she is certainly connected – or on out-of-the-box, creative thinking. She trades, rather, on her little black book. Within its pages are the contact telephone and fax numbers providing access to everyone who is anyone in fields as diverse as fashion, art, business, the media, politics, sport – the list is endless. In the words of her friend, interior designer Robin Anderson: 'She does know the world. If someone mugged her and took her filofax they'd have the best entrée into everything.'

Whether it's organizing an art exhibition opening or the revamp of a restaurant, Liz Brewer knows exactly how to get the right cast along. Attendees are chosen to provide all the complementary elements required to make the event a success – glamour, buying power and publicity, to name but a few. Then the whole thing is merchandized to a breathless world via the media (Nigel Dempster, the country's most famous gossip columnist, is Brewer's number one media confidant). By arranging that the right people will appear in the right places at the right time, Brewer's influence extends well beyond that of a party organizer, which is how some of her detractors like to describe her. If 'third-party endorsement' is a key part of public relations, then there can be no greater success for a new restaurant than to have it heaving with celebrities on its opening night – all duly reported in the *Daily Mail* next day. These are the kinds of events which define what's hot and what's not, who's in and who's out. And, importantly, they are the perfect environment in which to launch a new star.

Take the case of poor, rich Mona Bauwens. The daughter of a wealthy Palestinian businessman high up in the PLO, blonde bombshell Mona first came to national prominence when embattled Cabinet minister David Mellor turned out to have received luxurious hospitality in Europe at the Bauwenses' expense. Mellor, who was already reeling from disclosure of his affair with actress Antonia de Sancha, was now shown alongside photographs of the young and attractive Mona, who clearly relished the media attention. In fact, asked several years later how it felt to be out of the public eye, she retorted emphatically: 'Horrible! I like to see myself plastered on the front page. Give me two years and I will be legitimately on the front page.'

It was Liz Brewer who gave Mona the metaphorical leg-up towards achieving her dream. Brewer had, in the past, helped Mona publicize a play, at a time when her ambition was more inclined towards that of theatrical impresario. Now Mona called on her friend and fixer to help her get ahead in the world of newspaper publishing. Specifically, she had set her sights on becoming contributing editor to *ES*, the weekly lifestyle magazine published every Friday with London's *Evening Standard*. The role of contributing editor is a rather nebulous one. The title sounds grander than 'freelance journalist', although that is, in effect, what contributing editors usually are. In most cases they tend to bring something to the party that extends beyond an ability to write – a glamorous lifestyle, social contacts or an expertise in some promising area – which was where Mona needed Liz Brewer's help.

Brewer had to provide a platform for Mona's future progress, and decided to do this by underlining Mona's interesting past. On the day that *ES*'s editorial team were to decide whether to use Ms Bauwens' services, the *Sun* ran an exclusive story on the subject of how David Mellor had asked Mona to marry him. This happy coincidence was masterminded by the glamorous Liz, who was filmed that morning in her sumptuous four-poster bed advising her client not to speak to the ex-Minister of Fun, who had telephoned her incandescent with rage. That same day, Brewer had arranged a lunchtime gathering of 'Women Achievers' at the fashionable

Belgravia club Mosimann's, to which Mona Bauwens had, naturally, been invited – as had a posse of journalists and photographers from the national press, falling over each other to give Mona even more publicity. All of a sudden, Mona was back in the news. She was all the more interesting for her previous involvement in a *liaison dangereuse*. That afternoon when her name came up on the *ES* agenda it didn't take the editorial panel long to make their decision: Mona Bauwens was in.

Others who have had reason to be grateful for Brewer's services include Richard Branson, Ivana Trump, Peter Cadbury, Soraya Khashoggi (ex-wife of Adnan) and Robin Anderson – not forgetting the indefatigable Nigel Dempster. Like other PR operators whose clients are household names, Brewer prefers to operate in complete anonymity. Working from her Belgravia home, such is her reticence that she doesn't even have a work telephone number listed in the telephone directory, and requests for interviews must first go through her lawyer.

Liz Brewer, Max Clifford, Matthew Freud and Mark Borkowski may be distinctly bristly about appearing in the same sentence as one another. But in the broadest of terms they, and celebrity spin doctors like them, have three main functions in common. The first is to create celebrity. Whether the candidate is a circus no one has ever heard of, a contributing editor wannabe or an artist who pickles dead sheep, it is the job of the celebrity PR adviser to create maximum interest in the right circles – which usually includes the media – to launch his or her client on the trajectory of fame.

The second is the protection of celebrity. Celebrity, as we have already noted, has a value that can be translated into wealth, and preserving that value, by keeping it current and stamping out stories that might detract from it, is a vital part of the PR function. Because the third function is making celebrity pay. By a range of means including setting up sponsorship deals, making endorsement agreements or selling media interviews, the celebrity spin doctor is there to help make his clients even richer. The bigger the audience, the wider the appeal, the more money there is up for grabs.

In the next four chapters we will look at examples of all three of these functions and at how spin doctors manipulate the media on behalf of their famous clients. In the first instance we will look more closely at the tabloid press, because this medium, above all others, is the true province of celebrity PR. Yes, there are national radio stations with massive audiences – but there are no commercial stations with the financial muscle of the mass market tabloids. Television, the most powerful medium of all, is ripe with opportunities for celebrity marketing, though mainly through advertising, which falls outside the remit of celebrity PR. It's true that news broadcasts, chat shows and documentaries offer sought-after opportunities for exposure; but the medium providing the greatest scope for financial exploitation allied to huge markets remains the tabloid press. Yet ironically, despite their constant presence in our lives, the workings of the tabloids are only poorly understood.

'drugs priest in palace sex romp':
the wacky world of the tabloids

American writer Elbert Hubbard made the now famous remark that newspaper editors are people employed by newspapers to separate the wheat from the chaff and to see that the chaff is printed. While one would be hard pressed to defend the application of this rather testy aphorism to Britain's so-called 'quality' national newspapers, today's mass-market tabloids – the *Sun*, *Mirror* and *News of the World* – are very different matters. In fact, 'chaff' seems altogether too gentle a word for the unremitting outpouring of sleaze, sensation, violence and human impropriety which constitutes their daily fodder.

On the information–entertainment spectrum, while journalists on the quality papers regard themselves as messengers and commentators on world affairs, their counterparts in the news-rooms of the tabloids are driven primarily by the need to entertain. One might regard the *Financial Times* as occupying one end of the British newspaper spectrum, other broadsheets and the *Mail* and the *Express* occupying the mid-market, and the *News of the World* placed firmly at the entertainment end. And what a coincidence that the *FT* has one of the lowest circulations of any national news-paper, while the *News of the World* is the biggest-selling newspaper in Britain! As Piers Morgan, editor of the *Daily Mirror*, explains: 'Nobody buys the *Sun* or the *Mirror* for hugely intelligent writing. The old days of the newspapers breaking the news are long gone.

We are far more in the entertainment industry. We print the stories behind the stories and gossip. We know that if we put an *EastEnders* storyline on page one, we will sell more papers.'

Since their inception, mass-market newspapers have flourished and multiplied as purveyors of prurience. (And it is usually the case that where the tabloids lead, the qualities will surely follow, frequently adopting a morally superior tone, castigating the tabloids for their disgraceful reporting of a story while naturally repeating the salacious details for the benefit of their readers.) Four themes, in particular, provide a constant backdrop to tabloid editorial agendas: sex, celebrity (especially royalty), crime and sport. Where two or more of these can be combined in the same story, the result is a heady cocktail designed to appeal to the most jaded palate – as with successive disclosures of Princess Diana's relationships with various male friends (Hewitt, Gilbey, Carling, Hoare – and, of course, Dodi Fayed), allegations of match-fixing by Bruce Grobbelaar (subsequently overturned) following a secretly videotaped 'sting' operation, drug-taking by bad-boy novelist Will Self on the Prime Minister's election campaign plane. The perfect tabloid banner headline, combining the maximum number of the key ingredients of a sure-fire tabloid exposé, would be something along the lines of 'Drugs Priest in Palace Sex Romp'.

The very reverse of this approach to constructing a newspaper story is the adherence to verifiable, if rather dull, facts at what former *Sun* editor Kelvin (Macca) McKenzie has labelled Britain's 'unpopular' newspapers – and the contrast is nowhere better reflected than in the respective styles of headlines. While researching this book I was told what may turn out to be an apocryphal tale about how newsroom journalists at the *Financial Times* ran a competition one year to see who could succeed in publishing the most boring story. The writer of 'Bolivia earthquake: few injuries' thought he'd be the clear front-runner. Alas, his peers decided he had been pipped to the post by the reporter who came up with a piece entitled 'Senegal elections: no surprises'.

If it were the case that the tabloids simply reported arresting stories with a few colourful adjectives thrown in for good measure, there would be little cause for outrage, pretended or otherwise. But, except when a story is sold to a newspaper on an 'exclusive' basis, it is often the case that what ends up in print bears scant resemblance to reality. Distortions, deletions and blatant fabrications are the stock in trade of mass-market tabloid journalists, who are frequently reluctant to let facts get in the way of a good story.

But while tabloid journalists need to be experts in the black art of innuendo, there is one particular area in which even they have to tread with care: libel. As Philip Hall, editor of the *News of the World*, told me in December 1996, 'People believe that we print any kind of rubbish – but that simply isn't the case. We check our facts thoroughly – we have to be extremely careful. We're the biggest-selling newspaper in the world and are seen as a libel target – that's why we check what we print. And we haven't been sued for libel in seven years. There are not many other newspapers that could say that.'

Would that other editors in the News International stable were so punctilious about adhering to the truth, the whole truth and nothing but the truth – or even intending to. Kelvin McKenzie, who under Rupert Murdoch's proprietorial eye was largely responsible for creating the *Sun* in its present image, is quoted as having exclaimed during a typical Macca-esque outburst: 'We haven't had a libel writ in a week. And what we've got is a bloody awful newspaper.'

Another feature of tabloid reporting which frequently attracts public censure is the way in which these papers come by their stories in the first place. Tabloid journalists are well practised in the technique of approaching potential news sources in disguise, be it as a bank clerk, a hospital manager or even, ironically, a writer from one of the quality nationals. Their duplicity plumbs even greater depths when, through a combination of overwhelming charm and sheer persistence, they win the trust of naïvely un-suspecting individual members of the public, only to betray that trust the moment they have extracted their story, without any regard for the public humiliation, destroyed careers and wrecked relationships they leave in their wake.

Such is the cut-throat environment in which the mass-market papers compete for stories that duplicity and blandishments – among an arsenal of techniques surveyed in this chapter – are likely to remain permanent features of the tabloid landscape. The means by which tabloids obtain their stories, in short, is as contentious as the treatment of the stories themselves. Process, as well as content, is frequently perverse.

So what is the effect of day-in, day-out exposure to the output of tabloid newsrooms? Christopher Browne, author of *The Prying Game*, an exposé of the workings of the press, is in little doubt: 'We tend to believe almost everything we read or hear, as we have no means of contradicting it. Each day we are the unwitting victims of propaganda, half-truths, make-believe, stories that are hyped up and facts that are deliberately designed to mislead. We may be better informed, but we are also becoming the innocent pawns of the news media.'

This issue is at the core of the mixed feelings many self-respecting middle-class folk have about the mass-market tabloids, on the one hand decrying their crude sensationalism, on the other unable to escape the fact that the majority of their fellow news-paper readers choose to buy them. And out of these mixed feelings have arisen a number of serious misconceptions about the tabloids and how they operate.

only yobbos read tabloids

The first misconception is about who actually reads tabloids. 'Uncouth yobbos' might come the reply from 'Disgusted' of Tunbridge Wells, who has taken the *Telegraph* for the last thirty years. But the image of the British construction worker bent over his labours, buttock cleavage revealed and rolled-up tabloid shoved in a back pocket, though persistent, is hopelessly inadequate as a means of defining tabloid readership. For the simple if surprising fact is that several mass-market tabloids are actually more popular among the upper and middle classes than are some of the qualities.

To use the language of media analysis, *News of the World* is read by 11 per cent of Britain's A/Bs (readers in professional or management positions) compared to only 4 per cent of A/Bs who read the *Financial Times*, and 4 per cent of A/Bs who read the *Independent*. The table below illuminates this point further.

circulation of national newspapers

	Copies sold	% of A/Bs who are readers
Dailies		
Sun	3,834,892	9
Daily Mirror	2,369,351	6
Daily Mail	2,211,673	15
Express	1,224,850	7
Daily Telegraph	1,110,816	15
Daily Star	734,431	2
The Times	761,040	11
Guardian	410,641	7
Financial Times	319,766	4
Independent	263,716	4
Sundays		
News of the World	4,422,633	11
Sunday Mirror	2,290,518	7
Mail on Sunday	2,179,269	19
People	1,924,541	5
Sunday Times	1,330,542	20
Express on Sunday	1,169,844	8
Sunday Telegraph	890,915	12
Observer	455,779	6
Independent on Sunday	282,019	4

Source: Mediacom (September 1997).

Of course a fair amount of multiple newspaper readership goes on, suggesting that when many A/B readers have finished the worthy business of reading their *Telegraph* or *FT*, they will turn to the *Mail* or *Sun* for a little light relief. Many A/B homes take more than one paper and a tabloid–quality double-act is a popular combination. Tabloids, far from being the exclusive domain of the factory floor and the building site, have an entrenched penetration among Britain's 'chattering' classes.

And, given their massive circulations, their importance as revenue earners should not be underestimated. It is this fact, combined with his well-known populist streak, that explains why Rupert Murdoch, probably the world's most powerful media tycoon, chooses for the walls of his office at Twentieth Century Fox in Los Angeles not major scoops from *The Times* or *Sunday Times*, nor even scenes from his major motion pictures, but rather front pages from the *Sun* and the *News of the World*.

things have never been worse

To illustrate the next popular misconception about tabloids, which is held by many tabloid readers themselves, we revisit a particular story from the *News of the World*. The piece concerns a stunning seventeen-year-old, Emma Monkton, who visits her local pharmacy in Lambeth to collect some medicine for a sick child. While waiting for the prescription to be made up, the pharmacist, one Edward Morse, offers her a drink which Emma, in her naïvety, accepts. You can guess what happens next. The first thing the poor girl remembers is the horror of being dumped in a canal. Fortunately, two labourers catch sight of her in the water and scramble to her rescue, saving her life. It is too late, of course, to save her virtue; Emma has been violently raped.

As tabloid stories go, this offering, with its combination of violent crime and sex, might be regarded as typical of the low ebb to which the tabloids have sunk in the late 1990s. But it is, in fact, a story taken from the very first issue of the *News of the World*, published in October 1843.

Editorially speaking, little has changed in the last hundred and fifty years. Of course language has evolved, reporting has become more explicit and today's page layouts bear little resemblance to the tiny print and cramped columns of earlier times. But the main editorial interests – sex, celebrity, crime and sport – have remained consistent. The popular misconception, however, is that the tabloids have 'got worse'. Never have we been besieged by so much sleaze and sensationalism – thus runs a commonly heard refrain; and the media (it continues), by constantly thrusting aberrant human behaviour in our faces, is rotting the very fabric of society and eroding our sense of values. It is ironic that society has changed a lot more in the last century than have editorial interests. What's more, the incidence of crime, sexual deviance and murder is, in many cases, far higher in countries with a much more conservative press than Britain's. The declining standard of tabloid reporting is, therefore, more apparent than real, an example of the curious British compulsion to believe that 'things have never been worse', despite overwhelming evidence to the contrary.

blame it on the editors

A third misconception about tabloids is how their editors decide what to put in the papers and what to keep out. Perhaps because of the larger-than-life personalities of editors like Kelvin McKenzie and proprietors like the late Robert Maxwell – who frequently wrote the *Mirror*'s front page himself – it is generally supposed that tabloid editors are a robust breed of monstrous egotists who dictate editorial policy on the basis of personal whims and prejudices. If it wasn't for the perverse instincts of these pedlars of sleaze, goes the argument, the British public would enjoy a more wholesome reading environment.

Of course, it is the case that ultimate responsibility for what appears in a newspaper lies with its editor and that an editor's personal judgement is constantly called upon, especially with regard to the way that big stories break. But to say that editors foist their own world view on the reading public is an inversion of what is really going on. The reality is, in fact, more chilling. There are many who believe, like author Christopher Browne, himself a journalist, that 'The news media is reluctant to find out what the public really wants to see, read or hear or to assess its role as a responsible communicator.' However, the fact is that newspaper editors are constantly finding out what their audience wants to read about, and what appears in the papers is their best attempt to deliver what the marketplace wants. All the major national newspaper groups conduct media research among their readers on a continuing basis, and some individual newspaper titles have permanent teams of market researchers monitoring the tastes and preoccupations of their readers. Quite simply, the first objective of a newspaper, like any other business, is to make profit, and the more readers it can attract and retain, the more profitable it can be.

A model example of this process is the *News of the World*, the most popular newspaper in Britain. Its editor, Philip Hall, says:

> We run readership surveys all the time. We do focus groups among readers to find out what they like. We ask ex-readers why they no longer read the paper. We track where our circulation is going up and down among men and women, among different age groups, social categories and regionally across the country. If we find readership is going down in a particular grouping, we do something about it. For example, when our female readership started to decline, we launched a separate magazine specially for women.

Even when editors have found out that readers want a fresh direction, they will test-market the revised product before launching it more widely. 'Dummy' copies of new-look features, columns or newspaper sections are shown to groups of readers selected by market researchers to reflect the audience to which they are intended to appeal. It is a carefully controlled process and little is left to chance.

Editorial judgement, then, is far less a matter of the personal predilections of an editor than most people suppose. Even so, the best-informed editors can still make mistakes. A particularly vivid example of this was the coverage given to the Hillsborough stadium disaster by the *Sun* and the *Star*. The 1989 FA Cup semi-final, held at Sheffield between Liverpool and Nottingham Forest, turned into tragedy when police diverted football fans arriving for the match through an extra gate manned by only one policeman. The huge pressure of a crowd desperate to get into the stadium led to the collapse of the milling board and barricades. A vicious stampede broke out, the mob trampling fans underfoot and fights breaking out between rival supporters. Ninety-six fans were killed and hundreds injured.

The gruesome spectacle of death and mayhem hardly required sensationalizing; but the *Sun* ran a major article under the banner headline 'The truth', accusing Liverpool fans of being drunk, beating up police officers and looting the pockets of the dead before urinating on them. The *Daily Star* ran a similar piece headlined 'Dead fans robbed by drunk thugs'. As Kelvin McKenzie, then the *Sun*'s editor, later admitted, most of the story was speculative and there were no named sources. When an outraged *Liverpool Echo* challenged the Fleet Street version of events, neither the *Sun* nor the *Star* was able to provide any justification for its treatment of the story. The net result was that furious Liverpool newsagents cancelled their orders of both papers: the *Sun*'s circulation in Liverpool dived by almost 40 per cent, from 524,000 copies to 320,000 copies a day. It was several years before Merseyside's circulations of the two tabloids fully recovered.

The Hillsborough episode illustrates just how fine is the line that editors have to tread between delivering the sensationalist coverage demanded by their audience and risking alienation of part or all of their readership. The pressure is always to go as far as possible, to sail as close to the wind as they dare. And this pressure is a direct result of a ruthless struggle between the tabloids in the continuous battle for readers. The feverish quest for a front-page exclusive which will snatch readers away from rival titles is a constant feature of life in all newspaper editorial offices, not just in the tabloids. However, while *The Times* or *Independent* relishes delivering scoops on corporate scams or professional malpractice, tabloid exclusives are altogether more personal. And tabloid journalists will stop at nothing to get them.

blandishments and bribery

In his book *The Good, the Bad and the Unacceptable* Raymond Snoddy, then a senior journalist with the *Financial Times*, describes how:

> In post-war years, tabloid journalism was, in its own way, every bit as competitive as now, with reporters racing in fast cars to be first to a story in Reading or Basingstoke. If the item was sensational or bizarre enough there would be the buy-up – paying for an exclusive – and the person involved would be whisked off to a hotel to protect the paper's investment and ensure no other reporters got near. Tyres of rivals would be let down. On really big stories a paper like the *Daily Express* would send four cars – three of them to block the road while the lead car got away with the quarry.

It is remarkable, really, how little has changed. These days key protagonists at the centre of kiss-and-tell stories are regularly dispatched by the *Mail* or *News of the World* to hidey-holes in the country, or perhaps the south of France, before major exclusives are broken, to ensure none of their rivals gets so much as a look in. Competitor titles will instead pursue anyone closely connected with the quarry – ex-lovers, parents, children, neighbours – relentlessly door-knocking, phone-calling and waving wads of cash to buy their own exclusive, designed to undermine the credibility of the person who kissed and told. We will look at a particularly vivid example of this phenomenon, the Mandy Allwood case, in the next chapter.

Buying up rival story angles is all part of well-established tabloid drill. Today's *Sun* news source is rubbished by the *Mirror* and *Mail*. Tomorrow's *Mirror* news source is rubbished by the *Sun* and the *Mail*. For the journalists involved it is all part of a perpetual game of cat and mouse as they out-buy or out-smart their rivals. At stake are huge readership figures and the advertising revenue these generate.

Unfortunately for most individuals caught up in a tabloid story, it is a game with which they are completely unfamiliar and for which they are hopelessly unprepared. During the course of researching this book I approached a number of people who had been, for their metaphorical fifteen minutes at least, the focus of media interest, as tabloids either bullied or bribed them into blurting out things they would never, in calmer, saner moments, have dreamed of saying. None of them wanted to talk about their experiences on the record. For all of them it had been, without question, the biggest mistake of their lives.

One woman who was persuaded by 'a friend' at a tabloid into selling the story of her affair with a showbiz celebrity found that, far from having her name buried in a much larger article on the celebrity's extra-marital love life, she was thrust to the centre of a two-page article, photographed, captioned and, of course, misquoted. Any hopes she might have had that her parents, who live in Australia, would be spared the misery of seeing their daughter thus embarrassed were short-lived. The nature of the media being what it is, local reporters in Sydney were quick to pick up the story and splash it all over the Australian media, with the additional spin that one of the city's daughters had fallen into international notoriety.

'I hurt my parents and everyone I cared most about,' she told me. 'It was hell when I went home – it took me months to begin to repair the damage. Some of my friends will never trust me again and I can't say I blame them. What I did was stupid and inexcusable. It happened at a low point in my life, though I'd never have gone along with it if I'd known what a big thing they were going to make of it. But I was incredibly naïve and had no idea how powerful the media could be.'

Different versions of these same sentiments have been expressed to me time and again by those who have found themselves on the receiving end of tabloid attention. And there are, regrettably, thousands of anonymous members of the public, busying themselves about their lives at this very moment, who will in the future come to rue the day they ever agreed to speak to a tabloid journalist.

It is one thing to cave in to blandishments or bribery and give an interview; quite another to wake up and find oneself propelled into the headlines with accusations of criminal wrongdoing. Such is the cut-throat struggle to out-scoop their rivals, however, that tabloids are prepared to run the most damning 'revelations' on public figures without a shred of evidence to support their case. Such was the fate that met Peter Bottomley – husband of the now more famous Virginia – when, as minister of transport in May 1989, he was featured in a front-page *Mail on Sunday* story saying he had recently been formally interviewed by the Obscene Publications Squad and suggesting he was a paedophile.

The accusations were a shock for Bottomley who was horrified by the *Mail*'s accusations. 'There was my face and the headline which could effectively destroy everything I'd done in thirteen or fourteen years as a Member of Parliament and had the potential to wreck my family life and destroy my reputation. My whole world had fallen apart. In two or three seconds I could see everything that mattered to me going – my work with voluntary organizations concerned with family welfare and child welfare, my family, my job, my chances of future alternative jobs – everything just torn up and thrown away.'

The shell-shocked Bottomley immediately carried out a damage limitation exercise, contacting broadcast and press media and saying that legal action was being taken and would swiftly follow any repetition of the libellous accusations. Scotland Yard put out a statement denying that it had formally interviewed Bottomley, who immediately instigated legal action against the *Mail*. The *Mail* did not instantly retract the story or apologize. They showed signs of contesting the matter in court – until four months later, when a front-page apology admitting the mistake was published. A substantial out-of-court settlement followed.

By then it was late as far as Bottomley was concerned. The damage had been done. He could have already lost the trust of constituents in what was only a marginal seat. His wife was informed by members of the public that her husband was a pervert. Such is the power of the media that one single article could have destroyed his most precious asset – his reputation.

Such are the huge readerships reflecting the populist energy of the tabloids that, like a force of nature, they represent a power to be respected, if not feared. Ranged against an individual, they exert such overwhelming influence as to transform a reputation overnight, leading to financial ruin and personal disaster. Correctly harnessed, they provide one of the most effective means of changing attitudes, selling products or making money. The need to manage relationships with the tabloids is particularly intense in the case of celebrities – especially those who harbour dark secrets in an unknown closet, who would rather their personal life remained unknown, or whose sexual proclivities would be damaging were they ever to see the light of day.

In such cases the need for a professional media relations manager is especially acute. Whether it's a question of breaking a positive story or – more likely – concealing a negative one, having a powerful advocate who knows the tabloids better than they know themselves is a decided advantage. And when it comes to celebrity PR and cutting deals with the tabloids, one name looms above all others, that of the ubiquitous showbiz PR who has become a showman in his own right. He is, of course, Max Clifford.

max clifford: white knight or sultan of sleaze?

Max Clifford is unquestionably the most famous and controversial spin doctor in Britain. The man who brought us Antonia de Sancha, Bienvenida Buck, Mandy Allwood, O. J. Simpson and the Jerry Hayes scandal is loathed by many Tories who saw him as a malevolent predator during the Major era, intent on destroying their party by assassinating the reputations of individual ministers. He is despised by a vociferous lobby of PR practitioners who believe he is dragging the industry into a mire of disrepute. He is abhorred more generally as a mercenary sleaze-merchant who will sell anyone's secrets for a fast buck. How many of these perceptions withstand critical analysis we will discover. But, as one might expect when dealing with a creature of the tabloids, beneath the two-dimensional, sensationalist hype, the real Max Clifford is far more interesting.

Clifford was born and brought up in Wimbledon, south London, one of four children whose father had been ostracized by his family because of his socialist beliefs. A willingness to forfeit approbation as the price of firmly held convictions is clearly something Clifford inherited from his father – along with a hatred of the class system: 'I am anti-establishment. The more I see of the establishment, the more hypocrisy, double standards and corruption I see. I'm very much a Labour voter.'

This background didn't prepare Clifford well for his first job. On leaving school aged fifteen, he found work in a department store frequented by 'snooty old ladies from Wimbledon Village' who expected a level of servility Clifford felt unable to provide. Suffice it to say he didn't last long. Moving on to become a trainee reporter for the local *Merton and Morden News*, he found himself in an environment much better suited to his natural talents. It was in his humble capacity as local newspaper reporter that Clifford first discovered the power of PR – and also had his first foray into spin-doctoring, albeit of a somewhat different kind. At this time he had his own pub disco, and the events he managed as DJ made rapid leaps in popularity after his act came to the attention of – you guessed it: the *Merton and Morden News*. Shamelessly plugging his own disco in the local paper, Clifford was already exercising his combined abilities as media man and spin doctor that were to suit him perfectly for his next role.

In 1962 he became a press officer for EMI Records, where one of the bands he promoted was the talented new group The Beatles. Joining a colleague from EMI who set up his own PR agency, over the next few years Clifford handled some of the biggest names in showbiz, including Bob Dylan, Jimi Hendrix, the Bee Gees, Tom Jones and Engelbert Humperdinck. Early exposure to stardom inured him completely to working with big names: 'Very few stars are nice people,' he says. 'Most of them are totally obsessed with themselves. Jimi Hendrix was out of his head most of the time and Bob Dylan was a miserable sod. You'd set up interviews for these guys and they're not there because they're in a heap on the floor somewhere. A lot of these stars were unbearable.'

In 1968 Clifford set up his own company, Max Clifford Associates, through which he has continued to work for some of the biggest names on both sides of the Atlantic. Despite the constellation of stars that is his client list, and an income that some in the industry have estimated as being between £800,000 and £1 million a year, Clifford has always lived modestly and shunned the high life. His home for the past twenty-five years has been a modest, three-bedroomed semi in Raynes Park, south-west

London, from which he would only like to move to provide his handicapped daughter with a ground-floor bedroom. Unlike nearly all his PR industry peers, he has a relaxed working lifestyle – building up an empire to immortalize his name is clearly not a priority. Most working days he arrives at his New Bond Street offices only in the late morning, and he regularly leaves at 6 p.m. He's never in on Wednesdays, which he spends playing tennis or going shopping with his wife Liz: 'I lead a healthy lifestyle, playing tennis and swimming three or four times a week. I enjoy going down to my local workman's café just as much as dining at Claridges. The two are quite different, and I get just as much pleasure eating a smart meal as I do having bacon and eggs locally.' Tales of how Clifford, who is a teetotaller, has entertained megastar clients in his own favoured haunts are legendary. He once took Marlon Brando to his local Chinese restaurant, while Muhammad Ali was treated to a transport café: 'I like to do things that are different.'

stars on their knees

Clifford's unflappable down-to-earthness, old-fashioned courtesy and considerable charm are no doubt reassuring for the stars who call on his services – usually in their hour of need. Exactly whom he represents at any one moment is a closely guarded secret because, contrary to popular belief, he insists that the vast majority of his time is spent keeping clients out of the papers: 'I only spend 10–20 per cent of my time on the big splash stories people know me for. The rest of the time I'm working for my regular clients. I can't name names. If people don't know I'm involved, so much the better. Some of these people already have PR advisers who don't even know I'm involved.' Several of Clifford's tabloid contacts confirm all this to be true.

In nearly three decades of running his own company, Clifford has never pitched for business. 'The relationship has to be on the basis that they need me more than I need them,' he says.

Very often when stars come to me it's because they're in trouble and they don't want to be found out. It's very important, right at the outset, to lay down the ground rules. I'll listen to their position and tell them how I would deal with things. If they're not prepared to do what's needed then I say 'good luck and goodbye'. The biggest problem is always ego. But once they agree to a course of action then we get results. And the more results we get, the easier it becomes.

It is all to do with trust because I'm in the business of protection. As a media adviser you have to know everything about a star to be prepared. You get to know a lot more about them than their wives, lovers or mistresses. You play a close part in their lives and have to understand what makes them tick. Sometimes stars don't care about the person they're married to, but don't want to part with £50 million to get rid of them.

His clients' sexual activities cause Clifford some of his greatest headaches.

The bigger the star, the bigger the risks they like to take. This is especially the case with sex. When you are a really big star every sexual fantasy you can imagine is presented to you on a weekly basis. It's there all the time. So you're always looking for something different.

The key to keeping them out of the papers is anticipation. If one of my clients likes having sex with hookers in his car, then I would find a madame whose discretion is assured, to look after him. It might seem far-fetched but it isn't. You really have to control areas of weakness. If the media get hold of a story you can sometimes kill it off by offering something bigger and stronger, but that is the exception.

It is ironic that the man who is notorious for exposing the shameful double lives of the high and mighty spends more of his time doing the very reverse. As *News of the World* editor Philip Hall says: 'We tend to approach PR people like Max Clifford and

Matthew Freud, rather than the other way round. Max protects a lot of people and spends a lot of his time keeping them out of the media.'

No doubt if he were to break his clients' confidences Clifford could provide enough material to keep the tabloid mills churning feverishly for months. Although he won't talk about it on the record, there is little doubt that he has come by information that would rock the monarchy, the House of Lords and the careers of many more MPs, not to mention megastars of stage and screen. But, contrary to public perceptions, Clifford is very much a man who keeps the lid on things. When offered a kiss-and-tell story by someone of whom he is suspicious, he will actually tip off the intended victim. And he has been known to pass up opportunities to represent big-name stars about whom he has doubts – Michael Jackson, for one.

The 20 per cent of client work for which he is best known – the kiss-and-tell stories – also come his way unsolicited. Usually, the first inkling Clifford has that a story is in the offing is when he is telephoned by a lawyer, agent or friend of someone who is in a corner: 'There is usually no time for meetings and meetings about meetings,' he says. 'You have to think on your toes, understand the problems and work out a solution.' The process by which such stories come into the public arena is probably best revealed by a behind-the-scenes look at one of the most controversial cases Clifford has handled in recent times: the Mandy Allwood story.

The first Clifford knew of the existence of Mandy Allwood was when her solicitor Michael Waldridge contacted him to say that his client had undergone fertility treatment and was pregnant with eight babies. She knew her position would arouse media interest – though just how much, at that point, she couldn't possibly have guessed. She needed advice on how to deal with the media – and how to generate company sponsorship to help her bring up her huge, instant family. Clifford agreed to meet Mandy and her boyfriend Paul in Wimbledon Village, where they were to end up buying a house:

I liked Mandy and I explained that the best thing for her was to do a deal with a single newspaper. That way she would be taken care of by the paper, kept away from the world's media and do what her doctor said was important for her to do, which was rest. In time we could start structuring other deals with manufacturers of baby products, that kind of thing.

I was just about to go to the States for a fortnight and I told them they should say nothing about the pregnancy for the time being. Then Paul told me he had already approached Central Television – the commercial TV station where they lived. That was unfortunate. If only they had come to me before anyone else knew. We'd have struck a deal with a paper and there would have been no publicity until just a few weeks before the birth. I would have dictated the timing of the world exclusive and run the whole thing.

But, as Allwood admits: 'When we started on this we didn't have a clue how the media worked.' Had she had a clue, events would probably have turned out very differently.

Clifford did warn her what lay ahead. He told her that for the newspaper that got it, the story would be One To Touch Your Hearts. For the many that didn't it would be The Story That Shames A Nation. He told her that each and every skeleton in her and her boyfriend's closets would be discovered and hauled out for public inspection. Anything even resembling a skeleton would be exhumed and shown in its most hideous aspect. And there were skeletons aplenty, including her embittered ex-husband whom she'd left for Paul, dodgy property deals from Paul's past and, most unsatisfactory of all, the fact that Paul himself was also involved with another woman, Maria Edwards.

There was no time, however, to bury these skeletons – if such a thing had been possible. For Mandy Allwood and her boyfriend, if they didn't work out something soon, they would have the world's media quite literally camping on their doorstep and be facing journalistic harassment on a scale usually reserved for scandal-struck royals or politicians.

Clifford had to move fast, and he quickly got in touch with

Philip Hall, working out the deal which was later to become the subject of heated national debate. Hall was later quoted in the *Daily Mail* as saying:

> Mandy's been very clear – she's looking for the money to help bring up the children, she doesn't want to gain financially for herself. So if she doesn't have the children, she doesn't want to make money out of it. We've agreed a sum should she give birth to eight children, and we've agreed to discuss the situation with her should it change. If she loses two or three of the children, we are still very interested in her story. If she had a miscarriage or changed her mind about going through with the pregnancy, we would pay her a small amount, but certainly we're not going to pay a large sum of money and she's aware of that. The *News of the World* isn't a charity.

Exactly how much the *News of the World* agreed to pay her if she had all eight babies no one will say. Clifford maintains the deal he made was for the story of a woman who was pregnant with eight babies – not for the mother of eight children. 'Media insiders' were often quoted as estimating a top whack of £800,000–£1,000,000 if Mandy had all eight babies. The £1 million figure was also the basis for claims that the *News of the World* had offered to pay her £125,000 per baby born. Whatever the amount that was paid, Clifford took a 20 per cent cut – his standard charge for deal broking.

When the Allwood story broke, it instantly became the subject of an unprecedented national furore. Not only was it seized upon with gusto by the tabloids, which it provided with so many related issues for sensationalist exploitation (as we will see); it set off arguments which raged on prime-time television and radio chat-shows, in pubs, restaurants and sitting rooms, not only in Britain, but throughout the world. Clergy, gynaecologists, politicians and right-to-lifers all found matter for comment in the potent cocktail of issues that the case presented. But, the more the story unravelled, the greater the quantity of misinformation that was disseminated. Despite the fact that she had been warned by Clifford to brace herself for the worst, Mandy Allwood watched all this, from the retreat provided for her by the *News of the World*, with a sense of disbelief and outrage. As she later commented to me: 'I can't believe the way the media manipulate things. The only way to make sure what you say is reported without being twisted is to appear live on television.'

So what were the facts of the Mandy Allwood story? In a nutshell:

- Mandy Allwood married Simon Pugh in 1986 when she was twenty-one. They had one child, Charlie, in 1991. Mandy became pregnant again in 1993, but following a car accident had to be treated with drugs which doctors advised her would damage her baby: she was forced to terminate the pregnancy.

- Her marriage, which had always been rocky, came to an end when she met Paul Hudson, a Jamaican, in 1995. Hudson, a would-be property tycoon of unusual charm, already had a complicated love life. He'd left former long-term lover Jenny Edwards with mortgage debts which she claimed totalled £160,000; and he had two children by Maria Edwards, with whom he was still involved and whom he had no intention of leaving. Mandy was, nevertheless, besotted with Hudson and fell pregnant to him in October 1995. However, she lost the child through a miscarriage on Christmas Day that year.

- Next, Mandy went for fertility treatment – but didn't tell Hudson. But rather than the one desired foetus she conceived eight.

- She consulted Professor Kypros Nicolaides, head of foetal medicine at King's College Hospital, London, who warned her of the complications of continuing with the pregnancy and the near-certainty that there would be no survivors. He did not, however, suggest she should selectively abort any of the foetuses.

- Mandy decided to keep all the foetuses and continue with the pregnancy. She told Paul the situation and the two realized they had a story to sell to the media – they had no idea how much they might get for it, but hoped it might be enough to help offset the huge bills they anticipated should the

pregnancy be successful. Both of them were out of work at this
time.
- Hudson contacted Central TV with the story, but had come to no
arrangement with the station when the couple, on their lawyer's
recommendation, approached Max Clifford

The *News of the World* broke the story as a 'World Exclusive'
under the headline 'I'm going to have all my 8 babies' on 11
August 1996. The paper devoted five whole pages to the 'full
amazing story', covering every aspect from Mandy's pregnancy to
Hudson's love life, the medical debate on how many babies she
should carry and an interview with Max Clifford on the money she
could make from the deal.

all aboard the gravy train

While other newspapers had caught wind of the eight-baby story
and run it the day before under headlines like 'Abortion dilemma',
once the *News of the World* had identified the players in the drama
they all swung into action in earnest, chequebooks at the ready.
What makes the Mandy Allwood story such a classic case of
publicity deal broking is the sheer speed and scale with which a series
of knock-on deals was struck, with most of those connected to
Mandy and Paul Hudson scrambling for their share of media money.

The Mirror Group lost no time in signing up Simon Pugh,
Mandy's ex-husband, a plasterer now living with another woman.
For a rumoured £25,000, he told the *Mirror* how Mandy had
wanted to abort their first child, Charlie, and that it was only
when, with tears in his eyes, he begged her not to that she decided
to have the child. Pugh's credibility suffered a dent, however, when
he admitted to a journalist: 'The more you pay me, the more dirt I
can dish on her.'

The two other women in Hudson's life were also quick to enter
the fray. Maria Edwards, by whom Hudson had two children, sold
her story to the *Sun* for around £25,000. According to the *Sun*,

Maria had had no inkling that Paul was involved with Mandy Allwood and 'threw a fit' when the eight-baby story broke. Under the headline 'Unfit to be a dad' she described how badly he treated their two sons. Meantime Jenny Edwards (no relation of Maria), the lover Hudson had left in debt, managed to extract a more modest sum from the *Mirror* on the subject 'King Rat. He left me £160,000 in debt.'

Hudson's mother, Sybil Wheeler, who branded her son a 'shameless opportunist', sold her story 'exclusively' to the *Daily Express* for £5,000 and then to the *Daily Mail* for exactly the same amount – resulting in payment by neither. And while Mandy's parents were among the few to keep their own counsel, her sister Jackie haggled with different media groups before accepting the *Sun*'s £15,000 offer, and brother Phil did a deal with the *Mirror* on the subject 'My sister's rat slept all over town'.

Meanwhile, on the central topic of Mandy's pregnancy, every national newspaper was interviewing eminent gynaecologists who variously suggested she should abort two or more of her babies to raise her chances of keeping the others. Anti-abortionists, meantime, piled in on her behalf. Clergymen mused over such blatant tinkering with the stuff of life, while sociologists questioned the ethics of giving fertility treatment to unmarried mothers in uncertain relationships. Except for *News of the World* readers, who got Mandy's version of her life as she had told it, the public was given the impression through this coverage that Max Clifford had behaved reprehensibly in selling her story to the *News of the World*, and that Mandy Allwood herself was foolish or greedy or both.

The term 'media circus' barely seems an adequate description of the goings-on during the week the Mandy Allwood story broke. And once broken, it lived in the media and the public imagination for week after week, in ever-changing permutations. Then, on 1 October, in her nineteenth week of pregnancy, Mandy had the miscarriage which most expected, losing three sons; the following day, she lost the remaining five babies.

The final, bitter, sting in the tail came when Max Clifford was accused by Allison Pearson in the *Evening Standard* of inviting the media horde to the babies' funeral. It was an accusation that rankled with Clifford who had, in fact, turned down countless offers of huge sums of money from media groups wanting exclusive coverage of the event, and who had tried to minimize press attendance by inviting only Press Association reporters, on the basis that their coverage could be accessed by all media groups. When he wrote a letter to Max Hastings setting the matter straight, his first such epistle in thirty years, the *Evening Standard*'s editor refused to publish it. Clifford had to resort instead to the *Guardian*, in which he wrote: 'I can cope with most things they throw at me with regard to Mandy Allwood: that's not a problem . . . But to claim that I engineered a media circus at a moving and private ceremony is just obscene.'

All of which brings us to the question of the much-maligned Max's role in the whole affair. What are we to make of the, in this case, very visible persuader? He was roundly condemned for handling the story by journalists, clergymen, medics and much of the public. The argument against him goes along the lines that by negotiating a hugely lucrative incentive for Mandy to have all eight babies, Clifford encouraged her to go against medical advice and her own better judgement and keep them all – a decision whose disastrous consequences were inevitable.

The reality, of course, was that Mandy had decided to keep all eight babies before she even spoke to Clifford. As she asked Clifford in a private moment: 'How can I decide I should kill this one or that one?' Moreover, at no point did Mandy's medical consultant suggest she should abort any of her babies – that was the advice of other consultants questioned by the *News of the World*'s rivals. Take Clifford out of the picture, and where would that have left Mandy? Still pregnant with eight babies, a good deal poorer, and subject to untold media harassment. Hardly an improvement, whichever way you look at it.

scoops minus max

A brief glimpse into the lives of those who have hit tabloid head-lines without the benefit of a publicity agent confirms the swift viciousness with which they've been dealt. Lottery winners are among a relatively new breed of instant, if short-lived, celebrities, who are usually poorly equipped for the media fate that awaits them. Of course the lottery organizer, Camelot, does offer con-fidentiality to those who want to keep their multi-million-pound prizes secret. Not that Alasdair Buchan, a one-time winners adviser at Camelot, would opt to go down this route himself: 'The neigh-bours of one secret winner still haven't found out, nor have any of his relatives. So he's done well keeping it a secret – but mentally he's in a terrible state. He's scared to buy a new car or people will ask questions. He thinks people are following him. He suspects all strangers. He can't sleep for ghastly and ghoulish dreams. His life has been turned upside down. He's gained nothing – except money in the bank.'

But what of the alternative? The biggest lottery prize won in Britain to date, £22.5 million, was claimed one Sunday morning by Mark Gardiner, aged thirty-three, who walked into his shop in Hastings, scarcely able to believe his luck. But, says Hunter Davies, author of *Living on the Lottery*, 'What happened next has to be considered a world class achievement for the tabloid press. Never has so much dirt been gathered in such a short time by so many hacks working on the same story at the same time, yet all starting from scratch, on a Sunday, with so little to go on.'

Within two hours there were forty reporters and photographers camped outside Croft Glass Ltd in Hastings, the firm owned by Gardiner and his partner Paul Maddison, who had jointly bought the lottery ticket. Camelot quickly whisked the two men and their partners away to a luxury hotel, but this absence didn't put an end to their media troubles. If anything, it precipitated an even more intense investigation of anyone connected with the two men. And the muck was soon being raked. Gardiner's adoptive mother described him as 'a feckless drunkard, womanizer and thief', adding: 'I hope he drinks himself to death with the money . . . I wish he was dead. He has been nothing but a curse to this family.' Someone identifying himself as Gardiner's 'best friend' told reporters: 'He's the scum of the earth.' Variously depicted in tabloid headlines as 'Lotto Rat' and 'Drunken Monster', the thrice-married Gardiner's three former spouses were only too happy to relate tales of his wife-beating, serial womanizing and drunkenness. Former wife number three was particularly obliging, sporting half-naked for Page Three of the *Sun*.

Had Gardiner known about the workings of the tabloids and done a deal, he would have been able to neutralize at least one of the news channels pumping out a stream of invective and taken himself out of play to the others. But he was unversed in the ways of the tabloids and he didn't have a hand on his shoulder to guide him through the sleaze. As it happened, subsequent press stories revealed him to be a model father and a very much more affable soul than earlier reports suggested. By then, Gardiner may well have felt it was a bit late.

Yet it is for performing the function of deal broker and media chaperon that Max Clifford is so vilified – particularly by the Tories. The kiss-and-tell client for whom he is probably best known is Antonia de Sancha, on whose behalf he sold the story of her affair with cabinet minister David Mellor to the *Sun*. Once again Clifford was consulted only after the story was already in the media domain – on that occasion leaked by the owner of the flat in which Mellor and de Sancha used to have their love trysts. De Sancha was being subjected to enormous media harassment and Mellor wanted to have nothing to do with her – she had become an embarrassment and threat to his political career.

'She was being attacked in the media for kissing and telling. She hadn't, in fact, said a word,' says Clifford. 'At that stage I didn't know anything about David Mellor, but I decided to find out about him. Time and time again people told me the same thing: Mellor just uses people, then dumps them.' While Mellor was setting up family photographs to try to restore his 'family values' credentials, following a discussion with Sir Tim Bell, Clifford arranged for de

Sancha to be whisked out of the cauldron to Spain, where the *Sun* paid her £100,000 for her story.

Bienvenida Buck's story of her affair with defence chief Sir Peter Harding, former Cabinet minister Alan Clark's alleged affairs with both Valerie Harkess and her daughter, and MP Jerry Hayes' alleged gay relationship with Commons researcher Paul Stone are some of the other big splash stories Clifford has handled in recent years. Hardly surprising, really, that he is a hate figure of the Tories. His use of the word vendetta to describe his activities against the Major government was greatly publicized, as was the primary cause of his disillusionment. His daughter, Louise, has been severely disabled with rheumatoid arthritis since she was a child and has had a dozen operations. Every night, last thing, Clifford has to carry her upstairs to bed: 'I've watched the Conservatives destroying the NHS,' he says, 'and I despise what they've done.'

Less well publicized are Clifford's remarks making it clear that he has turned down stories about the private lives of several politicians in both main parties: 'Providing they are doing a good job for their constituents I don't think I should have anything to do with it – all I do is mark their card.' What's more, he says he would have brokered the same deals if they had been about Labour Cabinet ministers: 'It is not so much about Labour or Conservative as it is about exposing people who say one thing in public and then behave completely differently when they think they can get away with it,' he says.

Clifford has been labelled 'the sleazeball of sleazeballs' by David Mellor, who has said about him: 'It's disgusting that such a man can be accepted by newspapers as a witness of truth.' Edwina Curry has referred to him as 'that little turd'. And it's not only politicians who bestow such unflattering epithets. The *Evening Standard* – which, since Max Hastings was installed as editor, has taken a particularly strong line on Clifford – described him famously in an editorial on 7 January 1997 as 'that haemorrhoid on the back passage of our society'. Strong words indeed. But, once again, one has to question what, exactly, it is in Max Clifford to which Tory grandees and their friends in the press object. That he exposes those who proclaim 'family values' as adulterers? That he makes money for undeserving human flotsam and jetsam? Or that he himself, horror of horrors, benefits financially from the deals he brokes?

It is an incontrovertible if inconvenient fact that the newspaper-reading public do want to know about the extra-marital affairs of their MPs. Even if Max Clifford – and, indeed, other deal brokers – didn't exist, newspaper groups would continue to pay handsomely for such stories. Whatever one personally thinks of public attitudes towards morality, given the media environment in which we all live there is only one way for MPs to ensure that news of extra-marital affairs never becomes public: don't have them!

clifford v. bell

So much for what his targets think of Clifford – but how is he regarded in the PR community? Because he works very much on his own, little is actually known about Clifford by his PR peers – which is not to say that most of them don't have a view on him. Given the controversy aroused by his deal-broking activities, many are unaware that he spends any of his time doing pretty much what they do. There are many who admire his success as a publicity agent. But there are also some who take the view of Caroline Hamilton Fleming of Chatto PR, who wrote to the industry organ *PR Week*: 'What has selling sleaze to the highest bidder to do with the Institute of Public Relations' statement that "PR is the planned and sustained effort to establish and maintain goodwill and mutual understanding between an organization and its public"?' Clifford's response to Hamilton's question is straightforward: 'The kiss-and-tell deals involving Tory MPs weren't just one-offs. They were part of an ongoing campaign to reveal the sleaze associated with the Tories. I did this because I'm angry about what they've done to the NHS. I don't think many would argue that I haven't been successful.' Ms Hamilton went on to say: 'Whatever his [Clifford's] motives, he can only influence the public's perceptions of PR for the worse and we should have nothing to do with him.'

This is the critical point. Is it, in fact, the case that the public see Max Clifford as typical of the PR industry? Quentin Bell, in his time as chairman of the Public Relations Consultants Association, took on the challenge of distancing the industry from Clifford. Says Bell: 'If you have a person like Max Clifford who is ubiquitous in the media you can either ignore him or say, "If we are legitimate PR people, we mustn't let him ruin our reputation by default. Reputation is our most precious asset."' While in the PRCA chair, Bell arranged several head-to-heads with Clifford on radio and in the press. 'I had nothing personal against Max,' he says, 'it's just that he is in the business of marketing sleaze. We are more like management consultants. I wanted to get that point across.'

Unfortunately for Bell, he lost the set-piece industry debate he arranged. Clifford's frank admission that he lies to the media on behalf of clients – for example, telling journalists a pop record has sold a million copies when it has only sold 100,000 – struck an empathetic chord with his audience of PR spinners. After the Bell/Clifford contretemps was over, celebrity spin doctor Mark Borkowski's view, shared by many, was that 'Bell came out of it looking inexperienced. It didn't do the PRCA any favours either – these days the industry regards it as a glorified Rotary Club.' As for Clifford, he wrote a cheeky letter to *PR Week*, thanking both the publication and Quentin Bell 'for the time and effort put into promoting and establishing me as an acceptable part of the British public relations industry . . . if I get the opportunity to help turn the media spotlight on to either Quentin Bell or his wonderful organ, then rest assured it will be my pleasure.'

Is Max Clifford ruining the reputation of the PR industry by association? No market research has been done on this question, so it's impossible to answer with any degree of certainty. But, turning for a view from the street to that source of no-nonsense enlightenment, I asked my London cabbie what he thought of Max Clifford. There was a considered pause before the answer came: 'Well, he's got his own niche, hasn't he? He sells all them stories. That's what he does and there ain't no one like him.'

let them eat cake: PR and the royals

Spin doctors and senior journalists are a motley crew of rugged individualists, with strongly held views and, in the case of journalists at least, no fear of controversy. So it is extremely unusual to find any measure of unanimity among them regarding any subject you care to mention. There is one, however, about which they all speak with a single voice: royal PR. Everyone I interviewed while researching this book, from the editor of the *News of the World* to the editor of *Tatler*, from street-smart consumer PR-ettes to the most august of City advisers, agreed: royal PR is a shambles. Even more astoundingly, everyone agreed why royal PR is in the state it's in.

But first, before launching into the subject of contemporary royal PR, a reality-check. Tabloid headlines would frequently have us believe that various royals have dragged the monarchy into a state of disrepute such as has never existed before. The media have never been so bold in attacking our ruling family. The republican debate has intensified, and as blunder succeeds royal blunder, the royals' popularity, and thereby their constitutional position, continues to weaken. Or so it is commonly thought. But consider the following passage, from an article which appeared in *The Times* in 1830 on the death of George IV:

> There was never an individual less regretted by his fellow-creatures
> than this deceased king. What eye has wept for him? What heart
> has heaved one sob of unmercenary sorrow? . . . If George IV had
> a friend – a devoted friend in any rank of life – we protest that the
> name of him or her never reached us. An inveterate voluptuary,
> especially if he be an artificial person, is of all known beings the
> most selfish . . . Nothing more remains to be done or said about
> George IV than to pay – as pay we must – for his profusion.

It would be inconceivable for such damning words to be written about any of our current royals, especially about the present Queen. If the monarchy as an institution has recovered from a media nadir such as that of George IV's reign, it does not seem unreasonable to argue that the current difficulties with which the royals are afflicted can, in time, be overcome too.

From a PR perspective, the royal family presents us with a host of paradoxes. Its members are meeting and greeting a wide cross-section of people all the time – but all too often say things which betray that they are out of touch with public opinion. They are concerned, sometimes to the point of paranoia, about what gets said about them in the media – but whom do they appoint as media managers? Army officers and other establishment figures with no understanding of the grubby media world and little desire to deal with it on its own terms. Prince Charles, who benefits from a life-time's training as a royal as well as the support of the royal PR machine – such as it is – remains far less popular than his late ex-wife, who up till the age of twenty had no experience of the royal goldfish bowl and who had to struggle actively *against* the royal machine. And then there are Charles's views on issues like the environment and the unity of all religions which, although reflecting significant elements in contemporary thought, hold far less popular appeal than his mother's constant and often anachronistic round, receiving banners from dukes and distributing Maundy money.

Understanding what is wrong with royal PR helps get to the heart of these paradoxes. First and foremost is the perhaps obvious but nevertheless important fact that the royal family is, in many ways, out of touch with the reality in which most of its subjects live. This is hardly surprising when one considers the exceptionally cosseted lives of the major royals, whose exposure to the realities of day-to-day life is almost always stage-managed. It has been said before that to the Queen the whole world must smell of fresh paint. The same could be said for most of her family. Living as they do in a hermetically sealed bubble of hereditary wealth and power, to them the outside world is more intellectual concept than the product of visceral experience. Yes, they meet tens of thousands of people every year – far more than most of us. Yes, they canvass eminent leaders from every field of human endeavour for their views. But how meaningful is this contact? And why are such important misjudgements made?

The Queen misjudged popular sentiment when she expected the public to foot the bill for repairs to her private home, Windsor Castle, after the 1992 fire. Again, after Diana's death, it took four days and countless newspaper editorials to prompt her to give voice to the unprecedented outpouring of national grief. Prince Philip is famous for saying the wrong thing at the wrong time, whether it's castigating those out of work for complaining – after all, they wanted more leisure, didn't they? – at a time of peak unemployment, to saying that cricket bats are just as dangerous as handguns, shortly after the Dunblane massacre. Perhaps most misjudged of all was Prince Charles's commissioning of TV journalist Jonathan Dimbleby to produce the now-notorious TV programme in June 1994, followed by a biography in which he admitted to three separate affairs with Camilla Parker Bowles and further admitted that he had been forced by his father to marry a girl he did not love. It was, according to a member of the Queen's own household, 'the most vindictive royal revenge since Henry VIII cut off Anne Boleyn's head'. With public sympathies already siding so strongly with Diana as the injured party, it seems incredible that Charles could have embarked on such a self-defeating course of action. Not only did it show how out of touch he was with public feeling; it is symptomatic of how badly he was advised.

no place for PR at the palace

It could be argued that many of Britain's captains of industry also inhabit worlds which are detached from mundane reality by money and status. But the main difference between most of them and the royal family in their approach to PR is that they recruit communications professionals to deal with reputation, image and the media. The royals appoint army officers, civil servants, administrators and faithful secretaries who, for the most part, have little theoretical understanding of their role and no practical experience of dealing with journalists. And it shows.

'The Press Office at Buckingham Palace are appalling,' says Philip Hall, editor of the *News of the World*.

> If you phone them with an enquiry, they don't look into things on your behalf. They just put you off with this line: 'We have no knowledge of it.' They have no knowledge of anything! When you say, 'Are you saying that X, Y or Z isn't the case?', they will say, 'No. But we have no knowledge of it.' It's almost a conceit to treat the media that way.
>
> The royal family are so arrogant they are oblivious to the way their press officers deal with the media. The public pays massive sums to the Queen and deserves more open treatment. The problem is that they don't have professional people. They have military people, establishment people. What does an army commander know about dealing with the media?

Cynics might argue that the editor of the *News of the World* would say that, wouldn't he? But most other editors say it too, including Jane Procter, editor of the ultimate in up-market magazines, *Tatler*: 'Most editors have contempt for the Palace PR machine,' she says. 'They show constant contempt for journalists and treat them as though they're stupid and don't notice things. But journalists are trained observers. The Palace press office just aren't professional.'

Why, one might well ask, does the most famous family in Britain, perhaps the world, appoint such a patently unqualified crew to guard its most precious asset – its reputation? It doesn't take a royal kremlinologist to work out that the royals, in fact, have little appreciation of the role of PR; it is understood that they don't even see themselves as needing it. They see the purpose of their courtiers as upholding the monarchy – as distinct from the royal family – an institution which Palace insiders believe is un-PR-able. They believe in the principle that 'ye shall see me by my works' – good as far as it goes, but a climate which is hardly conducive to well-managed communications. They refuse even to comment to journalists about stories they consider to be 'rubbish' – the very stories that journalists most write about. As one royal correspondent on a national newspaper puts it: 'The press office at Buckingham Palace is completely hamstrung. As part of the court system it is restricted by its rules. Many of the staff are not held in confidence, they are always involved in damage limitation.'

Royal PR people are functionaries rather than decision-makers. Like the adulterer's wife, if that's not too close an analogy, they are often the last to know about the plans and intrigues of those whose images they spend their working hours trying to protect. Often, the first they hear of the latest twist in the royal soap opera comes in a call from the press. It's scarcely surprising that they are constantly on the defensive, caught between the devils of the press and a deep royal-blue sea.

As in any royal court, not all servants are treated equally, and this holds true of the royals' media advisers – the result being a hotbed of intrigue and scheming which militates against good communication. In his book *Diana: Her New Life*, Andrew Morton revealed how at the height of the War of the Windsors one Buckingham Palace official admitted: 'I'm delighted I'm going on holiday. It's like a snake pit in there.' The Duchess of York was furious that her decision to leave the royal family had found its way into the press, and was so convinced it had been leaked by a Palace official, plotting to discredit her, that she offered an exclusive interview to the journalist who would 'out' the royal mole. She never got to the bottom of it.

Ironically, the Duchess herself was later accused of leaking news of Prince Edward's romance with Sophie Rhys-Jones. Inflamed passions and a family conference at Windsor Castle were followed by a letter from Prince Edward to Prince Andrew demanding he keep his estranged wife under control and away from the press. 'This', says Morton, 'is but a snapshot of the prevailing climate of routine paranoia inside the royal family. Indeed, these days Prince Edward actually employs a senior courtier to detail all the news stories about him and then list all those who could possibly have leaked information. Bitter inquests and acrimonious investigations, occasionally involving police officers from the Royal Protection Squad, are a regular occurrence.'

So, the royals appoint the wrong people to PR positions of enormous responsibility, and then frequently keep them in the dark, treating them as functionaries, in an atmosphere that breeds conflict and disloyalty. But what if they were to decide the time had come for change? What if they were to go out on to the open market, recruit a team of spin doctors – either in-house or as advisers – and put their PR on a professional footing?

To begin with, there is one perhaps surprising obstacle they would have to surmount – money. Their current press officers are appointed to senior positions on salaries which, it is understood, are the equivalent of those paid to junior or middle-ranking consultants in the real world of PR – £20,000–£35,000. They are expected to do this for love of Queen and country and, if they are lucky, a free car-parking space at Buckingham Palace. Companies from which the royal household solicits design and print tenders are always reminded that their charges should reflect the prestige of possible appointment (which actually means the opposite of what instantly springs to mind!). But prestige and free car parking are not, as will have been amply demonstrated in this book by now, what makes the PR world go round. As leading entertainment spin doctor Mark Borkowski puts it: 'For a PR person, taking on the royal family is a pointless exercise. They swamp you with work. They keep you in the dark. And they pay peanuts.'

Borkowski might have well had Jane Atkinson in mind when he made this remark.

the atkinson experiment

Jane Atkinson represented a bold break with royal tradition on the part of Princess Diana, who appointed her as press secretary in January 1996. The former joint managing director of Eighties PR firm Granard Communications and founding partner of Atkinson Courage, Atkinson was a senior practitioner in the industry with a background in looking after blue-chip corporate clients. Her experience in business rather than celebrity PR provoked some comment in the press at the time of her appointment. But so did supposedly bonding similarities between Atkinson and her famous client – blond hair, an interest in fitness, clothes and aromatherapy, and a failed marriage (although that was twenty-five years ago in Atkinson's case). At the time of her appointment, Atkinson told *PR Week*: 'The view by the people who appointed me [was] that I would get on with the Princess professionally. I am extremely sympathetic with what she wants to achieve.'

From the word go there were those in the PR industry who thought Atkinson was mistaken in accepting the appointment: 'She'll be eaten alive,' said Brian MacLaurin, whose company briefly employed Sophie Rhys-Jones, Prince Edward's girlfriend. 'She can't have any idea what she's taking on. I know from my days with Sophie Rhys-Jones that your offices get besieged by the press and the company grinds to a halt.' But for Atkinson, who was by then a happily married mother of three living in Chiswick, west London, the royal appointment must have seemed like the crowning recognition of a career which had seen her meteoric rise from her first job as a secretary more than twenty years before.

Within seven months, it was all over: Atkinson resigned. Instead of a two-days-a-week role working as confidante and strategist to the Princess, Atkinson found herself deluged with media calls every day of the week, starting at six-thirty in the morning and frequently continuing long into the night. Press enquiries ranged from the weighty to – far more frequently – the banal and outré; during Wimbledon week, she found herself fielding calls from the world's media wanting to know if Diana was hiring English tennis star Tim Henman to give lessons to William. Such were the over-whelming demands of the job that to keep her other Atkinson Courage clients happy, Atkinson had to recruit more staff; hard to justify when she was being paid only £35,000 a year for services rendered to the Princess of Wales (barely enough to pay, accom-modate and equip a fairly junior consultant).

As for strategy, she soon found that that was Diana's depart-ment. The Princess of Wales set the agenda, whether it was orchestrating photo-opportunities togged up in surgical cap and gown to watch operations or resigning as patron of over a hundred charities. 'It was not my job as media adviser to tell her what to do,' Atkinson says simply. However, when the press decided the Princess was 'ghoulish' for wanting to watch heart operations, or 'petulant' for resigning her charity commitments, Atkinson was criticized for her inability to retrieve the situation.

As well as attracting criticism for media events which went wrong, Atkinson soon discovered that being too successful brought its own difficulties. Having stage-managed media coverage of the Princess's highly successful trip to Chicago in June 1996, Atkinson found herself mentioned in dispatches: 'Jane Atkinson, Diana's new press officer, did more for her client's profile than a hundred *Panorama* interviews,' wrote Tobyn Andreae in the *Daily Express*. Others in the media welcomed the openness of the Princess's new adviser and she quickly built up a powerful new network of friends in the press. Being far more accessible than the Princess, Atkinson was frequently quoted in the media – but more and more the media began to intrude into her life. Photographers sprang out at her when she was walking the dog. A mundane trip to the shops with her children couldn't be undertaken without the ever-ringing mobile telephone. The crunch came on the night of her forty-ninth birthday.

On the morning of her birthday, Atkinson woke up to find pho-tographs of Diana and the Duchess of York at their holiday retreat in the south of France plastered all over the *Daily Mirror*. Not long afterwards the two royals were on the phone to her, wanting to lodge a complaint with the Press Complaints Commission. After a day of toing and froing with the PCC, Atkinson may have been looking forward to an undisturbed birthday dinner party she had arranged for a few friends at her home that night – but it was not to be. As her dinner guests arrived she was kept on the phone by an 'animated' – her word – Duchess of York and her sister-in-law discussing a formal letter to the PCC which Atkinson had drafted. When the time came for Atkinson to fax her a revised draft of the letter of complaint, Diana asked for Atkinson's husband George to go upstairs where the fax machine was kept, to guard against curious dinner guests, while Atkinson remained downstairs on the phone. The 'top-secret' arrangement descended into farce amid a volley of shouting between Atkinson and her husband two floors away, alerting the bemused dinner guests to what was going on.

A week later Atkinson resigned, though her return to a more private lifestyle was delayed somewhat when she returned home to find forty journalists camped on her doorstep wanting to know the reason why; she managed to give them the slip, disappearing to France until the brouhaha abated.

Within months Atkinson had also left Atkinson Courage, the firm she had launched with colleague Robin Courage only eighteen months earlier. At the time the reason she gave for the move was a desire to pursue 'strategic PR consultancy with high-profile individuals' – which was out of line with Atkinson Courage business plans. The reality is that six months of near-total immersion in a £35,000 a year account could hardly have helped her side of the business. Interestingly, she decided to join Sir Tim Bell at Lowe Bell Communications; among her new colleagues were none other than Patrick Jephson and his secretary Nicky Cockell, also émigrés from Diana's office at Kensington Palace.

all dressed up and no place to go

Because the royal family don't see themselves, or the institution they represent, as needing PR, they don't have a PR or communications strategy. Princess Diana herself admitted to Andrew

Neil when he was editor of the *Sunday Times*: 'The Royal family is not streetwise. They have no strategy and do no thinking ahead. They just blunder from day to day.' UK chairman of Hill & Knowlton, Anthony Snow, says: 'My disappointment with royal PR is that it doesn't seem to follow a plan. The perception of the monarchy is extremely mixed as to its value and its future. It has begun to be perceived as a set of individuals but needs to return to an institution and explain its relevance. Quick fixes on a personal basis will not work.'

Given that the monarchy has survived for well over a thousand years without the benefit of anything as grandiose as a public relations strategy, it might well be asked why it needs one now. What's more, the overwhelming tide of national grief expressed after Diana's death, and support for her two sons, might lead one to believe that future royals will remain firmly in the public affections. Such a view is, however, dangerously complacent. Perhaps the overriding reason a royal PR strategy is needed is because the media have developed, in terms of both speed and intrusiveness, to the point where the public is now instantly informed on any and every nuance of royal behaviour. This is something with which previous generations of royals never had to cope. Going back to the damning piece written about George IV in *The Times* in 1830, today's journalists wouldn't have been content to describe him as the modern equivalent of a 'voluptuary' and 'profuse'; instead, there would be a graphic summation of his clandestine affairs and extravagant holidays. What's more, they would have been reported to the public, in prurient detail and complete with paparazzi pictures, the moment they were discovered.

For most of the 1980s the House of Windsor worked with the media to successful effect; but when the two royal marriages started to come unstuck, it became apparent that, having let the TV cameras into their lives, the royal family couldn't simply shut them out again. Media attention is not a tap that can be switched on or off as required. A strategy for dealing with it needs to be decided, or the result is the situation that currently exists: a highly defensive Palace press corps denying all knowledge of the matters that really interest the media, and trying instead to feed them stories about state visits which are of little interest.

It would be so much more convenient for the royal family if they were allowed to retreat behind the veil of mystique which protected them in the past, when the Disraelian maxim 'never complain, never explain' served them well. There are still those who believe that by battening down the media hatches and plugging away at their ceremonial and charitable concerns, the royal family will over time regain the respect and affection of the Queen's subjects. But this simply isn't an option – especially with so much of the family's glamour, internationalism and populist appeal lost with Diana. Not only must the royals reach out to the people, they need to be *seen* to be reaching out. And, as consumer and celebrity spin doctor Nick Fitzherbert says: 'Most organizations can call on a multitude of different marketing disciplines to promote themselves, but the royals have only public relations at their disposal. The reality, therefore, is that the royals need the media more than the media needs the royals.'

There is little doubt in the PR industry as to how the royal family should go about developing a strategy. The classic, three-stage approach to strategic planning – Where are you? Where do you want to be? and How do you get there? – is endorsed by most. The big question is: would the royals collectively be willing to go through the process and agree on a course of action?

The first, fundamental step would be for the royal family to re-evaluate its role in today's society and decide what it stands for. The Queen's 'Way Ahead' group is probably a recognition of this need, although its deliberations seem ponderously slow at present. With centuries of tradition weighing heavily on the shoulders of all concerned this is understandable, but few could doubt the general direction, which must be to move from an outmoded empire-style towards a more European-style monarchy. This state of affairs will come about through a process of natural attrition in any case – in twenty years the royal family will be considerably slimmer than it is today.

Within this overall repositioning, roles must be found for royals major and minor. The War of the Waleses, as Charles and Diana each sought to turn public opinion in their favour, had a polarizing effect, which ultimately didn't help either of them and which certainly damaged the monarchy. The first Andrew Morton book about Diana (*Diana: Her True Story*), which, the author revealed amid much controversy in September 1997, had been written on the basis of taped interviews with the Princess herself, contained the most damaging revelations about life in the royal household in recent times and presented a highly unflattering portrait of Prince Charles. In response Charles's camp, instead of embarking on a programme of containment, went several steps further. The Prince's sympathizers let it be known to the press that Diana's suicide attempts, detailed in the book, were nothing but 'amateur dramatics'. Penny Junor, Charles's biographer, wrote a long article portraying Diana as temperamental hot-head on the edge of a nervous breakdown, and the *Evening Standard* carried a profile which said of the Princess: 'She has become an egomaniac convinced of her world importance and even her healing powers. Prince Charles's friends are bitter and frustrated at the prospect of the royal family held to ransom by a spoilt and increasingly spiteful woman.'

As long as Charles and Diana continued to undermine the credibility of each other, they undermined the credibility of the royal family as a whole. Complaints that the royal family have taken on the aspect of a soap opera can be firmly laid at the door of the royals themselves. For the fact is that feuding royals make great newspaper copy – but extremely poor PR. Like any other organization, be it a company wishing to woo investors, a political party seeking votes or a charity drumming up funds, the royal family has to be seen as united, coherent and singing from the same hymn sheet, albeit different parts.

The notion of a well-oiled royal PR machine orchestrating complementary programmes of activity for its cast of players in common support of a renewed royal 'brand' is, of course, a PR man's fantasy. At the moment, some individual royals find it impossible to behave in their *own* best interests. And there are a number of issues which, so long as they remain unresolved, will continue to make the royal family's dealings with the media extremely difficult.

from empire monarchy to european royals

The most serious of these is the cost of the royal family, an issue which continues to bubble beneath the surface of public opinion, erupting whenever fresh evidence points to what many of the Queen's subjects regard as the colossal misuse of public funds in propping up Britain's most wealthy family. The debate first became particularly explosive during the 'annus horribilis' of 1992, when the Queen assumed her subjects would pick up the bill for repairs to her private wing of the fire-damaged Windsor Castle. Retreating in the face of overwhelming opposition, she agreed to open up Buckingham Palace to tourists in the summer months to recoup the costs.

Then, in 1994, the House of Commons Public Accounts Committee released details of the £20 million annual cost of running the royal household. Breakdowns of costs for telephones, electricity, gas, furniture, water rates, and grace and favour apartments for some 300 families once again provoked an outcry from public and media alike. In a country still gripped by the 'feelbad' factor, traumatized by recession and worried about job security, house prices and other aspects of personal and family finance, how was it possible for any single family to justify making such massive demands on the public purse?

There are, of course, the balancing arguments. Twenty million pounds is an utterly insignificant amount in the context of total government expenditure, and amounts to less than one pound a year from every taxpayer. It is even less significant when compared to the upkeep costs of comparable heads of state, most notably the President and ex-Presidents of America, who cost American taxpayers far more than the royal family costs Britons. And then there is the notion of the royal family as an 'invisible export', drawing tourists in huge numbers who wouldn't otherwise come to Britain. It is difficult to prove the validity of this much-aired defence, let alone quantify it, but few would argue against the fact that the royals do contribute indirectly, to some extent or other, to the nation's financial well-being.

Nonetheless, the headline figures, like '£20 million', inflame public opinion. The Queen may not be demanding a replacement royal yacht, but she and her family still have castles in Windsor and Balmoral and spectacular residences in Sandringham, Buckingham Palace, Kensington Palace and St James's Palace. There is no question that the pace of reform at the Palace has quickened since Diana's death. In November 1997, in an unprecedented move towards greater openness, Buckingham Palace sanctioned Simon Gimson, their former Policy Unit head, to speak to *Panorama* about the lesson the royal family was learning from public response to Diana's life and death. It is interesting that Buckingham Palace could not, yet, bring itself to allow a current member of its household to speak on national television. Gimson assured viewers that the royals are both sensitive and responsive to public opinion. For example, if the public wanted the royals to give up Kensington Palace, he seemed to imply, then give up Kensington Palace they would.

However, the overall impression created was that the royal family are reluctant reformers. We should not expect any surprise announcements from them about slimming down their imperial-style trappings. And therein lies the problem. Until they become more proactive in proposing such measures, they will continue to be – and be seen to be – constantly on the defensive, reacting to public complaint rather than leading by example. And, what's more, they will continue to provide their opponents with a stick with which to beat them every time they come under attack on quite unrelated issues.

camilla v. joe public

The main public relations challenge facing Prince Charles is Camilla Parker Bowles, although he is beleaguered with other image problems too. Poll after poll shows that most people in Britain are opposed to Camilla formally sharing the Prince's future when he becomes King. While public attitudes may be gradually thawing, overall opposition to an official recognition of Camilla will be difficult to change as long as the memory of Diana remains so powerful an influence on public opinion. Since her relationship with the Prince was made public, Camilla herself has been the model of discretion and dignity. She is a far more obvious soulmate for Charles than Diana ever was, sharing his intellectual interests and love of country life. But Diana, who in life was the most celebrated and, many would say, glamorous woman in the world, and probably the most popular royal after the Queen, in death has transformed to near-saint status, which makes it more, rather than less, difficult for Charles to introduce Camilla to his public life. Had Diana returned from her trip to Paris and gone on to find happiness in a second marriage, it is probable that public resistance to Charles's future with Camilla would have declined steadily. But Diana's untimely death stopped the clock on the dynamics of their relationship. When she died, Diana was still regarded as the moral victim of Charles's duplicity, with Camilla hovering unseen in the wings. It is from this position that Charles must find his way – and it will not be easy.

Here we come up against a particular difficulty in introducing strategy into royal – and, for that matter, celebrity – PR. If one were advising the chairman of a PLC that one of his subsidiaries was having a persistently adverse influence on City opinion, he would set about divesting the company of that subsidiary forthwith. Telling Charles to get rid of Camilla is, however, not an option. In the words of his aides, her presence in his life is 'non-negotiable'. As long as the Queen remains on the throne and Charles keeps his relationship with Camilla out of the public eye, the inconvenient romance remains a latent rather than an active problem. But, unless there is a significant change in public opinion, it is conceivable that Camilla could prompt a major royal crisis in time.

Prince Charles's other PR headaches are far more manageable than an affair of the heart. But the Prince's reluctance to take the advice of communications professionals is well known; one royal adviser famously told a journalist that 'he [Charles] doesn't even like PR people' – an unfortunate admission, given that the journalist in question was reporting for industry journal *PR Week*! Instead of hiring PR professionals, the Prince consults with civil servants and friends who have little experience in dealing with public opinion. The results are plain to see. His previous attempts to own up and open up backfired badly. Instead of winning a place in the nation's affections, he unleashed a storm of public censure, laid his judgement open to question and was seen by many as a self-pitying whinger who had to be told by his father when to get married and by his mother when to get divorced.

Of course, it is all too easy to see these mistakes with the wisdom of hindsight. In 1996 Prince Charles appointed a PR man from the real world, Mark Bolland, to act as a communications adviser. Whether or not Charles will listen to him, of course, remains to be seen. But most of Charles's inner circle remains staunchly establishment: Tom Shebbeare, Stephen Lamport, Sandy Henney and Julia Cleverdon – all are worthy, forty-something products of the Civil Service and/or quangos – and it shows. The Prince's recent campaign to revive his popularity as a 'People's Prince' is foolish and misjudged. His advisers should be exhorting him to desist in this course of action, rather than encouraging him to continue. Prince Charles is altogether too formal, cerebral and introspective to be a prince of the people. In the words of Dr David Starkey, the constitutional historian: 'He is not the sort of personality who easily acts as a vehicle for public relations. He is knobbly, prickly and arrogant.'

Charles also frequently shoots himself in his PR foot by airing controversial views on a variety of esoteric subjects. While these views are clearly sincere and strongly held, they do not strike a chord with large swathes of the population, and are merely used by the tabloids as fodder to beef up the Prince's undeserved image as an eccentric nutter who talks to his plants and dabbles in foreign philosophies.

His sensitive and dignified response to Diana's death did much to repair the damage of previous miscalculations, however. And with the spotlight off Diana, his public appearances have been more relaxed and engaging. His trip to South Africa with Prince Harry in late 1997 was a particular triumph, encounters with Nelson Mandela and the Spice Girls boosting his populist credentials by association. Since then, behind-the-scenes glimpses of his charity work have portrayed him in a more emotionally accessible light than hitherto. The longer-term strategy will see Prince Charles working more closely with the Queen, symbolized by the transfer of his office from St James's Palace to Buckingham Palace. Certainly he would stand to benefit from sharing more of the Queen's public duties and continuing with his more open approach. But Charles's positive advances in PR terms may be jeopardized at any moment so long as the Camilla time bomb continues to tick . . .

the princess and the paparazzi

The announcement of Diana's death on Sunday, 31 August 1997 was accompanied in the world's media by descriptions of her last car journey from the Ritz Hotel in Paris with Dodi Fayed – and their high-speed chase down a curved underpass in central Paris pursued by members of the paparazzi. As people throughout the world came to terms with the news, there was a fierce backlash against the paparazzi, who were seen as directly responsible for Diana's death (this was before revelations about the state of the driver were made). Mourners who made their way to the gates of Buckingham and Kensington palaces responded angrily to television crews, making clear their bitterness towards those who they believed had hounded their princess to her death. Bemused radio reporters were told in no uncertain terms that they too were in part to blame for the tragedy. Meanwhile, the national press's newsrooms worked feverishly to assemble special editions for the following day, hastily assembling images from their picture archives to illustrate Diana's life and work.

On Monday 1 September sales of the tabloids rocketed. Most

tabloids had produced special supplements which proved popular with a public hungry for any news about the Princess that could help bring them to terms with what had happened. Such was this appetite that the *Sun* alone added 1 million copies to its circulation.

Media-watchers could only wonder at the grim and incredible irony of it all. Here was a public blaming the paparazzi for Diana's death while pouring huge sums of money into the coffers of the paparazzi's paymasters. At the same time, TV and radio crews, who have absolutely no connection with paparazzi, were being tearfully denounced in the streets.

There is, of course, an even greater irony in the media's role in Diana's life and death. Had it not been for the media, most notably the tabloids with their massive circulations, Diana would never have developed into a figure of such compelling popular appeal. It was *because* of the media that she became part of the national psyche. The media provided the necessary conduits for her to engage people's affections, to become a fashion icon, role model, charity worker, issues manager – and to seek fulfilment as the nation's queen of hearts. However, it is the view of many, including the Princess's brother, the Earl Spencer, that the media must take at least part of the responsibility for her death.

At the time that this book goes to press, the trial of the paparazzi cameramen who pursued Diana in Paris has yet to be held. But whatever the outcome of the trial, there can be no disputing that, even before the final horror of her car journey in Paris, Diana's way of dealing with the media was fraught with contradictions. For, unpopular as the notion may be, Diana was as much a manipulator as a victim of the media, and frequently tried to use her feminine wiles to turn the media to her advantage – often to disastrous effect. Photographed by a member of the paparazzi as she drove millionaire art dealer Oliver Hoare into Kensington Palace late one night, Diana tried to stop the photograph appearing in the *News of the World*, who bought the photo, using a friendly contact at the *Daily Mail* to suggest the photograph was a fake – two companions in the back of the car had been masked out. Of course this wasn't true, and the *News of the World* duly ran the photograph anyway. And when an exclusive appeared in the *Daily Mail* in which 'a close friend' of Diana told the paper about the Princess's recent 'bloody awful weekend in Spain' being harassed by unwanted media men, it emerged the next day that the 'close friend' was none other than a media man himself – *Daily Mail* reporter Richard Kay – whom the Princess had met, bizarrely, in her Audi in Beauchamp Place, Knightsbridge. Such blatant collusion with one of their competitors raised the ire of every other national newspaper, and the next day the *Sun* ran a story under the headline 'Two Faced Diana' alongside a photograph of her assignation with Kay.

Diana's attempts at a cover-up after the episode of the 'nuisance calls' to Oliver Hoare provide yet another example of her 'do-it-yourself' approach to PR. Countless calls had been made to the Hoare residence, but each time when the phone was picked up the caller remained silent. The calls were traced by the police to Diana's private Kensington Palace apartment and her private mobile phone. Once the news became public, Diana got the long-suffering Kay to phone tabloid rival Clive Goodman, *News of the World* royal editor, to claim that a member of the Princess's house-hold was responsible for the calls. Given that her special relationship with Kay had already been exposed, it was a mission doomed to backfire at the very time she needed to cool down, rather than inflame, the media row developing around her.

On other occasions she has manipulated the media with far greater skill. One of her more outstanding successes occurred on the night when Prince Charles appeared on national television with his confession of adultery. Diana had an engagement at the Serpentine Gallery that evening and knew that the national press would be in full attendance. So she chose to wear a replica of a dress, and even the accompanying choker, in which Camilla Parker Bowles had recently been photographed. Of course she looked absolutely stunning, and sure enough, next morning the national press delivered what she was after – photographs of the two women in a comparison which did Camilla no favours at all. This, and countless other examples of similar calculation, are quoted by royal correspondents and newspaper editors. Interviewed some months before Diana's death, Philip Hall, editor of the *News of the World*, said: 'Diana is highly manipulative of the media. She has been known to phone up editors in tears about a story, then five minutes later they hear she's gone out somewhere, laughing with friends.'

How much of this fickle behaviour was play-acting, and how much the product of a volatile temperament, is hard to detect. But in the Princess's defence, she had to cope with media intrusion on a scale that few could possibly imagine. *Dicing with Di*, a photo-book produced by two paparazzi and published long before the accident in the underpass, is a 200-page, blow-by-blow account of their relentless scrutiny of her every move outside Kensington Palace. Using that hackneyed justification 'we're just doing our job', a particularly shabby excuse for freelance photographers, Mark Saunders and Glenn Harvey explain how they sold photo-graphs of Diana for a living. Far from respecting any sense of privacy, the more intimate the moment the higher the price they got for the photograph, whether it was a private meeting with her son at Eton or close-up inspection of her legs for signs of cellulite. Explaining, with adolescent glee, how they frequently provoked Diana to angry outbursts – known between the two as 'loon attacks' – or alternatively reduced her to tears, the effect of their harassment was summed up by the Princess herself during an encounter in Leicester Square after she had taken her two boys to see *Jurassic Park* which is related in the book:

> It was Diana, but this was a Diana I had never seen before. It was her face but it was now red and twisted. She was racing towards us through the crowds. Her eyes were fixed on us and then she let out a scream like a wild animal. The hundreds of milling pigeons took to the sky. The shocked tourists stopped walking and looked our way. William and Harry rushed up behind to see what the bel-lowing was. No monster's roar they'd heard in the film could have scared them as much as this one, 'You make my life hell!' she screamed, 'You make my life hell!'

Next morning, the *Daily Mirror* published a cartoon showing Diana's head atop a Tyrannosaurus rex spitting at cowering photographers – the Princess's moment of torment merchandized for the benefit of over 3 million readers.

The paparazzi, or 'stalkerazzi' as they are known in America, would argue that the Princess used them as much as they used her – not only at moments like her appearance at the Serpentine Gallery, when she counted on their presence, but to showcase herself as the devoted and fun-loving mother of the two young princes, whose 'normal' lives with her were portrayed as a million metaphorical miles from the stiff formality of the rest of the family. And she would go for a swim in the knowledge that a rooftopful of photographers would be flashbulbing her every move, later commenting to one of them: 'Were you one of the rooftop boys? I always make sure I have a nice swimsuit on for you.'

With her two sons Diana felt at her most vulnerable, the cameras heightening her maternal protective instincts. It is ironic that Diana, the more informal of the two parents, was far less relaxed in the presence of the media. As Glenn Harvey noted: 'Watching Charles's reaction to the media presence in comparison to Diana's, there is a fundamental difference between the two: Charles couldn't care less who is watching when he plays with the boys, whereas Diana feels she has to protect them from the cameras and exposure.'

This same love–hate attitude was clearly apparent in Diana's dealings with the media away from the cameras. There were times when she went on a charm offensive. Apart from her much-publicized meetings with the *Mail*, she also had her friend Lady Stevens, wife of the chief executive of Express Newspapers's Lord Stevens, arrange meetings with Nick Lloyd and Eve Pollard, the husband-and-wife duo who edit the *Express* and *Sunday Express*. Such was the personal warmth and sincerity she could bring to bear on anyone in her presence that these meetings, like tête-à-têtes with other key influencers, resulted in a change of editorial policy at the *Express* – at least for a while.

The late John Junor, himself a former editor of the *Sunday*

Express and a columnist for the *Mail on Sunday*, and one of Diana's most strident critics, found himself on the receiving end of a session of her famous 'love-bombing' after bumping into her on Kensington High Street – and a dramatic turnaround in the way he wrote about her followed. 'My own views of Princess Diana,' he admitted, 'have been the subject of change. But, on one aspect of her character, I have never been in any doubt. She is on the side of the angels. She is a warm, compassionate person who lights up every room she enters. She cares about people. And the people have come to care deeply about her.' And Lord Fawsley, much-quoted constitutional expert and friend of Prince Charles, had a similarly Damascian experience on meeting Diana, saying afterwards that he had misjudged her.

Diana's charm was certainly one of her most powerful attributes, and even though it was keenly felt during her life, few, if any of us, could have appreciated just how universally she was admired, respected and loved. Writing in the *Evening Standard*, Christopher Hudson commented how not even the deaths of George VI or Churchill stopped the clocks the way that Diana's death did. The queues to sign condolence books at St James's Palace and the oceans of flowers laid outside palace gates represented to many spontaneous gestures of bereavement that as Hudson commented: 'There's no longer any doubt that something of bewildering significance is taking place. I feel, as many journalists must do, that somewhere along the line we missed a trick.'

The Princess's warmth, compassion and appeal to ordinary men, women and children all over the world became most clearly evident only after she died. As did the void she left, which the royal family will find difficult to fill. One of the greatest PR challenges facing the royals over the next few years will be to engage some of the overwhelming public feeling that was focused on Diana. That she was irreplaceable is not in dispute. But the royals need to ensure that at least some of the 'Diana effect' remains with the family.

Already there are signs of a public transference of affection to Princes William and Harry, with William, the eldest and heir, and the more closely resembling Diana, enjoying particular support. To return to the well-worn theme of this chapter, however, the stakes for the royals, including the two princes, really are too high for them to leave their future public relations to chance. They will need to appoint the right PR advisers – and stop taking media advice from the wrong ones. They will need to ensure that they move ahead according to their own agenda, rather than engage in end-less fire-fighting. They would certainly benefit from the services of a professional spin doctor. But who? Jane Procter, *Tatler* editor, nominates Sir Tim. 'They should put themselves in his hands,' she declares. 'He's one of the few people in London who can stop editors running stories.' Philip Hall believes Sir Tim's longstanding business associates, the brothers Saatchi, would do the trick: 'They would transform their image,' he says.

As the most famous family in the world, and as a historic and much-envied institution which provides our head of state, the royals have a duty to manage their relationships with the media more astutely. Whether they like it or not, the media are the means by which public sentiment towards them, and towards the future of the monarchy, is shaped. Through the media, they are present in all our lives. 'If you live by the media, you should die by the media,' the Bishop of Peterborough once prophetically paraphrased. For too long now the royals have been avoiding the issue, much less dealing effectively with it, but if there is one legacy Diana leaves to the royal family, it is the need to find a way not only to live with the media, but to manage it effectively. There is already evidence that the Dianafication of the royal family is underway. It is perhaps the greatest royal irony of all that, through her death, Diana has forced a change of approach, and thereby improved public feeling towards the family that was the cause of such deep unhappiness to her in life.

CHAPTER ELEVEN
media alchemy and making celebrity pay

America is the land of celebrity – indeed, celebrity might be seen as an intrinsic part of the American dream. Money on its own isn't enough. Status, too, must be witnessed by the length of the limo (preferably an import), social acceptance by 'the right kind of people', and, as media theorist Douglas Rushkoff suggests, the amount of air time occupied. The fast route to celebrity, as every midwestern prom queen and young blood knows, is to be found in Hollywood – notwithstanding the countless articles about the Greyhound-loads of young hopefuls who find themselves on the boulevard of broken dreams, and the plethora of documentaries starring waiters, couriers and reluctant gigolos, whose cameo appearances are the only ones they're destined to make in front of rolling cameras. But here's the rub: what happens if you do become a star? What, even, if you get to be one of the biggest stars in history? What if you're more famous than you could ever possibly have imagined, with every studio head in town on his knees, begging you to work for him? What then?

Well, then it's time to open a chain of diner restaurants. Launch a new perfume bearing your name. Or perhaps start your own health and fitness organization. In short, it's time to cash in on the fact that your name is now a 'household brand'. Enter the celebrity spin doctor who will guide you, as a 'franchise celebrity', through a hall of media mirrors carefully angled to show off both you and your endorsed product to best effect. It is a world where you will be expected to bare your soul, in carefully scripted five-minute soundbites, to a dozen journalists in quick succession. You will be required to strut your stuff in clothes you would have been embarrassed to wear in the Seventies. And you will find yourself going to parties, not so much to enjoy yourself as to take part in extended photo-shoots, together with other celebrities, with whom you will appear to have been lifelong buddies.

Turning the ephemerality that is fame into a seven-figure bank balance in an offshore account is one of the great conjuring tricks of celebrity PR. And whether it's hamburgers or handbags, your celebrity spin doctor will find a way of ensuring that the product you endorse merges seamlessly with your media persona. The closer your chosen product is to your real life and work, of course, the better. In that respect, Planet Hollywood probably represents the zenith of celebrity endorsement.

Planet Hollywood does for movies what the Hard Rock Café did for music. Operating in dozens of cities worldwide – there will be 100 restaurants in the chain by the twenty-first century – the company already has a market capitalization of a staggering $2.5 billion. Not that it's market capitalization that brings the punters in. It's 'eatertainment'. Planet Hollywood is owned by Sylvester Stallone, Arnold Schwarzenegger and Bruce Willis, everyone knows that, and stories are legion of out-of-towners from the provinces visiting London of a Saturday for the Oxford Street–Planet Hollywood–Harrods routine, rounding the corner to their lunch table to find themselves face to face with none other than their all-time favourite Hollywood hero.

The throngs who flock to Planet Hollywood don't do so on account of its outsize portions of burgers, salads and cheesecake. What brings the pilgrims in is the opportunity to touch stardom. And even if Sly, Arnie and Bruce aren't there on the day you go, you can always console yourself, as you munch your way through the apple strudel cooked to Arnie's Mum's recipe, by looking at the exhibits from all those movies of the past – the little silver guy from

Star Wars, Kim Basinger's handcuffs from *Nine and a Half Weeks* – or by spending up a storm in the branded franchise shop conveniently located near the exit.

Celebrities always turn up for opening nights, of course, and when Planet Hollywood opened in Moscow, over ten thousand people waited outside to catch a glimpse of greatness; two fans died after falling off a roof to which they'd resorted. The first night in London, orchestrated by celebrity spin doctor supremo Matthew Freud, was memorable for all the right reasons. Over £2 million was spent in one evening, with eighteen stars flown over from America to make the opening bonanza a more glittering array of fame and glamour than any film premiere or awards ceremony Britain had ever seen. It was on the front page of all the national papers, the talk of every London radio station and featured by Michael Aspel on Carlton Television (the producer being obliged to ensure that the Planet Hollywood logo appeared for thirty-four of the fifty-one minutes the show was on air).

One more demonstration of just how much more the media needs celebrities than celebrities need the media. So badly, in fact, do the media need them, that they will roll over and let the likes of Matthew Freud tickle their collective tummy in circumstances which would otherwise have them growling ferociously about editorial integrity. At no point during the opening of London's Planet Hollywood did the media say: 'You're just opening a restaurant in a city of ten thousand restaurants.' Instead, the message, conveniently for Planet Hollywood, was: 'All the stars in the galaxy were there.' Subtext: Planet Hollywood is the most glamorous place to eat a burger in London. No amount of advertising could have communicated the message to quite such effect.

In many ways the whole media image of Planet Hollywood is a PR conjuring trick of which the late Alfred Hitchcock would have been proud. Because the chance of the Bloggs family running into their Hollywood hunk is, in truth, extremely slim. Even the perception that Sly, Arnie and Bruce 'own' Planet Hollywood is mistaken. They're not even majority shareholders. That privilege belongs to Robert Earl, B. S. Ong and Keith Barish, three gents who would fail to muster so much as a second glance should you bump into them as you kit yourself out with a branded sweatshirt in the Planet Hollywood shop, but who are the real Planet Hollywood heroes (Robert Earl's personal shareholding in Planet Hollywood is worth around $800 million, placing him nineteenth on the *Sunday Times* 'Rich List' for 1997).

However, such is the voracious appetite for celebrities that the media are happy to go along for the ride, whatever the nature of the vehicle carrying them. This simple truth not only underpins the work done by celebrity spin doctors, it is well understood by those promoting consumer goods (and often there is a high degree of cross-over between the two roles). The basic maxim might go something along these lines: 'If you're in a fix with a product or event that is completely un-PR-able, then rent a celebrity.' What's in it for the celebrity is a large pile of cash. Sly, Arnie and Bruce may not be majority shareholders in Planet Hollywood, but even their modest holdings are worth immodest fortunes – all for the price of an upfront investment and guest appearances around the world when new restaurants open.

smart people, smart products: the sumptuous world of aurelia

Putting together smart people and smart products is an activity well understood by Aurelia Cecil, whose client list includes brands such as Versace, Krug champagne, TAG Heuer Watches, Mappin & Webb, Lalique, Jaeger Womenswear and *Country Life* magazine. Based in offices with a suitably aspirational Chelsea address, Aurelia's PR portfolio includes a *PR Week* award for 'Best Small Consultancy', together with congratulatory letters from Patrick Lichfield and a top Versace executive in Milan. A less *Absolutely Fabulous* person you could not, however, hope to meet. Aurelia Cecil personifies what she describes as 'a new breed of PR people: focused, professional and strategic in approach'. Her neat, elegant form encased in designer chic, Aurelia herself is clearly a young woman in a hurry, with no time for chit-chat about celebrities, irreverent humour or false modesty: 'We are the number one specialist in fashion and luxury goods in England. We're in our eighth year and represent beauty and fashion companies at the top end of the market.' Selling her agency to advertising group Abbott Mead Vickers in August 1997, she closed the deal with £4.25 million at the tender age of just thirty.

'The perceived value of a brand', she says, 'is integral to a high-price sale. In the Eighties there was a lot of money around. It was all labels and people didn't care how much things cost, they had to have them. In the early Nineties there was a move to grunge. It was very insular, very depressed. Now we are seeing what we call the "connoisseur consumer boom". People are buying luxury goods again, but not indiscriminately. They have to be made well and the brand value has to have integrity.'

Giving a brand value 'integrity' clearly means more than simply ensuring the stitching doesn't fall out of your new Armani frock. It also has to do with image and association – which is where celebrities come in. Take the opening of jeweller David Morris's store in New Bond Street. Wanting to drum up maximum publicity for the occasion, he put himself in Aurelia's capable hands. She realized it would take more than champagne and canapés to put the David Morris shop on the map, and duly commissioned Patrick Lichfield to take portrait photographs of a bevy of society gels modelling a variety of diamond rings, bangles and necklaces. Camilla Parker Bowles' daughter Laura was one of the models, whose photographs were duly placed exclusively in the *Sunday Telegraph*. The Hon. Mrs James Lowther, Lady Victoria Harvey and twin sisters Mrs Ben Sangster and Mrs Rupert Cordle were other willing subjects for Lord Lichfield's lens.

So when opening night finally arrived – celebrated not *in situ*, but at a cocktail party at the Ritz – the media had more than a bray of Sloane Rangers to fuss over, they also had plenty of photographic material showing off David Morris's artistry to perfection. The choice of Laura Parker Bowles as a model was inspired: both parents arrived to support their daughter who then confessed –

newsworthier still – that she and her father had had 'a massive row' when she complained that her dress was falling apart. Mother Camilla, meanwhile, wore a split skirt which revealed rather more thigh than she had hitherto exposed to the British public, whipping up even greater media excitement. The *Evening Standard* had to look no further for its page three splash.

Among the Parker Bowleses, Palmer-Tomkinsons, Moores and McShanes, there were enough celebs to ensure that coverage appeared in most of the national press. Says Aurelia: 'We got in 80 per cent of the national newspapers the next day. That's not bad for the opening of a single shop.' Indeed it isn't. Not that one would expect anything less of an upmarket consumer goods spin doctor who knows that designer labels attached to designer celebrities represent a far more marketable proposition than labels attached to jewellery, ballgowns, or any other fashion accessory.

From time to time spin doctors are helped in their task when celebrities in different fields, who really are pals, offer to help each other out. Before he was gunned down in front of his Florida mansion in July 1997, Gianni Versace had formed, with Elton John, one such high-powered duo. Versace kindly loaned his Old Bond Street shop to Elton for a party to raise funds for the Elton John AIDS Foundation. Reported *Tatler* breathlessly: 'In a nutshell it was a star gazer's paradise – much what one would expect from a party hosted jointly by Gianni Versace and Elton John and co-ordinated by Aurelia Cecil.' And the rock star returned the favour a few months later, bravely modelling one of Versace's women's dresses – a gender-bending event of such magnitude that Aurelia persuaded the *Sunday Times* to feature it on the front page of its magazine, as part of a much larger feature showing off the fashion king's latest creations. Did money change hands? Aurelia couldn't possibly comment. About all such matters she retains a Sphinx-like silence.

virgin on the ridiculous – the secret of branson's celebrity appeal

Of all British businessmen, one has clearly succeeded in making an impact on the collective psyche where others have failed. He knows exactly how to manage the media to deploy his celebrity to best effect, whether it's to launch a new soft drink, airline, vodka or record store. And with the launch of every new venture, his celebrity as an entrepreneur grows greater still. A survey conducted on behalf of the *Sunday Times* by polling company NOP found that Richard Branson is the best-known businessman in Britain – 35 per cent of people spontaneously named him as one of the country's most prominent businesspeople. On the surface of things this is, perhaps, no great surprise – as the *Sunday Times* concluded: 'People's responses appear to have been heavily influenced by the amount of media coverage business personalities receive.'

But from a PR perspective it is highly revealing that a man who runs a large but by no means all-powerful commercial operation, in name-awareness terms completely dwarfs, for example, Sir David Simon and Sir Richard Sykes, neither of whom scored even a single percentage recognition point even though they run BP and Glaxo Wellcome respectively, two of Britain's biggest companies. Successfully running a major multinational corporation is clearly not enough to make any impression at all on the public. Which raises the question: does it really matter? So what if nobody has ever heard of you, as long as you effectively market good products or services? Would more people fill up at BP petrol stations if they thought as fondly of Sir David Simon and BP as they do of Richard Branson and Virgin? Well, of course they would, which is why Branson has been so successful at introducing new products and services into marketplaces as diverse as airlines, record stores and Personal Equity Plans.

Making celebrity pay is an art form in which few could teach Branson any lessons. He is famous as the country's favourite entre-preneurial hero, the consumer's champion who, time and again, takes on the establishment and shows he can deliver the same thing more cheaply. But more than this, it is his own personal endorsement of new Virgin products, via highly media-friendly stunts, which gets the message across at a fraction of the cost of advertising. What other chief executive would be prepared to dress in bouffant white drag to publicize the opening of his bridal stores? Or pour vodka on to his breakfast cornflakes to promote his new liquor brand? Of course, Branson's various hot-air ballooning exploits do much to promote his image as the fun-loving free spirit, not to be constrained by convention. But it is the calculated merchandizing of this celebrity which lies behind so much of Virgin's success.

Curiously, those who know Branson and his PR chief, Will Whitehorn, say that it is the latter who comes across as the more gregarious of the pair. In fact, Branson surprises some with his reticent personal style in face-to-face business encounters. But he certainly knows how to put on a good show for the media. Says Vicky Bolger, one of Branson's PR handlers at London agency GCI: 'Even if we phoned up a dozen journalists and told them "Richard Branson is having breakfast" they would turn up with photographers. He can always be relied upon for a good picture. He is hugely popular with the media because he always does something different.'

The launch of Virgin Vodka was a case in point and a signal lesson to other business leaders about how to slash advertising budgets by thousands through exploiting a higher personal profile. The launch day began with a photo-call in the garden of Branson's Holland Park home. Fifteen photographers from the national papers, key regionals and the marketing press turned up to photograph Branson pouring vodka on to his cereal and cavorting with nurses. The reasons for these two particular props derived from the PR idea central to the launch theme: Virgin Vodka is triple-distilled, a process which makes the alcohol so pure that it has the potential to be hangover-free. Morning breakfasts after a heavy night before need never be the same again. So confident was Virgin in its claim that a 'hangover test' was to be initiated that very evening under strict medical supervision.

The main event was the hangover test itself, for which GCI,

Branson's consumer PR agency, booked the prestigious Kensington Roof Gardens venue and invited over 200 journalists to participate in a thoroughly scientific appraisal of the effect of the triple-distilled Virgin Vodka. At 6 p.m., when most of the national press had arrived, enthusiastically joined by journalists from various radio stations, television and consumer magazines, they were all breathalysed in the interests of statistical rigour, invited to line their stomachs with ice cream, and provided with a golf-card-style 'Progress Chart' on which to record their intake of the miracle vodka. Branson once again entertained those present, appearing in Cossack dress and dancing on the tables before mixing and mingling, while other diversions during the course of the evening included 'walking the straight line', which was, in fact, distinctly crooked.

Poured into cabs at the end of the evening, journalists had good reason to feel grateful. Quite apart from a good night out and the chance to meet Britain's biggest business celebrity, they had photoshoot material plus a genuine news-hook – the triple-distillation concept. The 'hangover-free' idea was a nice, light-hearted support story.

The success of the launch quickly became apparent. In the guise of continuing the research exercise, GCI executives phoned those journalists who had attended the party the next day to enquire about their degree of hangover – and to give, where needed, a gentle prod in the direction of writing up the story. Within days, articles on Virgin Vodka were appearing in news outlets as diverse as the *Financial Times*, the *Sun*, the *Daily Mail*, the *Evening Standard*, *Loaded* magazine, BBC2 television, London Talkback Radio, and many more besides. The endorsement by Richard Branson of a product which claimed such major pharmacological benefits, even in the jokiest way, certainly befitted his positioning as 'consumer champion'. Celebrity endorsement had, once again, been used to powerful effect in communicating a message which wouldn't otherwise have been heard.

In fact, there was an underlying irony to the whole proceedings; those journalists who knew about it were happy to keep it to themselves, and those who didn't weren't unduly disadvantaged. For the truth of the matter is that almost all vodkas are triple-distilled. In this respect, if not in others, Virgin is no different from most other vodkas on the market. It is just that Virgin chose to focus on this particular product attribute, suggesting, by unspoken implication, that it represented a 'unique selling proposition'. The whole notion, therefore, of a 'purer' form of alcohol than had hitherto been available and of hangover-free drinking was built on a premise which could not have withstood even the most casual scrutiny. But, as will have become apparent by now, celebrity-led events aren't about investigative journalism, scrupulously researched analyses or balanced reporting. If they were, they wouldn't get into the papers at all, let alone on to the front page. They are about delivering celebrities, together with their attendant messages, to a reading, viewing or listening public which is trans-fixed by celebrity. They are about boosting newspaper sales, or viewing and listening figures, by giving access to those the audience hero-worships. Celebrity-led events are about the media alchemy performed by spin doctors in transforming something that has no news value into front-page material. And the celebrity spin doctor who has taken the practice of media alchemy to its highest form is, without question, Matthew Freud.

new-colour pop can – hold the front page!

On 19 January 1995 a major world event took place. You may not remember the date, but you will almost certainly remember where you were when it happened, just as you will recall where you were when Charles and Di got married and Nelson Mandela walked out of jail. For 19 January 1995 was the day that Pepsi went blue. The publicizing of Pepsi Blue was probably the biggest event in PR history. The endorsement by celebrity Cindy Crawford was central to an exercise with a huge PR budget. But the news coverage was even huger, and went far beyond what any advertising campaign probably could have achieved.

Let's go back to the beginning, when Pepsi called in their PR advisers to discuss the international relaunch of what's known in the trade as 'can livery'. Pepsi had already changed their can livery a dozen times in previous years. The proposed livery change, from red-white-blue to blue-red-white, was hardly revolutionary. And the drink itself was to remain exactly the same. In terms of news value, therefore, the livery change had very little going for it.

So Pepsi had a choice. Either they could send out photographs of the new Pepsi can to the world's marketing and consumer correspondents with a media release along the lines of 'Please find attached a copy of our new can livery'. Or they could pretend that what was happening was an event of the most phenomenal importance, and act accordingly. In the hard-fought cola marketplace, where a flurry of new entrants was fragmenting what was once a two-brand race, as far as Pepsi was concerned this was no choice at all. Thus began preparations for 'Project Blue'.

Freud and his team worked up a number of secondary properties. Cindy Crawford was signed up to make an appearance on the launch day for an estimated £100,000. A nice start, but was it enough? Then someone came up with the idea of painting Concorde blue. Air France were persuaded to go along with the scheme, for a small consideration, but only on the basis that the aircraft wouldn't be used for transatlantic flights; the dark colour over a journey as long as that would overheat the aircraft. But the blue Concorde could be hired for ten days of corporate hospitality, jetting at supersonic speed to less far-flung destinations. Another good idea – but still, was it enough?

To make sure the most was made of Cindy and Concorde at the media launch, Freud got hold of the Rolling Stones' staging company and Pink Floyd's lighting designer, who wired up more floodlights in the old Greater London Council building, opposite the Houses of Parliament, than were used at the last Pink Floyd concert. A blue newspaper with all the Pepsi news was published and, by way of a stratospheric throwaway, astronauts on the Mir space station were persuaded to hold up a banner congratulating Pepsi on its exciting relaunch.

The corporate hospitality mill was meanwhile humming at full tilt in preparation for the arrival of more journalists than had been seen together in any one place since the beginning of the O. J. Simpson trial. On the day of the event, over 700 reporters turned up at the press conference, from eighty different countries, some paying their own way, others hosted by Pepsi. Directly or indirectly, every media outlet in the world of any note was represented.

Interviews had been set up both with Cindy, who was also appearing in the launch advertising of the new can, and with Pepsi executives. To be exact, 400 interviews were set up over a period of two and a half hours, journalists being invited to 'cluster' interviews or, if they were lucky, five-minute one-to-ones in which they could ask Cindy anything they liked – as long as their questions had been cleared by Pepsi beforehand. They were also advised that although their interviewing of Cindy wasn't dependent on anything, strictly speaking, mention of the name Pepsi would be preferred – conditions to which almost all journalists readily agreed.

And so the big day dawned. At 11 a.m. on Wednesday 19 January, the old GLC building, dormant since its heyday as the epicentre of socialist plotting, became, for a day, the focus of a very capitalist intrigue. To quote Jonathan Margolis, the *Sunday Times* reporter who covered the event: 'As Kobe burned 6,000 miles away, as Grozny shuddered under Russian bombardment, as Bosnia suffered another day of terror – I could go on – the journalists filed in from as far afield as Thailand, Argentina, Lebanon, Korea, Egypt, Poland, Turkey and Bulgaria. Just a glimpse of Cindy, a word from her plump lips, was all they wanted. But first they had to listen to, Lord help us, The Presentation.'

Well, of course they had to listen to The Presentation. That was part of the deal. Because while British journalists followed the whole proceedings with a decided sense of *ennui*, their foreign counterparts took scrupulous notes, which would later appear as so many column inches in a hundred and one different languages. After The Presentation the new Cindy commercials were shown, followed by the appearance of Cindy herself, posing beside a fridge full of Pepsi, an image captured by a thousand flashbulbs, a face to sell a billion newspapers.

After which came the moment 700 journalists had dreamed of: a chance to meet Cindy. As Margolis continued in caustic vein: 'A Martian at this stage would have to have concluded that the pretty young woman in black jeans, who had flown in from a Miami film set for the day, was a sage, a wise woman, who clearly had different messages to impart to her followers, depending on where they came from. A non-Martian could only conclude that the world had gone mad.'

If other journalists came to a similar conclusion, they were keeping zipped up about it. Clamouring instead for intimate disclosures from Cindy on how she felt about ex-husband Richard Gere's name being linked to British model Laura Bailey, or for news of the Pepsi-girl's modelling and movie career, they were very much playing the media game. In exchange for Pepsi coverage, they were gaining access to a celebrity whose most closely guarded secrets, divulged during an exclusive interview, could now be shared with their readers. The fact that the exclusive interview lasted only five minutes, and was one of two dozen interviews Cindy gave that day, was not an aspect on which they cared to dwell.

And the results of the Cindy endorsement, Pink Floyd lighting, Concorde painting and all the other hype that was 'Project Blue'? To begin in Britain, a public awareness of a staggering 86 per cent within forty-eight hours of the fact that Pepsi had gone blue. And outside the UK? Just the highlights of worldwide press coverage, collated into ring-bound folders, had within days stacked up to a file in Freud Communications' offices that towered over two metres high. Across the world, rainforests of newspapers were devoted to the cause of Pepsi. A staggering thirty-one hours of television coverage were recorded internationally. From Bel Air to Bangladesh, from Zurich to Zimbabwe, the fascination with the amalgam of Cindy and Concorde and a blue can of cola could hardly have been more intense. All this coverage over an event which had no intrinsic news value whatsoever.

If that last sentence seems unduly harsh, consider the following. One month before 'Project Blue' was due to be launched on an unsuspecting world, the Pepsi team was horrified to discover that despite its best efforts to keep the livery change strictly under wraps, *Marketing Week*, the leading marketing industry journal, had got hold of the story. Worse still, the magazine had plastered an image of the new, blue Pepsi can across its front cover. A more disastrous turn of events would have been hard to envisage; all the marketing and media columnists on the national and major regional press read *Marketing Week* from cover to cover to pick up stories. The same went for consumer correspondents on radio and television. It was only a matter of time before the news burst out via other media, thus rendering the official launch, whatever its razzmatazz, decidedly old hat.

As new scenario planning hastily got under way, both Pepsi and its PR agency, Freud Communications, braced themselves for the inevitable barrage of media calls. But as hour succeeded hour and, in due course, day followed day, there weren't any calls from journalists wanting to write up the story. There weren't even news-flashes in the papers. Gradually it became apparent that, as far as the mass media was concerned, the change in colour of the Pepsi can might be big news in the marketing world, but it was a complete non-event so far as they were concerned. So much so, in fact, that it didn't merit even a single column inch.

Stepping back from Pepsi's big moment, one might well ask: what about the sales figures? Did Pepsi's massively promoted blue-ness turn drinkers away from rival colas? After all, isn't that the point of all marketing activities, including PR? The sobering reality is that, following an exciting moment around the time of the launch, sales figures for Pepsi have in fact declined. But it would be foolish to conclude automatically that the launch PR activity was therefore a waste of time and money: that would be to misunder-stand the purpose of PR. As an executive close to the Pepsi campaign told me: 'The PR activity had the same effect as if you stood at the top of a building with a megaphone and shouted "Oi!!" very loudly. For a moment everyone will look up. You have their attention. It's what you do with it next that matters. That's where PR has to pass the baton on to advertising – to sustain the messages and excitement of the initial event.'

PR, like any other aspect of the marketing mix, has its strengths and its limitations. Big splash events are exciting for as long as the waves keep rippling. But just as quickly as it is marshalled, editorial attention moves on to the next big thing. Sustained coverage depends on a sustained campaign – which is where PR works best, not only with advertising, but with direct marketing, sales promotion, sponsorship, corporate hospitality and other marketing disciplines.

To conclude, the relationship between celebrities and the media is much more of a one-way street than many people realize. It is not only in status-conscious America that celebrities are the focus of media obsession; every British tabloid editor knew that a photograph of Diana on the front page increased sales of that day's paper by tens of thousands of copies, which is why she had such a high paparazzi bounty riding on her head. It is too easy to blame the media for our own preoccupation with celebrities. If there is anyone to blame, it is ourselves. It is we, the newspaper-buying public, who vote with our wallets, day in, day out, in favour of the team of 'stalkerazzi' who relentlessly pursued Diana. It is our own insatiable appetite for sexual intrigue that rewards Max Clifford and his kiss-and-tell clients whose stories we relish reading. And it is our adoration of the stars of screen, showbiz and society which makes spin doctors rich and their clients even richer as they use their media pulling power to endorse everything from frocks to fruit drinks.

If a spin doctor's power is a product of the clients he represents, then celebrity spin doctors are, without question, the most powerful of all. Very few City PR consultants can guarantee the presence of photographers from every national newspaper, not to mention the broadcast media, by the simple attendance of their client at a particular event. It is not often that corporate spin doctors have the power to vet *everything* a journalist writes on a particular subject before it goes to print. In the final analysis, where other spin doctors wield the influence to hold the front page, celebrity spin doctors have the authority to write it. And more and more frequently, they do!

PART III: lobbying and political PR

CHAPTER TWELVE
lobbying: the three great myths of the westminster warriors

Edward Silke looked up from the animated dinner gathering and, with a barely perceptible nod, indicated to the waiter standing at his kitchen door that it was time to bring on the dessert. Drawing back from the table, he glanced around at his guests' candle-lit faces, aglow with fine claret and bonhomie; he had good reason to be satisfied. As he'd hoped, a lively rapport had quickly developed between his clients and the two MPs who had already proved so useful to their cause. In future weeks they would prove to be even more useful – of this he had no doubt.

The dining room of Edward Silke's house, conveniently located just up the road from Labour's media centre – 'Mandelson Tower' – on Millbank and within earshot of Big Ben, was one of the most popular dining venues among inhabitants of the Palace of Westminster – Commons or Lords. This was not so much on account of the *haute cuisine* or most agreeable wine list, although Silke's hired caterers always did a sterling job. Nor had it to do with the considerable charm exercised by both Silke and his 'personal assistant', the svelte and liberally aftershaved Graeme Henderson. No, the sense of anticipation which accompanied the arrival of an invitation to dine with Edward Silke, Britain's most powerful lobbyist, had to do with altogether more tangible considerations. Free holidays and foreign travel, the use of executive cars and lavish entertainment for the family or mistress were just some of the gifts bestowed by this veritable Santa Claus of Westminster. Even more sought-after were the anonymous brown envelopes containing wads of freshly minted £50 notes which Silke would discreetly hand to the favoured few when they left his house of an evening.

Tonight it was the turn of Patrick Holmes and Gary Burton, both Conservative MPs on the Commons Select Committee for Tourism. Holmes, whose constituency was in north London, was finding it particularly hard going at the moment. He had two teenage children at public school and a high-maintenance wife. 'Please, Edward, won't you do something for him?' one of his colleagues had beseeched Silke only last week. Burton, whose constituency was in the Midlands, was also finding things pretty tough. Like many out-of-town MPs, he'd had to buy a small place in London where he could stay during the week. One of the more active back-benchers, the time and pressure of his political career had taken its toll on his marriage, which was now more an electoral convenience than a real partnership; for the latter, he'd turned inevitably to his research assistant, the delightfully pert and obliging Alice Cadogan. But the cost of supporting two homes, propping up a failing marriage until the next election and romancing a mistress went well beyond Burton's £65,000 MP's salary. These days, when he wasn't fielding calls from his constituents, he was hiding from his bank manager.

Across the table from the two MPs sat at least part of their salvation. Terry McIntie, a large, florid Scot, had made it big in the package tours to Britain industry, and had built up an impressive £100 million a year business from nothing. Jeff Hailsham, quiet, grey and thoughtful, was CEO of the chartered airline Skytrack, which served much of McIntie's business. While personal financial problems weren't an issue for either businessman, there was another difficulty which vexed them. A bill was about to be introduced in the House which, if passed, threatened their mutual business interests. According to the new Travel Bill, incoming visitors to the UK would be subject to increased airport tax on their departure – to be reflected in the cost of their air tickets. While an extra £7.50 wouldn't make much impact on most business and personal travellers, in the cut-throat world of package holidays the extra amount could be seriously damaging. Britain was already an expensive destination, and many foreign travellers might now simply opt to holiday in a different country – and if they did, McIntie and Hailsham would find themselves high and dry. Unless, of course, the bill were amended so that the increased levy was waived for chartered air bookings. Which was precisely why they'd hired Edward Silke.

Silke had put all hands to the pump in his lobbying firm, generating lists of all the chartered airlines and package holiday operators who would be affected, compiling statistics showing the probable impact of the increased airport tax – and had developed a powerful argument showing that, unless the increase were waived for charter operators, the adverse impact on overall tourist revenue in Britain would be enormous. Now all he needed were advocates for the argument.

'So tell me, Patrick, where do you like to holiday?' asked McIntie now, his Scottish brogue considerably stronger after the benefit of two generous single malts and several glasses of wine.

A pained expression momentarily came into the MP's eyes. 'Well, you know, it's difficult finding the time . . . I like the countryside, great outdoors, all of that. My wife is more a city lass—'

'Smart hotels and shopping malls?' underlined Silke.

'Precisely,' nodded Holmes. 'As for the two kids, well, anywhere there's a disco . . .'

Laughter rippled around the table.

'Have you ever been to Cape Town?' queried McIntie.

'Only on a two-day fact-find.'

'It would probably fit the bill.' He gestured expansively. 'Plenty of opportunity to enjoy the beach, the winelands, the veld. Excellent hotels. And a buzzing nightlife.'

Holmes nodded enthusiastically. 'I've heard very positive reports.'

Not, of course, that he could do anything about them. Cape

Town might just as well be on Mars, given the state of his finances. Though Terry McIntie might be about to change all that. He visualized breaking the news to his wife – 'Darling, we have a holiday in Cape Town' – she'd be over the moon!

'Not worth going all that way for much less than a fortnight,' McIntie was saying now, 'there's so much to see. And if you're doing Cape Town you might as well take in a game farm as well. Mala Mala – now *there's* luxury in the bush . . .'

Across the table, Silke met his lover's eyes with a twinkle. He had charged Graeme with the task of finding out suitable holiday destinations over dinner, but McIntie had saved him the bother. Patrick Holmes was clearly interested in Cape Town, and Gary Burton would have his chance next. Silke could see the scenario unfolding: the two MPs would take trips to their various destinations, a few ministerial appointments thrown in at the other end to give them official gravitas. Meantime, questions would be asked in the House. Early day motions would be tabled. Papers would be circulated to the media and considerable pressure applied on the minister to make the required amendment. As members of the Commons Select Committee for Tourism, Patrick Holmes and Gary Burton were powerful chorus-leaders among their backbench colleagues. Some judicious lobbying in the darkened corridors of Westminster would make all the difference.

What's more, Silke had a trump card he hadn't revealed to either of his clients. During the last general election, he had handed over £10,000 to another Conservative MP, one Timothy Crawford, to help fight his marginal seat. It was a donation which, as Crawford had admitted, had made all the difference. And who was Timothy Crawford now? Why, the minister responsible for the new Travel Bill!

Edward Silke was therefore quietly confident that an amendment would find its way into the bill. The business interests of McIntie and Hailsham would be saved. For the cost of a couple of expensive holidays, and his own consultancy fees, the businessmen could carry on happily making their millions. And his two parliamentary colleagues would find temporary respite from their pressing financial worries. Everyone was a winner, whatever way you looked at it.

The above piece of fiction illustrates the received wisdom on how parliamentary lobbyists operate. Paying MPs cash for asking questions in the House of Commons, doling out 'sweeteners', including stays at sumptuous foreign hotels, awarding generous 'commission' to those who introduce new business – all these are regarded by members of a cynical media as intrinsic to the modus operandi of lobbyists – or public affairs consultants as they refer to themselves. MPs, particularly the Tories during the Major government, are widely believed to be engaged in all kinds of nefarious goings-on – if they weren't having extra-marital affairs, they were feathering their own nests with lucrative 'consultancy' contracts. Corruption, we were told, had struck at the very heart of Parliament.

But in reality lobbying in Britain isn't like that now, and was only very rarely in the past. The Edward Silke cameo may have a surface credibility, but those in the know would recognize it as a typical example of the nonsense that some elements in the media would have us believe about lobbyists. In fact, it is yet another of the many ironies of PR that lobbying has received such an appalling press when it is one of the least sinister disciplines in the industry. Many City spin doctors are guilty of far more heinous crimes than upgrading the air ticket of a Member of Parliament – a practice which, today, would have to be entered in the Register of Members' Interests. Celebrity spin doctors wield far more influence than public affairs lobbyists who, like eunuchs in a harem, can only ever advise others on how to go about doing what they cannot do themselves.

The loud and sustained vilification of the handful of MPs and a single lobbyist who were guilty of practices we find unacceptable today has, however, created the erroneous impression that a few isolated examples were representative of a more general trend. What's more, the cash for questions issue, unavoidable in any sortie into the world of public affairs consultancy – and to which the next chapter of this book is devoted – is undoubtedly one of the reddest of herrings of recent times. That lobbying has become synonymous with sleaze is not only tabloid fantasy – it completely misses the point of what lobbyists really do.

So what *do* lobbyists do, and why should their activities be included in a book on PR? Like other forms of PR, lobbying is an American import – in fact, its very name derives from the lobby of the Willard Hotel in Washington DC, where those seeking legislative change would wait in the hope of bending the ear of the President in a less time-pressured era. (Some believe the term derives from the Central Lobby in our own Houses of Parliament, where any member of the public can present himself to speak to his MP.) Like their PR peers, lobbyists describe their practice in a wide variety of ways; but, crudely put, their work entails monitoring all aspects of the legislative process on behalf of clients, advising them on how best to ensure their interests are effectively represented to legislators, and helping them develop a network of contacts and supporters for immediate or future reference.

the public affairs explosion

Like City PR, public affairs consultancy has grown from almost nothing into a £100 million industry in the space of the last twenty years. When Ian Greer started his first consultancy, Russell Greer, in 1970 he found himself ahead of his time – potential clients felt they had little need of his services: 'The occasional shoot with the constituency MP, or contact with a brother-in-law in the Lords, continued to dominate their approach to the briefing of parliamentarians.' Twelve years later, when he launched Ian Greer Associates, his time had come, and the consultancy took off rapidly. Michael Burrell, managing director of one of the largest lobbying firms in Britain, Westminster Strategy, notes the same development: 'Twenty years ago there were hardly any consultancies. Now there are quite a few. There are hardly any major companies that don't have someone in-house looking after public affairs.'

Despite this explosion in demand for its services, the lobbying industry is still very much in its infancy – for example, it was only in 1994 that a specialist self-regulatory industry body, the Association of Professional Political Consultants, was set up (it now lists fourteen members and claims to represent 75 per cent of fee income generated in the lobbying sector). And, as in other parts of the youthful PR industry, issues such as regulation and evaluation are problematic. Charles Miller, secretary of the APPC and managing director of the lobbying firm Public Policy Unit, maintains that the overall quality of lobbying is still poor.

> The system still tolerates low standards of work. It will bite its lip and be polite. If the system was less tolerant of unprofessional conduct – which is different again from unethical conduct – things would improve. There are still too many people in lobbying with no training. They have met a few MPs and think they know how the system works. As a result, many companies are being led a merry dance, producing glossy brochures, hosting lunches and facility visits which are a complete waste of time. We are held in low esteem by the system because the few firms that are good are being dragged down by the many that aren't. Many lobbying firms really should not be practising.

Improving the level of professionalism in the industry is clearly one of its most urgent requirements. So is cleaning up its image in the wake of the cash for questions scandal. Michael Burrell admits that the image of public affairs consultants is now decidedly tainted:

> Public affairs was little known until the cash for questions scandal. Now there is the widespread perception that what we do is illegitimate and the methods we employ are corrupt. But I feel strongly that what we do is central to the functioning of a healthy democracy. The right to petition for redress of grievance goes back to the Magna Carta. What we do is help people express their grievances as best we can. In a free society it is curious if people can spend

> their money on doctors, lawyers and accountants but not on issues
> where the future of their business is at stake.

A large part of the reason why lobbying has acquired such a sullied reputation no doubt has to do with the fact that, as Burrell suggests, many in the public were only really introduced to the industry when it was revealed in its darkest hour. Journalists took free advantage of the public's fundamental ignorance about lobbying, getting away with colourful and highly misleading accounts of what was going on. In particular, the media have created and embroidered three specific myths about MPs and the lobbying process which are now strongly lodged in the public consciousness, and which will take a great deal of work to dispel. These myths are that MPs are important influencers in the legislative process; that MPs are the focus of lobbying activities; and that money buys influence.

why MPS have little influence

Dudley Fishburn, former Conservative MP for Kensington and Chelsea, says: 'The idea that MPs have any influence is greatly misplaced – you vote with the party 99 per cent of the time. I was in Parliament for eight years and I can't believe I had an influence on more than three or four things.' Because Britain has one of the most heavily whipped parliaments in the world – far more so, say, than the US Congress – what any individual MP thinks about a particular subject is rarely of much consequence. True, there have been a few issues in the past in which the views of backbenchers have been decisive – most of them involving free votes on issues of conscience, such as the Sunday trading question and age of homosexual consent. But these are few and far between. And the influence of individual MPs is even less significant in parliaments with a large government majority, such as that returned in May 1997.

But what about the asking of questions in Parliament? And the tabling of early day motions? Any MP can do these, and surely they are influential? The truth is that the importance of asking questions in Parliament has been greatly exaggerated. Every year, 45,000 parliamentary questions are tabled. In many cases, the answers to them are barely worth recording. Civil servants strive to be as economical as possible in drafting answers to questions put to their ministers. Few things give the men from the ministry so much pleasure as providing, to a lengthy and detailed question, a response consisting of only a few words. In fact, it was rumoured that for a while there was a prize among officials at the Department of Transport for the first civil servant who was able to draft a response for the minister to a parliamentary question consisting of only a single word!

Such is the banality of answers to parliamentary questions that it has given rise to the oft-told Westminster joke about the two MPs who became hopelessly lost while driving through the country. Spotting a local, one of the MPs wound down the car window and asked, 'Where are we?' to which the local replied, 'In a car.' The MP was outraged at this impertinence. But his fellow traveller thought differently: 'A fine parliamentary answer,' he declared: 'short, to the point, and telling us nothing we didn't know already!'

Lobbyists' clients, however, often urge that questions be asked by MPs because it's a visible sign that something is happening. There it is in *Hansard*, in black and white, to be highlighted and sent up to the chairman's office. It can also be brought to the attention of journalists who, in theory, will regard an issue with heightened interest if it is the subject of parliamentary questioning. The resulting column inches, in addition to the original question, are intended to exert pressure on whichever minister is responsible for the legislation or policy in question.

While all of this is grist to the lobbyist's mill, the reality is that textbook-style questions-cum-column-inch double whammies resulting in some form of change are as rare as hen's teeth. It is one of the many ironies of the cash for questions scandal that despite all the many questions tabled by various MPs in support of Mohamed Fayed, he completely failed to derail the steam train hurtling towards him, stoked up by his business enemy Tiny Rowland. What's more, he failed to prevent the DTI investigating his takeover of the House of Fraser and the publication of their investigation, which reported that he'd lied his way to ownership of the stores group.

Another greatly exaggerated dimension of an MP's supposed influence is his ability to table early day motions. In theory, these are motions to be debated at an early date, but in practice they never are. What they do enable is the voicing of an opinion or even direct allegations under the protection of parliamentary privilege. They can also be one way to sound out the feelings of the House on a specific issue. Once again, EDMs are very rarely moments of great drama, with well over a thousand appearing in order papers at the end of each session. Like parliamentary questions, while EDMs can be helpful as a means of exerting pressure on the legislative process, their efficacy should not be overrated; they are regarded among lobbyists as the parliamentary equivalent of scribbling graffiti on the toilet wall.

MPs, in short, are not nearly so influential as most of the public, and indeed many aspirant MPs, actually believe. Backbenchers do not drive the legislative process, they can't single-handedly change the law and, as Mohamed Fayed has demonstrated, even when you have quite a number of them rooting for you, that's absolutely no guarantee that things will go your way. True, they can sometimes provide a route in to meet a minister who is otherwise difficult to buttonhole. But effective lobbyists know the limitations of lobbying MPs, and realize that if you're trying to influence the course of events, the House of Commons is often not a useful place to do it.

all hail to the men from the ministry

This takes us to the second great myth of lobbying: that MPs are the focus of lobbyists' attention. It is true that many clients, having bought into the myth that MPs are creatures of great influence, frequently demand that their lobbyists set up lunches and dinners at which they can hob-nob with those they fondly imagine handle masterfully the levers of power. But the reality is that those who are in a position to help them most effectively are usually to be found up the road from Westminster, at Whitehall. Senior and middle-ranking civil servants are the true legislative movers and shakers. The armies of faceless men and women, with their Tupperware lunch boxes and M&S suits, are those really in a position to influence legislation. As Michael Burrell says: 'A meeting in a scruffy office with an acne-ridden junior official may not have the same glamour as lunch with an MP at the House of Commons, but that is the person who will be drafting the bill.' Paul Twyman, chairman of Political Strategy, agrees: 'Clients are quite unsophisticated and even big companies waste money on activities geared at MPs when, for about a tenth of the price, you can achieve these aims by focusing on one or two civil servants and one minister.'

The most effective lobbyists don't waste their time talking too high, trying to influence MPs who don't know the detail. Instead, they will be building up relationships with the directors or assistant directors in the relevant government departments who are responsible for drafting policy and legislation. The latter are usually interested to know what someone with a genuine interest has to say. As Graham McMillan, public affairs supremo at Fishburn Hedges, observes: 'Once an issue has already gone to Parliament, from a lobbying point of view you're already too late. You need to wake up early and get in at the think-tank stage, before the Green Paper or White Paper is produced. Lobbying Parliament is the most inefficient way to influence legislation – it requires the most effort, with the least likely result.'

And so to the third great myth of lobbying: that money buys influence. This is a favourite conspiracy theory of some journalists – the notion that large companies with deep pockets can co-opt the legislative process so that it delivers the rules and regulations that suit them. It was on this assumption that the cash for questions scandal rested: here were British companies pumping money into the pockets of MPs to swing the rules their way. But the absurdity of the assumption should by now be apparent. Even if companies did attempt to pervert the course of legislation with freebies and bundles of cash, MPs were the wrong people to be bribing. And there would have been no question of trying to bribe civil servants – the system is too forensic. Moreover, in the civil service no one dares do anyone a favour as the resulting risk of exposure, particularly by the media, would simply be too great. Officials who draft legislation are terrified, in particular, of exposing their bosses, which is why a favour-based system just doesn't work. Britain is fortunate to have an incorruptible Civil Service; even accusations that, after eighteen years of Conservative rule, the Civil Service had become politicized soon turned out to be a nonsense when Labour took over in 1997 and found no lack of willingness on the part of Whitehall's inhabitants to work with their new political masters.

If MPs aren't the right target for lobbying and civil servants can't be bribed, how do lobbyists have any impact? Indeed, *do* they have any impact? Charles Miller is disarmingly candid: 'The use of lobbyists doesn't give big companies as much edge as people think. What gives them the edge is their size and the quality of their case. A good lobbyist will optimize a case, but can't turn base metal into gold. You can't make a credible case out of one that is poor.'

Putting together a strong case involves lobbyists in much the same activities as their public relations peers. It requires an issue to be looked at from all angles, creativity to be applied to produce compelling arguments, and the execution of activity to be well planned and implemented. One textbook example of effective lobbying comes from Westminster Strategy, whose client, Electronic Industries Association of Japan, found itself faced with a possible government levy on blank audio cassette tapes in 1988. Westminster Strategy soon marshalled all the reasons why the levy was opposed by cassette manufacturers. But more effective by far was the consumer card. Thinking about who else would be affected by the levy, a number of specific groups came to mind, including various consumer groups and university students. Of particular note, however, was the impact that the levy would have on the blind, who rely on cassette tapes for the vast majority of their 'reading' matter. Working together with the Royal Society for the

Blind, Westminster Strategy devised a highly impactful 'Hands Off Reading' campaign to roll out, not only to civil servants and the ministers concerned, but more widely in the media.

By drawing together a number of separate arguments behind a particularly compelling case, Westminster Strategy delivered a clear result. When the Secretary of State for Trade and Industry announced he was abandoning the levy, he said he had been persuaded by the strength of the arguments in general and by those on behalf of the blind in particular.

'The best form of lobbying', according to Dudley Fishburn, 'is spontaneous. For example, when the Common Market wanted to change the laws on homeopathic medicines some time ago there was an eruption of opinion. An enormously wide cross-section of people protested, from Rastafarians to middle-class housewives. The government had to recognize that.'

Indeed, it is a little-known fact that there are civil servants whose job it is to count the number of letters their departments receive about particular issues. Most lobbying groups know this, which is why they endlessly exhort their supporters to write to relevant officials. In America, so highly developed is this aspect of lobbying that some firms specialize in what has become termed 'astroturf lobbying'; instead of rent-a-crowd, the idea is to rent-a-group-of-apparently-committed-supporters who will write letters, march marches and activate their local media to create the impression of a nationwide movement – all for a small fee.

One of the most effective ways in which lobbyists can attract and marshal support for a cause is by using standard media relations techniques. Indeed, the dividing line between what is a public affairs issue and what is a public relations issue is so often blurred, or crossed, that many businesses consider their PA and PR agendas in the same meeting, and a single executive may well be in charge of both functions, the most common title for this position being 'corporate affairs director'. Similarly, most of the larger PR agencies also field a team of PA experts on the basis that they provide integrated communications solutions.

However, there is very often a certain tension between PR and

PA agendas, which can all too easily begin to march to different drums. To begin with, as Charles Miller notes: 'The vast majority of lobbying issues are decided by boring things like legal argument and submissions, not by whether the *Independent* has covered it that week.' Then there is the nagging fear that a newspaper might put an angle on the story which could be counter-productive to the sensitive negotiations going on elsewhere. As Nick DeLuca of lobbying firm APCO points out: 'The trouble with news journalists is that they are beholden to the news desk. However committed they are to writing up the story you have discussed with them in the way that you and your client would hope, they will follow like lap-dogs the line that their news editor – who will have had no direct contact with you or your client and who never reads press releases – chooses to put on it.'

Part of the reason why PA and PR people sometimes circle uneasily about each other has to do with the different cultures from which they spring. It is the natural impulse of the spin doctor to publicize any client victory as widely and loudly as possible. The lobbyist, however, has to be far more discreet. To go out to the media with the story that a bill has been amended in one's client's favour has a decidedly triumphalist odour about it which sensitive civil servants and egotistical ministers, trying to act in the public interest, find distinctly offensive. How will those same civil servants and ministers feel next time they are approached by the lobbyist, pleading a different case?

Crowing over victories, then, clearly has no place in the majority of lobbying cases. And, as Chris Butler, managing director of Grandfield Public Affairs, remarks: 'The nightmare scenario of the public affairs practitioner is some bright spark PR practitioner boasting about success in winning a concession from government before that concession is actually signed, sealed and enacted. Nothing is more designed to alert and outrage the opponents of any such concession.'

Having said all this, lobbyists do sometimes use public relations to powerful effect. Jessica Morris, an associate director of Fishburn Hedges, and formerly head of the press office at the charity Shelter, tells of how a well-targeted media relations exercise achieved instant success where all other techniques had failed:

> We were having a very cold wintry spell and I got a call from field-workers to say that homeless young people were frightened to go to sleep on the streets in case they froze to death. We contacted the Environment Department and they did nothing . . . until Sheila McKechnie, head of Shelter, went on the radio. Suddenly the government came up with extra cash and hundreds of extra hostel beds were made available that weekend to some of the most desperate of our homeless people.

The effective lobbyist will choose whatever instruments are best suited to the task, be they detailed discussions in some dowdy Whitehall office, the delivery of briefing papers to involved ministers, or pulling out all the media stops. Free holidays for MPs at foreign resorts would not be much help, even if they were allowed. Occasionally, like a conductor driving towards symphonic climax, he will require every instrument to weave its effort in with every other, building up to a single moment of orchestrated drama. One particularly compelling case of this happening concerns the activities of the PLA, whose interests are at the heart of a legislative saga which continues to unfold.

the road to hell is paved with good intentions . . .

The PLA, or Pre-school Learning Alliance, is a charity representing 800,000 playschools in Britain which are attended by 60 per cent of the country's three-year-olds and 30 per cent of its four-year-olds. Until 1990, the PLA was virtually unknown as an association and many of those who did know about it viewed it condescendingly as the schooling equivalent of the village fête committee – a tea-party-style association of well-meaning but amateurish women fiddling about on the periphery of the central educational debate. The PLA recognized these perceptions, just as it recognized that the whole subject of pre-schooling was set to leap up the educational agenda. Accordingly, it set about putting its house in order. In 1990 training courses were set up for all the mothers and others who ran PLA groups. (These proved so successful that over 50,000 adults now attend the courses each year.) Curriculum guides were developed to establish the groups as places where learning as well as playing went on. Best practice health and safety guidelines were produced, and the PLA pioneered the first 'kitemark' standards for nursery schools which provided better-than-minimum supervision and facilities. The PLA also set about revamping its image, commissioning a designer to reposition the charity as a professional, effectively run operation representing a massive, grass-roots constituency up and down the country.

The PLA had been right to divine that fresh emphasis was about to be placed on pre-school education. In 1994 Prime Minister John Major made a new commitment, guaranteeing a nursery school place to every four-year-old as a first step towards nursery education for all. Major set up a Civil Service task force to look at how this commitment should be implemented.

At this point the PLA was ready to spring into action. Meetings were held with civil servants in the Department of Education at which the PLA proposed that the best funding mechanism would be for a fixed amount of money to be paid for each child to whichever nursery school took him or her on. The PLA also emphasized the importance of their own members' work; teaching standards were high and parent-run playgroups were far more cost-effective than those run by the state – in some cases suitably trained parents were prepared to work for little or nothing to keep fees low. All these ideas were warmly received by the Department of Education. It seemed that, by being well prepared, the PLA had pre-empted any unwelcome legislative moves.

But they were in for a shock. In July 1995 the government announced that while the voucher system had indeed been adopted, it would allocate only £550 a year for each child going to a PLA group, while paying £1,100 per head to state schools taking on children of the same age. PLA members were, naturally, outraged at this discrimination – and the PLA's lobbying machine was thrust into action. 'We immediately held a press conference,' says PLA's Rachel Thomson, 'attended by all the main educational correspondents. Then Margaret Lochrie, the PLA's chairperson, was interviewed on the BBC's *Today* programme. There was coverage of our case in all the broadsheets and some tabloids, on radio and TV.'

But that was only part of the story. The PLA also sent out a press release to every one of its 20,000 members and 430 branches nationwide, urging them to lobby their local councillors, media and MPs. By this time the organization had 150 trained spokespeople to speak to local newspaper and radio stations the length and breadth of the country.

'It was a matter of harnessing an enormous strength of feeling that was already there,' says Thomson. 'For a period of about ten days there was a massive grass-roots bombardment by the millions of people who were affected.' Within a fortnight the government had backed down. It announced a fixed £1,100 voucher for every four-year-old, irrespective of whether the child was accommodated in the private or state sector. Victory? Yes – but in the battle, not the war.

'While we settled the voucher issue fairly quickly,' says Margaret Lochrie, 'we had other serious reservations. The government hoped that by putting a sum of money on the head of every four-year-old, the effects of free market economics would be to create more nursery places, bring more nursery providers into the market, and improve teaching standards. We agreed with these objectives, but realized that by not setting maximum class sizes, the legislation would have the opposite effect of what the government intended.'

Sure enough, no sooner had the £1,100 voucher per child scheme been announced than state schools and local education authorities, which hitherto had shown little interest in under-fives, suddenly started to create 'reception classes', hoovering up as many children as possible. Soon it became common to find as many as thirty children in one of these classes – compared to the maximum limit of thirteen per class allowed by PLA groups. 'As one of our spokeswomen put it, that's not teaching, it's crowd control,' remarks Lochrie.

So what on earth would induce parents to send their children into a state class of thirty, when there was a privately run group of thirteen just down the road? Two things. First, blackmail: some schools started to threaten parents that, unless their child entered a 'reception class', there would be no place for Johnny at school next year. Many parents, not wishing to start off the relationship with their children's school on a sour note, find this disincentive hard to refuse. Secondly, as a result of this practice the privately run group of thirteen just down the road may well have collapsed, most of its parents having sent their children to the local state alternative to guarantee them *their* places. This, of course, has had a knock-on effect for the parents of many three-year-olds, who have come to discover their PLA places have disappeared. 'Instead of increasing the provision of nursery places and improving teaching standards, the scheme actually had the reverse effect,' comments Lochrie. 'It was embarrassing for the Conservative government, a case of the "law of unintended consequences".'

After Labour won the 1997 election, one of their first actions was to scrap the nursery voucher scheme. Announcing a commitment to 'high-quality, inclusive early-years service built on active partnership between the state, private and voluntary sectors', the new government instructed local education authorities to draw up alternative plans. It is unlikely that any quick-fix solution acceptable to all sides will be easily found; with a new administration, in many respects the PLA lobbying machine had to rejoin the battle on behalf of its many members all over again. So its campaigning continues, using briefings with civil servants, relevant ministers and a massive grass-roots organization to deliver messages to the media in a way which does indeed constitute a 'petition for redress of grievance'. The full child-care tale has, of course, yet to unfold. But what makes the PLA case noteworthy is the way in which several different aspects of the lobbying process were successfully brought together into one cohesive campaign.

Were that all PA activities were so well marshalled and effective at delivering results. But, as Charles Miller comments, 'Ian Greer was assiduous in repeating "never promise results",' and, indeed, the lobbying world is one in which the tides of fortune can ebb away from one just as swiftly as they flowed in. Even if you are the biggest and most famous lobbyist in the business, the divide between high status and low disrepute can sometimes be only a few perilous headlines away – as the next chapter shows.

CHAPTER THIRTEEN
cash for questions: ian greer and the lobbying scandal that never was

Number 60 Park Lane is an impressive block of flats, built right next door to the Dorchester and overlooking Hyde Park. At 6.30 p.m. one evening in 1985 a diminutive, though immaculately attired, figure made his way to the entrance of the building, to find himself confronted by two sets of bullet-proof glass doors, between which he had to stand while a security guard scrutinized him on a TV monitor. It was his first visit to the building, and Ian Greer was surprised by the elaborate security measures. He couldn't help reflecting to himself that they would have been more in keeping in a military installation or Middle East embassy. Passing this first obstacle, he was shown to a lift and directed to a floor. During future visits, Greer would be pointed to completely different rooms on different floors – rooms in which bookcases would be slid back to reveal hidden doorways. All this was a necessary security precaution as far as the block's owner, Greer's potential client, was concerned.

Mohamed Fayed was a businessman with a problem and, on the recommendation of Lord King, chairman of British Airways and one of Greer's clients, he had decided to summon the assistance of Britain's best-known lobbyist. As Greer made his way up in the lift to his first meeting with the new owner of the House of Fraser and his brother Ali, little could he have guessed the eventual outcome of this meeting. For within a few months a series of events would have been set in train which were to lead to him being accused of corrupting Parliament, would see his reputation blown to tatters and ultimately would lead directly to the collapse of his multi-million-pound business.

The cash for questions saga is very much a story of the Conservative era. It is a story which has been the subject of such widespread and sensationalist coverage of such a long period of time and associated with so many sub-plots that many people are bewildered or understandably bored by it. This chapter is an attempt to clarify the essential elements of what happened, for, in the final analysis, the reality is decidedly at odds with the version portrayed in many quarters of the media – and the story provides a fascinating insight into the real world of public affairs lobbying. This is not intended as a blow-by-blow account of every relevant action – two whole books have already been devoted to that, and we will look at the different versions of what happened according to each side in the end-game. The book written by the *Guardian* team, entitled simply *Sleaze*, is a masterpiece of sensation and innuendo from the first chapter – four pages of the purplest prose describing the Hamiltons' stay at the Paris Ritz hotel. The other, *One Man's Word*, is written from Greer's perspective; while certain questions are left unanswered, it is no whitewash. Both books relate the same set of events, although, as we will see, this is sometimes hard to credit.

the 'dull and uninteresting' world of ian greer

To begin with, it helps to understand something of the man at the centre of the most disastrous episode in British lobbying. Ian Greer was born in London in 1933, the son of Salvation Army officer parents. When he was fourteen the family moved to Scotland, where Ian finished his schooling before getting a temporary job with the Scottish electricity authority. His first proper job, however, was as a constituency campaign organizer for the Conservative

Party, on £6 a week. Greer had always been drawn to politics and relished his work; he was soon brought in to work at Central Office where he was appointed the party's youngest agent.

Greer remained with the Conservatives for thirteen years before leaving to become director of the Mental Health Trust. According to the *Guardian* team, this career change was brought about after a succession of failed attempts to win a number of seats for Tory MPs as a Tory agent. Greer's own explanation is somewhat different: wanting to stand as a Conservative MP himself, when his application was rejected it became clear to him after an interview with the party's deputy chairman, Richard Sharples, that the fact that he was gay meant that future applications would also be turned down; he was destined never to become an 'honourable member'.

The contrast in explanations for why Greer left the Conservative Party is just one instance among many of ways in which the accounts of Greer and the *Guardian* team significantly differ. Indeed, the *Guardian*'s insistence on presenting Greer in the worst possible light at all times serves to weaken, rather than strengthen, its case, robbing it of even the pretence of objectivity. Take, for instance, the thumbnail sketch of Greer's personality presented at the beginning of *Sleaze*: 'Greer's estranged friends (of whom there are plenty) offer some insight into this curiously blank but clever mind. "He is a dull and uninteresting person" . . . Greer liked to present himself as genteel . . . Staff sat at bogus-antique tables . . . His own office was oppressively decorated in an ersatz country-house manner, with the affectation of a couple of poodles snoring on a sofa.' Several veteran lobbyists I spoke to laughed out loud when I asked them if they considered Greer to be 'a dull and un-interesting person'. By contrast, they said he was a very colourful person indeed who inspired huge loyalty among his staff and friends – a finding confirmed by several former IGA executives themselves.

Greer was two years at the Mental Health Trust before setting up his first lobbying consultancy with John Russell in 1970. Russell Greer represented something of a new concept, political lobbying still being almost unknown in Britain at the time. As a consequence, the firm found it hard to attract business and the early days were very lean. However, a trickle of clients did turn into a flow and Russell Greer came to represent names such as McDonnell-Douglas, Fisons, Midland Bank, the Government of Zambia and the Unitary Tax Campaign. It expanded to a staff of twelve and moved to Mayfair, although it never succeeded in making its two partners rich or even particularly well-off. Greer and Russell, perhaps inevitably, had become personal as well as business partners and seemed to complement each other well, Greer being the more outgoing of the two, Russell more the analytical backroom boy. After more than a decade together, however, the two began to differ on the direction in which they wanted to take the business; relations between them deteriorated and Greer decided the time had come to do his own thing. Taking out a £5,000 bank loan, he launched Ian Greer Associates with four of his employees from Russell Greer – Wendy Donavan, Rhys Manley-Sale, Charles Miller and John Roberts.

The world into which IGA was born was very different from that which had existed twelve years earlier at the launch of Russell Greer. By 1982, public affairs consultancy was no longer a new trade and increasing numbers of big, blue-chip companies were having to take seriously the legislative and regulatory environment in which they operated. Three years earlier Margaret Thatcher had led the Conservatives into power, and many of the faces on the government front bench belonged to people Greer had previously worked for while at Central Office. Not only was he extremely well connected politically, he had acquired a reputation as a highly effective operator at Russell Greer. It wasn't long before IGA had begun to acquire an enviable client list, as well as to hire more staff – including Andrew Smith who was, in time, to become its managing director.

freebies for the eighties

It is helpful at this point to consider the lobbying environment in which IGA came into being. Before rules established in 1996 by the Nolan Committee on Standards in Public Life, it was considered normal and even necessary for MPs to take on consultancies or non-executive directorships with companies, simply to make ends meet. As Greer says: 'Earning little over £30,000, and usually running two homes, for many it meant economic survival. What we would now consider to be outrageous perks were regarded by many at the time as little more than basic comforts.' What's more, MPs weren't shy to ask for freebies from the lobbyists seeking to bend their ear. Says Greer: 'There was a shamelessness in the actions of many MPs. In an era when City yuppies boasted of the size of their bonuses, in much the same way parliamentarians shared tales of their freebies.'

The Nolan rules changed all that in order to stamp out the possibility that MPs might be bribed for their support. Whether or not the rules have succeeded we will see later on. Whether or not MPs ever felt beholden to those who provided them with freebies is debatable – though one shining example of an MP who, in a sense, proved unbribable was, ironically, Neil Hamilton. If he had proved more amenable to Mohamed Fayed, IGA might well still be in business today.

While freebies and non-executive directorships were very much part of the parliamentary terrain in the politically incorrect Eighties, a less widespread practice was the payment of MPs for new business leads. This is something to which Greer openly admits and which was to prove disastrous to him later. 'Ian was a soft touch,' a former colleague of his told me. 'That was part of his undoing.' A company chairman would speak to an MP about a legislative worry and ask who could help him. The MP would suggest he contact Ian Greer. Contact would be made, and if Greer got the business he would pay the MP who made the referral. Viewed from our current perspective, commission payments look very slippery indeed. But Greer argues: 'There was nothing wrong in making such payment – nor in receiving it. The problem was that the rules on registration of one-off payments were unclear at the time.' It was up to the MP to register any such payment in the Register of Members' Interests – but many didn't bother. This point was confirmed by Sir Gordon Downey in his report on the cash for questions episode: 'There is a general obligation on Members to the effect: "If in doubt, register!"'

The laxity of the lobbying environment in the 1980s was such that when the *Guardian* began to probe the affairs of Ian Greer, it arrived at some unsavoury possibilities; but significant ambiguities remain. It is interesting, for example, to compare and contrast the two different versions of one MP's conversation given by the *Guardian* team and Ian Greer in their respective accounts:

> Grylls [Michael Grylls MP] would eventually admit that he went privately to Lord King and said, 'Why don't you approach Ian Greer Associates?' Grylls took money from Greer for doing so, and could subsequently be spotted with Mrs Sarah Grylls, in May 1985, occupying first-class seats aboard a sumptuous BA freebie to Rio de Janeiro. (From *Sleaze* by the *Guardian* team)

> John King telephoned my friend Michael Grylls virtually in despair one day ... Lord King was growing frustrated by the lack of government support for his ambitions for British Airways.
> 'I will shoot myself shortly. I'm getting nowhere with the Department of Transport!' he exclaimed. 'I've got some public affairs people called Shandwick, but they are not getting anywhere.'
> 'Why don't you meet a chap I know called Ian Greer? He's good,' Grylls suggested. (From *One Man's Word* by Ian Greer)

Did King approach Grylls, or was it the other way around? There is an important distinction between bounty-hunting and giving advice on request which may or may not result in a commission. And why should the *Guardian* team associate this business introduction with a freebie flight? Grylls was paid an introduction fee by Greer for the BA account – why would BA also feel obliged to reward him for the introduction?

The bitter irony for Greer is that even if he hadn't paid friendly MPs for putting business his way, his firm would undoubtedly have flourished. The consultancy rapidly gained an enviable reputation as the leading lobbyist in Westminster – and went on to open up offices in Brussels, Scotland and Ireland. In his book Greer describes how, at its peak, IGA would be organizing two or three lunches a day for clients to brief relevant ministers or peers, as well as a dinner most evenings. Lights would burn in the IGA offices until eleven or twelve o'clock most weekday nights. There was a frenetic buzz about the place, a Westminster equivalent of the 'money never sleeps, pal' energy of the City. Greer's team comprised political animals and throve on the adrenalin of trans-formation which characterized Thatcher's decade. It was hardly surprising that IGA was considered a 'safe choice' for the pitch lists of Britain's biggest corporate PA accounts, eventually winning as clients the likes of British Airways, Cadbury Schweppes, Midland Bank, Coca-Cola, Whitbread, Prudential, British Gas, Thames Water and the governments of Canada, Malaysia, Pakistan, Kuwait and Taiwan, to name but a few.

mohamed fayed: buying a name – but losing a reputation

When Ian Greer arrived at his first meeting with Mohamed Fayed and his brother Ali in October 1985, he was near the peak of his career, his consultancy a thriving concern. Fayed had also recently got what he wanted – but was at risk of losing it. He had spent £615 million to acquire the controlling interest in the House of Fraser, the department store chain with Harrods as its flagship. However, ever since the takeover, Fayed's rival in the battle, Lonrho's Tiny Rowland, had been using the media – including the *Observer* newspaper, which he owned – to suggest that the Fayeds had only borrowed the money needed to buy the House of Fraser from their pal the Sultan of Brunei, and that many of the claims on which their successful bid had been based were false. Fayed had, however, sold the myth of 'Al Fayed' to the City – that myth being that the Al Fayeds were a fabulously rich Egyptian dynasty, whose wealth, based on cotton trading, went back for generations. (As it turned out, the prefix 'Al', an Arabic title denoting noble birth, was one that the Fayeds adopted in the Seventies from much the same impulse, one imagines, that inspires those who buy titles off the back pages of *Private Eye*.) What's more, the undoubted wealth that the Fayeds had accumulated was more a product of the oil boom than of the ancient wealth they fabricated. But, like BA's Lord King, Mohamed Fayed hated to be thought of as a self-made man. He wanted to be seen as the scion of a dynastic, old-moneyed family – part of the establishment.

How had the Fayeds' bid for the House of Fraser come to be approved by the DTI? Basically, because the money used to effect the purchase was vouchsafed by top merchant bank Kleinwort Benson, whose director John MacArthur said on TV that the Fayeds' net worth was several billion dollars and whose prospectus stated that: 'The Al-Fayed family is an old established Egyptian family, which has interests in the USA, Europe and the Middle East which include in particular, shipping, construction, oil, banking and property. The shipping companies are based in Genoa, Piraeus, London, Dubai and Egypt.'

Tiny Rowland's media and political lobbying campaign against the Fayeds was soon prompting questions to be asked, both in the House and, more importantly, at the DTI itself. No angel himself – he was once denounced by Ted Heath as 'the unacceptable face of capitalism' – Rowland accumulated a dossier of evidence which he handed to the DTI and which he said showed conclusively that, by using the aura of money borrowed from the Sultan of Brunei, Fayed had impressed Mrs Thatcher and Trade and Industry Secretary Norman Tebbit, who had 'flung aside the rules for a cheat'.

While all this was still going on, Fayed knew he needed someone to fight his corner. Hence his invitation to Greer to visit him at his

Park Lane apartment – next door to the Sultan of Brunei's own London acquisition, the Dorchester. (It was at this first meeting that Fayed later alleged Greer told him, 'You need to hire MPs like London taxis' – one of a number of unsubstantiated allegations which were later to pave the way to the destruction of IGA.) In addition, Fayed had hired Brian Basham to fight his media wars for him; Greer was to find himself talking to Basham's office regularly in future months as many of the parliamentary questions which came to be asked on Fayed's behalf had no political purpose whatsoever, but were prompted purely for reasons of publicity.

From his very first meeting with Fayed, Greer was struck by the intense and personal nature of the Egyptian's hostility towards Rowland. Says Greer: 'In every meeting, every telephone conversation, in every single encounter I had with Fayed, four words would keep cropping up time and again: "honour", "dignity", "pride" and "family". He became obsessed with Tiny Rowland's assaults and thought about how to stop or avenge them every moment of the day.' Fayed's persistent preoccupations didn't stop at Rowland. Whenever government officials questioned his takeover of the House of Fraser, or related activities, he would use the same phrase: 'They are shitting on me from a great height.' The repetition of this phrase became something of a standing joke at IGA and Greer tells how, on his return to the office from an appointment, his staff would sometimes tell him: 'Big Mo's been on the phone. It's falling on him yet again.'

In his obsession with getting the better of his hated business opponent Tiny Rowland, Fayed had developed a related obsession, according to Greer – namely, with the need to ask parliamentary questions. From the outset, Greer explained to Fayed that parliamentary questions have only a limited value (as described in Chapter 12). But Fayed saw questions as a clear sign that he had got the ear of Government, as well as an opportunity for publicity. Fayed also entertained the whimsical notion that Greer should organize 'processions' in Parliament, suggesting, says Greer, that a line of MPs should march through the Central Lobby chanting his name in a show of support!

Greer, who at that point had no knowledge whether the allegations made about Fayed were true, agreed to take on Fayed as a client for a fee of £25,000 a year which, in lobbying terms, represents a steady but by no means large account. His first action on Fayed's behalf was to set up a meeting for him with the three officers of the Conservative backbench Trade and Industry Committee, who met with the Secretary of State for Trade and Industry every week. They were his old friend Michael Grylls, Neil Hamilton and Tim Smith. A lunch was duly arranged on the top floor of Harrods building, with fine food and wine laid on; Fayed needed no prompting to launch into a tirade about how Rowland was unjustifiably attacking his honour, dignity, pride and family.

According to Greer, Hamilton got on well with Fayed from the start of the meeting, having already met him once before. Both men adored Margaret Thatcher; Hamilton was an outspoken advocate of free markets, and Fayed was a free market success story. 'From the outset,' claims Greer, 'Hamilton did not need to be paid to ask questions helpful to Fayed. A convinced supporter, he just needed to be briefed on the key issues.'

Soon after the MPs' lunch, Hamilton tabled two questions helpful to Fayed – a process which was to be repeated frequently in the future as Hamilton and other MPs questioned the validity of Lonrho claims and related issues. The parliamentary questions could then be related by Basham to the media.

Greer recalls how keeping a leash on his impatient and retaliatory client was to prove a difficult task. Fayed would contact MPs directly. For every letter Greer proposed sending to opinion-formers, Fayed would want to send two. Like so many other successful entrepreneurs, Fayed seemed driven by passion rather than cool business logic, often precipitating action when in Greer's view silence would have served him better.

Two years after Greer had taken on Fayed as a client, the Egyptian told him that he wanted to show his appreciation for all those in the House who'd supported him by tabling questions or early day motions challenging the Lonrho version of events. Greer was duly charged with inviting six MPs on a private trip to Paris to inspect the Duchess of Windsor's former home in the Bois de Boulogne, a recent Fayed acquisition, and to stay at Fayed's hotel, the Paris Ritz. Alas, the trip was never to take place; no sooner had Greer issued the invitations than the Secretary of State ordered a DTI inquiry into Fayed's takeover of the House of Fraser. Greer hurriedly uninvited the various MPs, suggesting that the visit might be rescheduled when the inquiry was completed. But, by the time the DTI findings finally emerged, accepting Fayed's hospitality would have been the kiss of political death to the MPs concerned.

It is worth reflecting for a moment on what the announcement of the DTI investigation actually signified in lobbying terms. The bald truth is that it meant Greer's efforts to minimize the impact of the Lonrho campaign, and get across positive arguments in favour of Fayed, had comprehensively failed. All the parliamentary questions, early day motions and backbench committee briefings, combined with Brian Basham's media efforts, had done nothing to convince those whose views really counted – the Secretary of State for Trade and Industry and his advisers – that Lonrho's allegations didn't have something to them. This was in spite of the fact that Tiny Rowland's own reputation at Westminster was far from glowing and that, having failed to win the House of Fraser himself, Rowland was clearly far from an impartial observer of Fayed's own bid.

Why did all the lobbying fail? As discussed in Chapter 12 the idea that money can somehow buy political results is a nonsense. Fayed's money may certainly have helped open doors. Greer's lobbying resulted in *Hansard* entries which supported his client's cause. But at the end of the day, a silk purse could not be manufactured from a sow's ear. What the DTI would eventually confirm as the truth about Fayed's takeover of the House of Fraser assisted by false claims could not be suppressed by all Fayed's money.

the election fund 'bribes' that never were

A month after the DTI announced it was going to investigate Fayed, in May 1987, a general election was called. It was at this point that a new and critical development in the cash for questions saga was to unfold. Greer, who had frequently been in touch with Fayed prior to the disastrous DTI announcement, paid him a visit during the course of which the lobbyist outlined his plans for the general election. It had become his custom during previous elections, he explained, to act as a fund-raiser for the Conservative Party. Rather than raise money which would disappear into Central Office coffers, Greer's approach was to target Conservative candidates fighting marginal seats, where the donation would be most appreciated – and arguably where it could be used to best effect. Would Fayed care to make a donation?

As might be expected, Fayed was not enthralled by the prospect. He told Greer that he had, in fact, donated a massive £250,000 to the Conservatives a few months earlier, after a contact by Lord McAlpine, the Conservative Party treasurer. He was more than a little piqued that the party he was so generously helping subsidize was now launching an inquiry into his business dealings. And here was Greer knocking on his door asking for more. Greer explained how any money he raised would go directly to the Conservative front line, and Fayed wrote him a cheque for £12,000 (Fayed's brother, Ali, would soon add a further £6,000 to Greer's election fighting fund). In addition, Greer raised £11,250 from DHL International, another of his clients. Greer then divided up the joint proceeds and sent them to twenty-six constituency associations – none of which had any idea where the money had originally come from.

Greer's election fund-raising efforts, like his payment of new business commissions, were not illegal, but nor were they typical at the time. No other major lobbying firms I have spoken to seemed aware of this kind of activity – to which the cynic might reply: 'They would say that, wouldn't they?' With the clarity of hindsight, it was a stupid mistake which Greer could easily have avoided –

and should have. It took cosying up to MPs just one step too far. But while most lobbyists regard Greer's front-line fund-raising as ill advised, all of them scoff at the suggestion that, by contributing £2,000 to an MP's fighting fund Greer could cause that MP to feel under some kind of obligation to him. 'People who think that are living in cloud-cuckoo land,' said one lobbyist. 'You can't buy people for that kind of money.' Greer's fund-raising was, therefore, a way of scoring brownie points, of ingratiating himself with those who might be in a position to smooth his path in the future. It was rather like helping teacher carry her books in from the car park – an appreciated gesture, no doubt, but of no bearing on your end-of-year exam results.

The *Guardian* team, however, construed his actions in a very dark light indeed: 'Fayed believed he was simply being asked to pay more bribes to Government politicians . . . In fact, none of the MPs who were subsidised by Greer, whether they were required by the existing rules or not, ever chose to make the fact public. Every one of them, with the possible exception of Greer's personal con-stituency MP, knew that they were getting campaign funds not from a local supporter, but from a political lobbyist.'

Later, according to Greer, Fayed told the *Guardian* that the £18,000 he'd paid Greer was to be forwarded to Hamilton and Smith for their parliamentary support, and it was on this allegation that his libel battle against the *Guardian* would be fought. The fact that Greer had never told MPs where the so-called 'bribe money' had come from, and didn't ask them for any favour by way of return, didn't seem to bother the *Guardian*. It was only after the collapse of the libel trial that Fayed's own spokesman, Michael Cole, told ITN's *News at Ten* the truth of the matter – that the money had been paid into an election fighting fund for various MPs. By then, of course, it was much too late for Greer. The *Guardian*-led media assault had already gone to town on his activities, combining the allegations of 'bribes' together with revelations of the commissions he paid MPs for new business referrals, not to mention the central cash for questions accusations; it all added up to a deeply sinister portrait of sleaze.

Meanwhile, the prospect of a free stay at the Paris Ritz, once lodged in the mind of one MP, was to prove both irresistible and, ultimately, politically catastrophic. Neil Hamilton asked for the six-night freebie – or was invited to stay by Fayed, depending on whether you believe the *Guardian* or Greer version of events – in September 1987, during a visit he and his wife were making to France. So much has been written about the now notorious hotel stay that nothing is to be gained by rehearsing the details here. Suffice it to say that Neil and Christine Hamilton clocked up a notional bill of £3,602 over a six-night period, dining every night at the hotel restaurant and generally taking such unstinting advantage of Fayed's hospitality that, in light of Hamilton's later actions, the businessman was to feel deeply aggrieved.

What does Greer have to say about the Hamiltons' stay? 'It was probably bad judgement on their part. Most people, I think, would have been embarrassed to stay there that long. In the eyes of many, they were greedy. But that does not mean they were corrupt. Corrupt politicians tend not to brag about their gains.' Certainly, by not registering the trip Hamilton broke the obligation on MPs to record their interests, as noted by Sir Gordon Downey. Even if he wasn't greedy, he was nonetheless extremely unwise.

the DTI investigates

As noted above, it was in 1987 that the DTI began its investigations into Fayed's takeover of the House of Fraser. The inquiry was, as is the nature of such things, an extremely protracted exercise, taking the better part of two years to reach the final report stage. As it turned out, publication of the DTI inspectors' eventual findings was to be not by the DTI itself but by the *Observer*. A special midweek edition in March 1989, timed to coincide with Lonrho's annual general meeting, leaked the contents of the report, which could not have been more to Rowland's liking: 'Exposed – the phoney pharaoh' the headline ran. It was a spectacular coup for Rowland; the report contained lines which vindicated many of his claims over the preceding years. The public, many of whom received their special *Observer* edition free, were amazed to read confirmation from no less a source than the DTI that

> The Fayeds dishonestly misrepresented their origins, their wealth, their business interests and their resources to the Secretary of State, the OFT, the press, the House of Fraser Board and House of Fraser shareholders and their own advisers.
>
> During the course of our investigations we received evidence from the Fayeds, under solemn affirmation . . . which was false and which the Fayeds knew to be false . . . in addition the Fayeds produced a set of documents they knew to be false.

Rowland's publication of the report's findings caused the government deep embarrassment – and Fayed even deeper shame. Greer counselled him to maintain a dignified silence, but Fayed could only keep this up for two days before, according to Greer, exploding at a charity tea being hosted at Harrods for 400 Cubs, Brownies, Scouts and Guides. Wearing a tiny Cub's cap, he told a band of jostling reporters following him through the toy department that no one had the right to question where he'd got his money from, and that his acquisition of Harrods had been completely above board. Greer says that 'for the first time IGA began to doubt whether everything Mohamed had told us about his background and his wealth was true. But we still stuck by him.'

While the DTI didn't deny that the report appearing in the *Observer* was the real thing, at the same time none of the allegations was yet officially endorsed. When the DTI finally announced that there would, in fact, be no prosecutions and that it would publish its report, IGA and Fayed's PR team swung into action with well-prepared rebuttals of the report and its authors. But it was to little avail. So damning was the DTI report that the press didn't need to resort to hyperbole to produce sensational headlines about how Fayed had cheated his way to acquiring the House of Fraser.

Fayed decided that rather than tough out the barrage of negative publicity, he would continue to fight. Despite Greer's advice to let the matter drop – he had, after all, succeeded in keeping hold of the House of Fraser – Fayed wanted the DTI report overruled, and now instigated a new and lengthy process to take the matter to the European Court of Human Rights.

hamilton's 'betrayal' – the beginning of the end

It was while this action was going on that John Major, who had succeeded Margaret Thatcher as Prime Minister and party leader in 1990, called the 1992 general election. Among the Conservative MPs who held their seats was Neil Hamilton, returned with a majority of almost 16,000 votes. Recognizing his previous work on the backbench Trade and Industry Committee, Major promoted him to the post of corporate affairs minister at the Department of Trade and Industry. From Fayed's perspective, Hamilton's new appointment may well have seemed, at the time, like a godsend. Here was the man he counted as a passionate supporter, who had lobbied on his behalf in Parliament and accepted his lavish hospitality in Paris, now positioned in a key role within the very ministry whose report he sought to overturn. In the past, Hamilton had told Parliament that the DTI inspectors' behaviour had been such a 'monstrous injustice' that it represented a 'twentieth-century Spanish Inquisition'. Now he was a minister and in a position of real power to do something about it.

Fayed sent Hamilton a letter at the DTI, congratulating him on his new appointment, telling him that he expected to win his case at the European Court of Human Rights, and inviting him to Harrods for lunch soon. But if he had hoped for a similarly friendly letter by return, he was to be sorely disappointed. For, now that he was a minister embarked on an upward trajectory, Hamilton had very different priorities. His job was to defend his department's position, not to rock the boat. Far be it from him to start his ministerial career by hauling out the hugely publicized report and saying that his department had got it all wrong and that the high-ranking Cabinet colleagues on whom he depended for future advancement had been utterly mistaken.

The fact that Fayed had written to him at the DTI, rather than at the House of Commons where his private secretary – who also happened to be his wife – would have opened the letter, caused Hamilton especial embarrassment. As it turned out, it was a civil servant who opened a chummy letter to the new minister from the man who was technically suing the department! Senior civil servants advised Hamilton not to reply to Fayed's letter. What's more, knowing of Hamilton's previous pro-Fayed sympathies, they suggested that the whole House of Fraser/European Court of Human Rights issue be handled by another minister, Edward Leigh, a recommendation Hamilton accepted after some delay.

When Fayed, awaiting a reply to his letter, or perhaps a telephone call to set up a lunch date, received instead the message relayed to him from his in-house lawyer, Royston Webb, that no reply to his letter should be expected and indeed that Hamilton wished to 'distance himself' from his erstwhile host, Fayed was livid. According to Greer, Fayed took Hamilton's snub as a personal insult to his honour. To make matters still worse, one of Hamilton's first tasks as minister was to reply to a parliamentary question tabled by the Liberal Democrat Alex Carlile, wanting to know if the President of the Board of Trade, Michael Heseltine, was satisfied with the outcome of the DTI investigation. While Hamilton's response was drafted by a civil servant, it came from his desk – and it described the DTI investigation as 'carefully considered and thorough'. This was, of course, in direct contradiction to the noises Hamilton had made as a backbench MP about monstrous injustice and Spanish Inquisitions. Feeling ignored and double-crossed by the minister to whom he had given so much, from that moment Fayed, it would seem, regarded Hamilton as a marked man.

Ever since his takeover of the House of Fraser, Mohamed Fayed had been beset by problems. Perhaps his ideal life-script might have gone along the following lines: take over House of Fraser; become acknowledged as leading international businessman from aristocratic Egyptian background; acquire British citizenship; move in the most influential establishment circles; become recognized as hugely generous charity sponsor . . . perhaps, eventually, a gong – arise, Sir Mohamed? But things had gone badly awry. Instead of being fêted as a tycoon, his integrity was assailed in headline after headline. Far from being accepted in establishment circles, he was ostracized and snubbed. Time and time again he found the doors slammed shut in his face, and unsurprisingly concluded that ingrained racism and snobbery were the causes. The nadir came when he had his application for British citizenship turned down, after what he believed was the personal intervention of Michael Howard. The government had shat on him one time too many – and Fayed's patience had run out. He decided to take matters into his own hands.

By 1993, the sleaze issue had been rumbling for some time. Indeed, Ian Greer had appeared before the Select Committee on Members' Interests as early as October 1988 to discuss the relationship between his firm and MPs, and in 1989 Andrew Roth, in his 'Parliamentary Profiles' publication, made it clear that IGA had paid Michael Grylls for introducing new business to the firm. Subsequently, the Select Committee, chaired by Dale Campbell-Savours, decided that Greer had done nothing wrong in paying MPs for new business introductions – but emphasized that MPs must list these payments on the Register of Members' Interests, which many had failed to do.

However, the issue of paying MPs cash to ask questions was a different matter entirely. It raised its head after Fayed, deeply aggrieved by what he saw as a catalogue of victimization by the Tory government, culminating in his rejected application for citizenship, met with the *Guardian*'s editor, Peter Preston, in July 1993. In one of the many ironies of this whole tale, the ruthless capitalist Fayed found his most valuable ally in the left-wing editor and his former critic Preston, whose newspaper was to become the vehicle for his revenge on the 'treacherous' Hamilton and unsuspecting Greer. Fayed claimed he had paid Greer tens of thousands of pounds to hand over as bribes to MPs for their support. He went further, identifying Hamilton as number one on a payroll of MPs he paid directly in brown envelopes containing £50 notes. In addition, he showed the *Guardian* team the bill for Hamilton's stay at the Ritz. High on the excitement of scandal, *Guardian* journalists followed up his allegations with Hamilton, who wrote them a strongly worded letter, copied to his lawyers Carter-Ruck and Partners, in which he stated, among other things, that his stay at the Paris Ritz had been the same as staying at Fayed's private address and therefore did not need to be included on the Register of Members' Interests.

Guardian journalists began phoning IGA staff members at their homes, as well as IGA clients, trying to uncover evidence of the payment of cash for questions and related evidence of corruption. When they finally asked to interview Greer, the lobbyist told them that someone had been filling their heads with wild ideas if they thought he got MPs to table questions by handing out brown envelopes stuffed with banknotes. Greer notes that when he met *Guardian* journalists David Hencke and John Mullin, it struck him that both of them *wanted* to believe the system was corrupt. They worked for a newspaper which was extremely hostile to the Conservative government: nothing suited their agenda better than to show that fifteen years of power had made the Tories corrupt to the very core. While Greer failed to provide them with any material with which to construct a conspiracy theory, there was one piece of information which surprised them – and which should have made them question the motives of their original source. When they described Fayed as a 'former' IGA client, Greer corrected them: Fayed still was a client. All the while he was pouring poison about Greer into *Guardian* ears, he still retained the lobbyist for parliamentary monitoring services.

But Fayed was not prepared to be identified as the *Guardian*'s source – yet. As a consequence, the *Guardian*'s first piece about Greer, entitled 'The power and prestige of Ian Greer', was a sly but muted affair, making no mention of cash for questions but hinting at the corruption of MPs through lavish entertainment and hotel

stays, and raking over the by now old story of new business introduction commissions for MPs. The article did no harm either to
Greer or to the two MPs on whom it focused – Hamilton and Tim
Smith. In fact, a short while after it appeared, Sir Tim Bell offered
Greer £2 million to bring IGA into the Lowe Bell Communications
group – an offer Greer has had plenty of time subsequently to
regret turning down.

Having failed to uncover any evidence that Greer was paying off
MPs, as Fayed kept privately insisting, David Hencke left the
Guardian to work for Central TV on *The Cook Report*. His
mission: to entrap Greer. In an astonishing twist to the saga, *The
Cook Report* hired two actors, 'Richard' and 'Ben', who were to
play the parts of a gay couple representing a group of Moscow-
based investors with £40 million to spend in the West, and a
particular interest in buying into the British government's privatization programme. Greer met with these 'businessmen' on several
occasions and was awarded a £10,000 contract, as *The Cook
Report* team attempted to entrap him. 'Ben', the younger of the
two men, even invited him round for a one-to-one session at his
Park Lane flat – an invitation Greer resisted – as the journalists
resorted to the very lowest cunning in a bid to tempt Greer, in a
moment of private intimacy, into saying something that could then
be aired on prime-time national television.

As it happened, *The Cook Report*'s attempted sting turned out
to be an expensive embarrassment. Despite having paid handsomely for the £2,000 a week Park Lane apartment, a £10,000
payment to Greer and actors' fees, not to mention substantial production costs, it failed to uncover any evidence of corrupt activities
on Greer's part. What's more, fearing that the undercover operation was about to be exposed for what it was, 'Richard' and 'Ben'
were forced to beat a hasty retreat to 'Moscow'.

The first that Greer and his colleagues knew of the operation
was when they opened the *Guardian* in May 1994, two months
after the sting began, to read allegations of how he'd 'boasted'
about his Westminster connections. Once again, there was no
damning evidence to mount against Greer – but, coming on top of

the *Guardian*'s previous piece, the innuendo and allegations were beginning to build up in an unnerving way. Greer realized somebody out there was gunning for him; little did he realize, at this point, that it was his own client.

fayed's loss – the *guardian*'s gain

Fayed's reluctance to go on the record with the *Guardian*, and deliver the *coup de grâce* he so vehemently wished upon his enemies, was attributable in part to his pending case before the European Court of Human Rights. It would have done his cause no good at all to be seen telling a national British newspaper how he'd bribed Members of Parliament for their support at the same time that the Court in Strasbourg was trying to decide whether he had lied his way to acquiring the House of Fraser. But two days before the verdict of the hugely expensive case was to be made official, in September 1994, it was clear to Fayed that he'd lost his case: so he asked Peter Preston to visit him. The *Guardian* team recalls: 'The fifth floor was not quite as the editor remembered it. There were fewer people around; it was somehow darker and chillier ... Mohamed looked a little dishevelled, shirt undone, jacket discarded, grim and upset.'

Fayed revealed to Preston the depth of his anger at those he saw as the authors of his misfortunes: Conservative politicians, and the lobbying system which had so grievously failed him. 'Now we show the bastards, now I right behind you,' Preston recalls him saying. But did this mean he was prepared to go on the record with his allegations about cash payments for questions and Neil Hamilton's Paris Ritz bill which to date had only been alluded to in newspaper articles? It did. With nothing more to lose, Fayed was now ready to deliver the *Guardian*'s scoop of the year – arguably of the decade.

On 20 October 1994 the *Guardian* broke its big one under the huge banner headline: 'Tory MPs were paid to plant questions says Harrods boss'. In the article, Fayed said he'd paid Greer tens of thousands of pounds to bribe MPs to ask questions in the House. Greer's monthly invoice would vary from £8,000 to £10,000 depending on the number of questions asked. Greer, said Fayed, had told him you had to rent MPs like London taxis – and Neil Hamilton and Tim Smith, both ministers, were two of the higher-ranking MPs whom he fingered. Even before early editions of the *Guardian* had hit the streets, all the other major news media had been alerted and were on to the story. A stunned Greer, scarcely able to believe what was happening, found himself suddenly at the centre of a media storm, the telephone constantly jangling and a troupe of photographers and TV cameramen trapping him inside his office building. 'The allegations are wholly and totally untrue,' he kept repeating like a mantra. 'My lawyers are issuing a writ for libel this morning . . .'

Once unleashed, however, Fayed's fury knew no bounds. As the hours elapsed, out came the story of Hamilton's luxury Ritz visit, and tales of brown envelopes stuffed with cash. In all of this Greer was presented as the fixer in the middle, the corrupt conduit of parliamentary sleaze. But the hysteria that accompanied the media repetitions of Fayed's claims led many to overlook the simple fact that the accusations didn't make any sense. As Greer himself says: 'No political lobbyist worth their salt would suggest anything quite as crass as paying MPs to ask questions. What is the point? Each year 45,000 questions are tabled. There are 651 Members of Parliament. I would not have been doing my job if I was unable to find one of them to ask questions in defence of Mohamed Fayed in 1985, one of Britain's leading businessmen . . .'

It was only much later, when Greer and Hamilton embarked on their abortive attempt to sue the *Guardian* for libel, that the newspaper quietly dropped its allegations that Greer had been involved in handing over money to Hamilton. It is significant that, in its reporting of its own ground-breaking article in the book *Sleaze*, the *Guardian* team does not repeat its original accusations. That's because by the time the book was published the *Guardian* had changed the focus of its attack, having failed to uncover any evidence whatsoever to support Fayed's claims about using Greer to pay cash for questions: now it was saying that cash payments to MPs were made directly by Fayed, and that Ian Greer had not been involved at all. In due course, Sir Gordon Downey was to clear Greer completely of any involvement in paying cash for questions. But that was many months later – and much too late as far as IGA was concerned. By then the damage had been done; Greer had lost his clients and IGA had collapsed.

No sooner had the *Guardian*'s cash-for-questions revelations been made than Tim Smith resigned his post as Minister for Northern Ireland, after admitting having taken cash for questions from Fayed. Greer was as surprised as anyone at this turn of events – as was Royston Webb, Fayed's own in-house lawyer. Greer had no idea that Fayed was paying off MPs, and he hoped that Smith would make this point quite clearly. But, infuriatingly for Greer, he didn't. Confronted later by Greer, the lobbyist says Smith told him that his letter of resignation was written 'in enormous haste. I was under great pressure. I should have said that, yes. I'm sorry.'

In the absence of anyone – except Greer himself – disputing the *Guardian*'s allegations about Greer, they began to become accepted as fact. What's more, the *Guardian* team was able to make a great deal of the various new business commissions Greer had paid Hamilton, Grylls and other MPs. Their cause was greatly aided by the way in which Greer agreed to pay some of his commissions to Hamilton. Instead of writing him a cheque he had, for example, allowed the MP to send him a bill from Peter Jones for garden furniture, and another bill from an art shop for paintings. Invoices for air tickets were also paid out of IGA coffers. As far as Greer was concerned, he didn't care how an MP was paid, once the amount had been agreed, so long as all commissions were recorded in IGA accounts. But viewed from the *Guardian* perspective, it all seemed very furtive and underhand and lent itself to the creation of a dark tableau. In its determination to prove that the Tory government was mired in sleaze, the *Guardian* published a highly colourful account of events. By way of illustration, let's take another quote from *Sleaze*, referring to what Fayed had allegedly paid Hamilton: 'This was Fayed's return for all the gourmet dinners, the bottles of fizz, the gift vouchers, the paintings, the plane tickets, the wrought-iron garden furniture, and the rolls of banknotes – the brush-off.' The fact is that while Fayed had handed out rolls of banknotes to various MPs, these had nothing to do with Ian Greer, while the paintings, plane tickets and garden furniture had nothing to do with Fayed – they were part of Hamilton's £10,000 commission for introducing two pieces of new business to IGA.

the collapse of IGA

The events that followed the tidal wave of media hysteria are already well documented. Hamilton found himself an embarrassment to the Government and his party for a number of reasons, not only because of the cash for questions charges which he continued vehemently to deny. Despite denying he had a financial relationship with Greer, when questioned by Deputy Prime Minister Michael Heseltine, he was thrown out as a minister, and later voted out as a Member of Parliament by his constituency, who rallied to the call of the 'anti-sleaze' candidate, BBC's Martin Bell, in the 1997 general election. Many of IGA's clients decided they couldn't risk being associated with the organization at the centre of alleged parliamentary sleaze, and inevitably the consultancy collapsed. There is now a diaspora of former IGA lobbyists in many senior positions within the public affairs sector, Ian Greer's most enduring legacy to the lobbying industry. As for Greer himself, he and his partner, Clive Ferreira, have set up a small, London-based international lobbying consultancy – International Government Relations.

When Sir Gordon Downey's report was published in July 1997, Greer was cleared of any involvement in cash for questions – the lobbying scandal that never was. He responded with the statement: 'I am delighted that the report has cleared myself and the staff of Ian Greer Associates of any suggestions that we acted as a conduit for Mohamed al Fayed's disreputable cash payments to MPs to ask questions.' Greer was not left completely unscathed by the report, which also commented on his role in making donations to election campaign funds. But on the central charge of cash for questions he was completely vindicated.

So what conclusions do we draw? It is a natural instinct to wish to depict people and events in black and white. In our yearning for simplicity, there must be good guys and bad guys, heroes and villains. The reality of the cash for questions story, however, is that no such easy distinctions can be made. The central players in the drama – Fayed, Greer, Hamilton and the *Guardian* – were all far from faultless; but Greer, in particular, became the target of accusations of misdemeanours he never committed, with disastrous effect. His consultancy, widely regarded as the leading lobbying firm in Britain, and for which he had recently been offered £2 million, became worthless within a matter of hours of the beginning of a vindictive media campaign which, in its central allegations, was without foundation. As such the *Guardian*, which was completely right to bring the public's attention to parliamentary sleaze, was equally wrong to destroy a company, and jeopardize the livelihoods of all those who worked in it, by making false allegations.

What of Mohamed Fayed? He says he was led by Greer to believe that you had to bribe MPs with cash to make headway – and there were certainly MPs willing to relieve him of bundles of it. Greer said he never proposed bribery as a strategy to his client. So who advised Fayed to pay cash for questions, and why didn't he double-check with other lobbyists – or, indeed, any of Greer's other clients – to find out if this was really the way things are done in Britain?

Of all the players in the drama, Neil Hamilton has unquestionably come out worst, having lost his status in the party and his constituency seat and having been found guilty by Sir Gordon Downey of failing to register Fayed's hospitality. On the crucial issue of cash for questions, Downey said: 'The evidence that Mr Hamilton received cash payments directly from Mr Al Fayed in return for lobbying services is compelling.' Interestingly, Downey stopped short of using the word 'conclusive' – and Hamilton immediately announced he was contesting the report, a process which has the potential to drag on for years.

the post-nolan world of lobbying

The parliamentary effect of the cash for questions 'scandal' is well known but not well understood. Prime Minister John Major called in Lord Nolan to investigate and prepare a report on standards of conduct in public life; the result might be seen as analogous to the Cadbury and Greenbury reports in the corporate world. Nolan rightly took the view that it was a lack of transparency, rather than the existence of corruption, which had shaken public confidence in the parliamentary process. It was confusion in the rules specifying what was and was not permissible which had allowed the media to paint such a misleading and damaging picture of what went on in the Mother of Parliaments. And so Nolan set down new ground rules. He put a strict ban on all forms of paid advocacy: 'No Member of the House shall, in consideration of any remuneration . . . advocate or initiate any cause or matter on behalf of any out-side body or individual.' However, parliamentary consultancy work is still allowed, so long as it is declared in debate and on the Register of Members' Interests.

What this means is that an MP can still work as an adviser, for example, to a large brewing company, and be paid by them for advice on how to lobby for a change in the rules. What he can't do, however, is lobby to change the rules himself. On the surface of things this seems a sensible division between advice and action – but it has unfortunate side-effects. As Dudley Fishburn says: 'Nolan was right on individuals – MPs should not take up a cause for money. But he was wrong in that many of those involved in a case are now frightened to speak about it. Debates are therefore less well informed.' If you are the MP advising a brewing company, a role duly listed on the Register of Members' Interests, and a brewing issue comes up in the House of Commons, you may well know a lot more about the issue than those debating it – but as it is strictly forbidden to take money for promoting a cause, you may not wish to contribute to the discussion for fear of being accused of taking bribes.

Another point about the Nolan rules is that they are difficult to police. Short of hiring a private detective to follow each and every MP, and setting up telephone bugging devices, there is no way to ensure that MPs do, in fact, register all relevant outside interests – the system depends on their honesty. As for making sure MPs don't actively lobby on behalf of client companies, that, too, is hard to enforce: an MP might simply ask a colleague to pose the question for him, or else ask it on behalf of a constituent.

There is no evidence that any underhand activity of this kind is going on at present. And, as emphasized in Chapter 12, underhand activity was rare in the past – although it was easy to create the impression of widespread deviousness for the sake of sensational headlines.

As for the lobbying industry, the formation of the Association of Professional Political Consultants in 1994 was partly a response to media allegations of lobbying sleaze. Ironically, one of the four founding members most keen that it should be established was none other than IGA. The APPC decided there should be a code of practice for its members and an annual report detailing which lobbyists represented which client companies made freely available to members of the government, and letters were sent to all MPs announcing the existence of the APPC. Included in the code of practice was a rule outlawing the payment of new business commissions and banning MPs from sitting on the boards of lobbying companies.

How much impact has the formation of the APPC had on perceptions of lobbying? Among MPs, very little, if the results of a survey conducted by the *Public Affairs Newsletter* are to be believed. The December 1996 edition indicated that 89 per cent of MPs wouldn't take any notice of whether a consultancy was a member of the APPC before dealing with them. As Greer remarks: 'The [lobbying] industry has . . . set up an organization to regulate itself, it has informed MPs of its existence and two years down the line it learns that MPs do not really care.' Outside Parliament and the lobbying industry, the APPC, like its PR counterpart the PRCA, is neither known nor respected. Both organizations suffer from a lack of teeth in that they can only enforce a code of conduct on their own members – and clients don't appear to care whether the consultants they appoint to advise them are members or not.

The broader issue facing the lobbying industry is how to re-habilitate a public image which has been badly damaged by media vandals. In the short term, Labour's 1997 election victory was part of the solution – at least on a perceptual level. Since the new government took office, Tony Blair's hard-nosed stance on parliamentary discipline and commitment to moral values have been to the advantage of the legislative process as a whole, and this can only be good for lobbying. In more concrete terms, too, the huge Labour majority in the House of Commons means that individual MPs are even less important and influential than they would have been with a smaller government majority: even if some Labour MPs could be persuaded to defy the Labour whip, the rebellion would be of no consequence. The focus of lobbyists, now more than ever before, is on Whitehall, and the realization that this is the case may gradually begin to spread more widely.

Lobbying, which is still really an industry of only twenty years' standing, will continue to evolve, with change driven in particular by the twin engines of power transfer and technology. 'Lobbyists go where the power is,' says Michael Burrell, managing director of lobbying firm Westminster Strategy, and with power moving to Brussels, Strasbourg, Edinburgh and Cardiff, the lobbying industry is already taking a different shape from its 1980s incarnation. Says Burrell: 'Lobbying as we do it is a very Anglo-Saxon phenomenon. The most effective lobbyists in Brussels are British and American – we dominate the consultancy scene there. Others are adopting our practices and we are able to bring about real change. For example, it was our idea of introducing Question Time to the European Parliament – it was a British import that an MEP should be able to cross-examine the Commissioner.'

While relationship-building will continue to be a key role of the lobbyist, his services as a monitor of information may well change as the Internet and other electronic communications systems become more sophisticated. While there will always be a role for the sifter of information, increasingly the direction of successful lobbying firms is towards strategic advice and away from tactical activities such as parliamentary monitoring and corporate hospitality. As Colin Byrne, head of Shandwick Public Affairs, says: 'Consultants will have to provide a deeper understanding of policies and what is driving them than perhaps the industry has been used to. Clients will expect added value in terms of understanding strategy, rather than just the cocktail party circuit . . .'

Lobbying will continue to evolve as a discipline in response to its environment, whether change is driven by geo-politics, technology or other imperatives. The unhappy chapter during which the industry acquired a largely undeserved reputation for sleaze is already starting to be viewed as belonging to a former era, part and parcel of John Major's troubled premiership, during which the ill-disciplined Conservative government seemed constantly embattled by allegations of sexual and financial misconduct. All of that was, of course, swept away in May 1997 when the British electorate voted in New Labour with a massive majority. While Britain clearly voted *against* the Conservatives, it also unquestionably voted *for* Labour, and in so doing demonstrated the power of yet another dimension of political communications: political party PR.

CHAPTER FOURTEEN
new labour: made in america

It was billed as a private dinner, so nothing the Labour leader said was to be quoted. The six journalists invited, including some of the more recently appointed political correspondents in the national media, were carefully chosen from *The Times*, the *Financial Times*, the *Guardian*, the *Daily Mirror*, BBC and ITN. With the election less than two months away, the journalists had responded to the invitation with alacrity. There was, after all, a very good chance that in a matter of weeks their host would be Prime Minister; what better way to get to know him than at an informal session in a Covent Garden restaurant?

Duly congregating at Luigi's, the journalists were introduced to the leader, his wife and his personal press officer – though the party's main media minder was surprisingly absent. The group sat down to their wine and Italian meal, and everything seemed to be going well until the leader started talking about the party's plans for national insurance. Up until that point, Labour had been in favour of a significant increase in national insurance contributions – but now the party's leader seemed to be toning that all down, talking about phased-in increases. Was this a major Labour U-turn?

Alison Smith of the *Financial Times* certainly saw it as a shift in policy and the following day wrote up a piece attributing her information to 'senior party figures'. It was due to appear on the newspaper's front page. While it was going to print, news of the policy shift had leaked out – Labour's media minder was soon fielding calls from the BBC and other journalists, and categorically denying there had been any shift in Labour policy.

But it was too late. The Tory director of communications and party chairman were already circulating a statement saying that Labour's tax plans were not worth the paper they were written on. Political writers from the Tory-supporting tabloids, who had not been invited to the dinner, laid into the Labour leader with a vengeance. The next weekend, the *Sunday Times*'s Andrew Grice wrote in detail about the dinner, pointing out that the Labour leader 'was apparently unaware of the impact his words would have'.

If this vignette of how *not* to conduct political PR doesn't quite ring true, that may be because the Labour leader in question was not Tony Blair but Neil Kinnock. The party media minder was not Peter Mandelson but David Hill. It is, in short, a tale of Old Labour rather than New and is symptomatic of why Labour was lost in the political wilderness for eighteen years. Such a dinner would have been unthinkable immediately before the 1997 general election. Five years after its defeat at the polls under Kinnock, Labour had become, quite literally, a different party. Its personalities, power base and attitude to policy-making had been transformed – and more than that, it now controlled the most devastatingly effective political PR machinery ever seen in Britain.

the clintonization of british politics

Without question, the biggest transformation to sweep Westminster since the mid-1990s has been the Clintonization of British politics. Labour, which stood to gain most from this approach, was the first of the main parties to identify the benefits it offered and to conduct root-and-branch reform. The Conservatives, who had won four elections in a row without resorting to the Clintonized approach, failed to recognize that the nature of the game had changed – and were hopelessly outgunned in the 1997 elections as a result. However else President Bill Clinton is remembered, his name will also be associated with what is, in effect, a new approach to political communication on both sides of the Atlantic, an approach which has transformed the methods and even the *raison d'être* of party politics, and in particular has changed the way in which successful parties manage their public relations activities.

The Clintonization of political party PR is essentially character-ized by three main developments. The first is the occupation of the centre ground of politics, requiring the abandonment of any historical baggage that makes the party beholden to forces associ-ated with political extremes. The second is the jettisoning of firmly held policy positions which may attract negative comment in favour of all-encompassing general statements which can be accepted by audiences with widely varying, and even conflicting, demands. (These all-encompassing statements are subject to change without notice according to public opinion.) The third development is the recognition that party campaigning is a con-stant process, rather than an activity conducted once every four or five years. The commitment to achieve power and/or stay in office is the guiding principle behind the formulation and presentation of all activity – all of the time.

The politics of the Reagan–Thatcher era, characterized by a rigid – perhaps too rigid – adherence to clearly spelled out ideals and principles, has given way to the new Clinton–Blair paradigm in which pragmatism has itself become the new ideal. Like her or hate her, the man on the Clapham omnibus would have had no diffi-culty identifying a handful of principles championed by Margaret Thatcher, but could the same thing be said for Tony Blair? It is doubtful. In the run-up to the 1997 election, when Labour's PR machine was at its most active, not even the national press was able to get a grip on Labour policy. Said the *Sunday Times* in its election guide supplement:

> Whenever this newspaper has tried to find out about prospective
> Labour MPs, for instance, a diktat has been issued from Millbank
> Tower stopping them from answering questions. And when policies
> are outlined, there is still waffle on education, the National Health
> Service, tax and our future in Europe. While Mr Blair is a decent
> man, we know little about what his party really thinks. We are still
> in a wonderland where disbelief is suspended while 'the project' is
> achieved: getting Labour into power.

Writer Barbara Amiel, who had spent an entire weekend with the
Blairs to gather material for a profile of the Labour leader, concluded in the *Daily Telegraph*:

> No British politician has ever been quite as spin-doctored as Tony
> Blair. The problem is not that he has a nasty nature (he hasn't), nor
> is he without principles or intelligence. He has both. What he
> doesn't have are ideas or policies. He and his team have seen that
> in this particular time in the Western world one needs to steer the
> middle course. So, they lift a moist finger to the wind and edge ever
> closer to the Tories. It must be easier to catch an eel than it is to
> find the policy core of the Labour party.

While one would hesitate before drawing too close a parallel
between Tony Blair and Bill Clinton in terms of their principles or
personalities, their rise respectively to the top of Labour and the
Democrats in the absence of any driving ideology is undeniable.
More significantly, the close similarity between the methods of the
Democrats in their successful 1992 campaign for the presidency
and those employed to such effect by Labour in 1997 is no coincidence. Labour sent over a group of agents to observe the
Democrats' workings at first hand; the result was a report which
formed the blueprint for Labour's phenomenal 1997 campaign. So
strong were the parallels between the political scenarios on
opposite sides of the Atlantic that, as we will see later in the
chapter, Labour was able to effect a direct and wholesale lift of the
Democrat techniques and even messages which had proved so

successful for Clinton, and apply them with equally resounding success in Britain.

Soon after New Labour came to power, President Clinton paid Prime Minister Blair and his Cabinet a visit; it was much commented upon in the British media that he seemed as *au fait* with Labour Party messages as the most conscientious of Labour Party activists. His understanding is actually less amazing than it seems, however, when one considers that the 'Labour' messages were actually Clinton's own. They were the self-same lines he'd repeated for month after month on the hustings back home in America!

The transformation of the Labour Party from the discredited wreckage of the late Seventies to the dynamic and ruthlessly effective New Labour of the new millennium was a remarkable achievement. It is probably fair to say that the process of change, begun under Neil Kinnock and continued during John Smith's brief stewardship, only really came to fruition once Tony Blair was elected leader in 1994. Despite strong and predictable opposition from the old-guard Labour ideologues, Blair was recognized by his party as the best chance they had of finding their way back from the political wilderness. But while the story of that metamorphosis is a fascinating one, the focus of this chapter lies elsewhere. Blair and his fellow Labour 'modernizers' were the targets of media attention throughout the transformation process and election campaign; our primary interest here is in how that attention was targeted, and who was the real architect of change.

One man, more than anyone else in the Labour Party, is credited with setting the agenda for the transformation process. There is very little about the external face of Labour, from its red rose icon, to the messages its leaders are permitted to utter, to its manifesto, that doesn't bear his hallmark. His efforts helped propel Tony Blair to the head of the party in 1994, and the Labour Party war machine which so spectacularly won the 1997 election was entirely of his making.

the rise and rise of labour's dark prince

Peter Mandelson was born in October 1953 and attended Hendon County Grammar School before, like Tony Blair, going up to Oxford University. While he and Blair were at Oxford at the same time – Mandelson reading PPE at St Catherine's while Blair studied law at St John's – the two men didn't know each other; at that point, Blair had little interest in party politics. After Oxford, Mandelson spent some time working in the Economics Department of the TUC, then moved on to the British Youth Council before, in 1982, finding his way into television. As a producer for London Weekend he was involved first with *The London Programme* before moving on to the weekly political programme hosted by Brian Walden, *Weekend World*.

It was Mandelson's understanding of how television and radio newsrooms operate, as well as his knowledge of the personalities of the various political reporters, which made him so attractive to the Labour Party. Although he was a producer, not a presenter, Mandelson quickly became acquainted with interview techniques and the cut and thrust of political debate; as he sometimes reminded journalists later, 'Brian Walden used to practise on me on the day before his *Weekend World* showdown.' Armed with this experience, Mandelson would later challenge journalists for being 'too soft' when interviewing Tory government officials, and would be relentless in criticizing journalists whom he felt had in some way overstepped the line in their reports on Labour.

But it was more than three years of TV experience that Mandelson brought to the party when he was appointed Labour's campaigns and communications director in 1985. In his book on politicians and the media *Soundbites and Spin Doctors*, BBC reporter Nicholas Jones observes: 'Mandelson's lasting value to the Labour leadership has been his understanding of the factors which motivate political journalists. He seemed to have a sixth sense: on seeing a group of them congregating in the members' lobby, or chatting away in the press gallery, he could guess, usually quite accurately, what the various reporters were up to and which of the day's stories they were likely to be discussing.'

One of Mandelson's first actions was to create a new icon for Labour. It was out of a review he commissioned that Labour's red rose emerged as the party's new symbol, with Neil Kinnock's ringing endorsement. The importance of this first act should not be underestimated. From the beginning, Mandelson had a keen appreciation of the need for Labour to disassociate itself from the iconography of its socialist past. He strove to reposition Labour as a party of the middle classes and to repackage its offering in a way that would appeal to those beyond its traditional support base.

All this required more than a new badge, and Mandelson set about transforming Labour's media management. Rejecting the traditional approach to electioneering, which involved cranking up a media machine once every four years, Mandelson knew that the Tories, with all the media advantages they enjoyed as the party in power, would only be ejected from office by a week-in, week-out assault. In presenting Labour's own views, he considerably broadened the scope of the party's media contacts beyond the ranks of the political correspondents to include reporters covering other areas. Weekly press conferences covering all manner of subjects were set up. Labour press officers were in constant contact with broadcast and press journalists. Even shadow ministers called up the newsrooms as Mandelson's media machine sought to exploit every opportunity for exposure.

Labour's new communications director not only transformed the party's media machine in quantitative terms; he also brought about a marked qualitative difference in the party's relationships with journalists. Mandelson quickly acquired a reputation for petulance and provocation, coming down hard on journalists whose reports he found offensive. Nicholas Jones relates in *Soundbites and Spin Doctors* how 'Labour's publicity staff would sometimes stand around open-mouthed, hardly believing that their director could ridicule reporters so publicly and still get away with it . . . At no point did he get cross or bang the table but instead made a succession of withering remarks. His show of total disdain tended to destabilise the journalists at the other end of the phone.' Known to reduce senior reporters to a state of such extreme irritation that in one incident a political editor grabbed him by the lapels, it is not for nothing that Mandelson has been described by those who have worked with him as 'a control freak'.

Within the party, Mandelson's forthright style and considerable influence made him enemies as well as friends right from the start: 'Peter is charming and great fun,' observes one of his supporters. 'He is also very mischievous in his dealings with the media, which is why he enjoys what he does so much.' Many on the left of the party, however, were decidedly unhappy about the direction in which he was taking Labour's PR, using the weight of his media relations machine to focus attention on party modernizers such as Blair and Brown while keeping the spotlight carefully off old-guard Labourites such as Michael Meacher, Bryan Gould and John Prescott. During the 1997 election campaign this focus was even more pronounced, prompting the *Sunday Times*'s 'TV Watch' correspondent, Nicholas Wapshott, to remark: 'John Prescott is a dream for television, loud, old Labour and larger than life; quite the opposite of the sanitised new Labour front-benchers with their smooth ways and rehearsed words signifying nothing . . . but this week he has been strangely absent from our screens . . . he has been marginalised.' The same observation might have been made of any on Labour's left – who can remember seeing Clare Short, Margaret Beckett or Frank Dobson during the 1997 campaign? Veterans of Old Labour, and far removed from the carefully manicured, telegenic New Labour image, they were kept firmly off-screen except when reading their carefully scripted lines.

Despite Mandelson's complete revamp of Labour's image in the mid-1980s, the impressive new media machine at the party's disposal and its tireless campaigning, come the 1987 general election the Tories swept back into a third term of office. The result was a severe setback both to Kinnock and to his spin doctor. The Tories had now won three general elections in a row and their position seemed unassailable. Under Margaret Thatcher, the political spectrum in Britain had shifted fundamentally, and it was becoming clear that unless Labour could well and truly detach itself from its socialist past then the party, unelectable, was doomed to extinction.

Mandelson stayed on as a communications director for three years until, to Kinnock's dismay, he resigned two years before the 1992 general election to stand as MP for the safe Labour seat of Hartlepool. Mandelson's reasons for making this move can only be guessed at: had he realized by then that no amount of effective communication could counteract the fact that most people in Britain, well accustomed by now to the gravitas of Margaret Thatcher, simply couldn't countenance the prospect of installing the 'Welsh windbag' at Number Ten? Another electoral failure would not only mean the end of Neil Kinnock, politically – it could prove a potentially fatal blow to his communications director too. Another element in Mandelson's calculations may have been the knowledge that he was despised by many on the left of the party, who resented the way he had squeezed their share of Labour's media voice, lavishing attention instead on the party's 'moderniz-ers'. Appointed by and answerable only to Neil Kinnock, he wielded considerable power as long as Kinnock was at the top; but as a party *apparatchik* he would be readily dispensable under any new regime. As a Labour MP, however, he would have a power base independent of the Labour leader – and would continue to exert a disproportionate influence on party communications by virtue of his contacts both inside the party and in the media.

With neither a formal party position nor a seat in the House of Commons, during the course of 1991 and 1992 Mandelson must sometimes have wondered what his future in politics held. He may have anticipated Labour's fourth successive general election defeat in 1992, and Kinnock's subsequent resignation of the party leader-ship, but no one could have predicted the untimely demise of John Smith, Kinnock's successor, struck down by a heart attack in May 1994.

It was a pivotal moment for Labour. Suddenly, the reins of power were up for grabs, and the result of the party leadership election would determine whether Labour had the will to transform itself into an electable entity under modernizers like Blair and Brown, or would slowly recede from the shores of political power under old-style Labourites like Prescott and Beckett. There was a tense moment as Blair and Brown, close friends as well as colleagues, determined who should step aside, although, of the two, Blair had been tipped a winner by the media from the start. No sooner had Gordon Brown confirmed he would let Blair take the revisionist lead than Mandelson was back at the centre of party communications strategy.

In his days as Labour's chief spin doctor under Kinnock, Mandelson had always 'talked up' Blair as a future leader, and flattering commentary about the shadow home secretary had long since been appearing in the newspapers. Blair certainly had cause to be grateful to Mandelson, and there was a recognition of mutual respect and dependence on the part of both men. However, Mandelson's role in Blair's campaign for election as party leader had to be entirely covert; because there was so much resentment towards him on the left of the party, if he was seen to be too closely linked to Blair's election team, it could harm Blair's chances of winning. Thus began Mandelson's secret media campaign, in which he would bleep broadcasters, alerting them to statements and speeches about to be made by Blair, while advising them that the conversation they'd just had had not taken place. Advance texts were disseminated to all the news media, with helpful bullet-point summaries up front. All the way through the leadership campaign, Mandelson advised Blair on how to pitch his ideas for maximum impact. And the output of all the news media was closely scrutinized – woe betide the journalist who said anything that fell foul of Blair's invisible persuader.

Once Blair had duly been installed as Labour leader, Mandelson assumed the role for which he was best suited, heading up the party's election campaigning, while Blair drafted in Alastair Campbell, a journalist from the now defunct *Today* newspaper who had been a tireless Labour supporter in the past. Tall, imposing, with a relaxed air that disguises a ruthless streak, Campbell is also fiercely loyal to his employers. One of the best-known stories about him in media circles is how, in his days at the *Mirror*, after the recent demise of Robert Maxwell he punched Michael White, political editor of the *Guardian*, for repeating what he considered to be a tasteless joke about his former boss – White retaliated with a punch of his own. Like Mandelson, Campbell had a reputation for coming down hard on journalists who proved to be spin-resistant, and he soon made it crystal clear that even the most casual contact with the new Labour leader would be controlled by him. With Campbell installed as his tough new media minder, Mandelson back at the centre of Labour presentation and a mandate from his party for reform, Blair now had all he needed to take his party through the Clintonization process in order to make it electable.

new labour, no lefties

'One of the Tories' greatest achievements is to have reshaped new Labour in its own image. It is this single irony that is the greatest threat to their survival in government.' Thus commented the *Sunday Times* at the start of the 1997 election campaign, reflecting the widespread view that, more than anyone else, the person Tony Blair had most to thank for his accession to leadership was Labour's old arch-enemy, Margaret Thatcher. Her extended period in office had moved the British political spectrum so firmly to the right that the Labour Party, in its previous incarnation, had been rendered unelectable.

While Blair reformed the party, Mandelson repackaged it. The most fundamental reform was, unquestionably, the rewriting of Clause IV of the party constitution, in which Labour pledged itself to common ownership of the means of production and a redistribution of wealth. While few but the most ardent Labourites had ever heard of Clause IV before Blair announced his intention to rewrite it in 1994, the fact that he was cutting the party free from its socialist roots in the highest-profile environment available to him – the party conference – sent out a powerful signal to the public. As Nick DeLuca says: 'It would be a mistake to understate the significance of eliminating Clause IV. In one step, Blair killed socialism. Labour was no longer about redistributing wealth. Once you've kicked that, you become a party of the centre.'

Dumping Clause IV also had the effect of pulling the rug from under the feet of the trade unions, which had exercised such unwelcome power over Labour leaders of the past: Blair made it quite clear that the days when the party leadership would accede to union demands were over. The Labour Party, he declared, had changed – now it was 'New Labour'.

Thus Labour rapidly negotiated the first stage of Clintonization – getting rid of unwelcome baggage from the past in order to become a party of the centre. The second stage, abandoning any policies which might attract negative comment, continued until election day in 1997 – even in the final weeks of campaigning, Labour undertook several U-turns which left media commentators open-mouthed. While the mechanics of Labour's election machine will be looked at in more detail later, it is worth noting at this point that the party's extensive market research programme, which included both focus groups and surveys, guided it in much of its policy review. Where policies were picked up on the radar screen of public opinion as being unpopular, they were quickly jettisoned. If, on the other hand, an idea played well in a 'pilot area', it would soon be introduced on to the national stage. And one of Labour's most enduring policy problems concerned tax.

Asked why the Conservatives won the 1992 elections, despite the sense of drift that was already apparent in the party, a Tory MP confided: 'First, we had Kinnock. Second, we had tax.' Tory advertising from that campaign, featuring Labour's 'tax bombshell', still lingered in voters' minds five years later, and getting rid of the 'tax and spend' image was one of the biggest hurdles in the way of Labour on the road to power. In an audacious move to distance itself from the high-tax approach – and, indeed, to occupy the traditional territory of the Conservatives – Labour mounted an attack on the Government for the tax increases the Tories had levied under the Mandelson-approved slogan '21 Tory Tax Rises'. 'As a technique this is very crude but very effective,' says Charles

Lewington, who was director of communications for the Conservatives at the time. 'It involves defining your line of attack, producing a snappy, alliterative phrase and getting everyone to repeat it, *ad nauseam*, at every opportunity.'

As Mandelson well knew, very few media commentators and even fewer members of the public would challenge Labour on what those supposed Tory tax rises actually were. The reality, of course, is that the slogan did not hold much water. The tax rises did not refer to direct taxation; Labour had looked at any individual item on which tax had gone up and labelled it a tax increase . . . The same methodology, looking at items on which tax had gone down, produced 25 Tory Tax Cuts . . . But by the time the Tories were collectively able to agree on this rebuttal, Labour had already stolen the initiative – 21 Tory Tax Rises was lodged in the public mind. And even though Conservative Central Office provided MPs and campaigners with the relevant 'attack phrases', unlike the ruthlessly disciplined Labour team many Conservative campaigners failed to sing the party chorus.

At the same time as it went on the offensive against Tory Tax Rises, Labour took the critical decision it would not increase income tax rates. It was known by the media that there was tension in party ranks, with Gordon Brown favouring an increase in the top rate from 40p to 50p. Blair and Mandelson, on the other hand, knew that adopting such a policy would be handing a stick to the Tories to beat them with; 'New' Labour could be portrayed as no different from the old 'tax and spend' Labour.

The way that Labour broke the news that it was committed to preserve existing income tax rates was typical of Mandelson's adroit and mischievous approach to media relations. Political correspondents in the national press knew that Labour was debating the issue internally, and would call Mandelson to get some kind of inkling as to the way the debate was going. Mandelson didn't deny that Labour might put the top rate up to 50p – the matter was still under consideration, he would say – even though the matter had in fact, to all intents and purposes, been decided. Ever in pursuit of the negative story, journalists began to report that it was probable that Labour would approve the tax rise – and when Mandelson didn't immediately jump on the phone to bite their heads off for the suggestion, they grew even bolder in their assertions. Mandelson deliberately allowed the consensus to grow in the media that Labour would put up tax – so that when the day of the announcement finally arrived, and he told them Labour was committed to keeping income tax rates where they were, journalists were stunned. 'You could see the shock on their faces,' says one Labour Party PR aide. 'Peter turned the announcement into a massive story which got far more coverage than it would have if journalists had been expecting it. He's very manipulative that way.'

At the same time, Labour went out with a big national poster campaign in which Tony Blair promised not to put up income tax in the next five years. Combined with Labour attacks on '21 Tory Tax Rises', this had the effect of putting the Conservatives on the defensive on tax for the first time. It was a radical departure from Labour's previous positioning and a significant factor in persuading the public that New Labour really was a new party. Like the '21 Tory Tax Rises', the poster campaign didn't, in fact, withstand too much scrutiny. Yes, Labour was committed to keeping *income* tax rates down, but what about other, indirect forms of taxation? Under cross-examination by David Dimbleby, Tony Blair admitted Labour hadn't ruled out any other form of taxation which would have the same effect of increasing the tax burden on individuals and companies. That was not, however, what stuck in the public mind. What stuck was the pledge not to increase income tax and the growing disillusionment with the Tories and their tax rises; for the first time, the Conservatives were not automatically being regarded as the party best able to safeguard the economy.

Labour applied similar techniques to remove other policies which constituted obstacles to their election – and to challenge the Conservatives on their traditional territory. Market research undertaken by the party showed that the aspect of crime the public found most offensive was the idea of ten-year-olds out on the streets at eleven o'clock at night throwing bricks through windows and stealing. In response, Labour came out with a strict commitment to tackle juvenile crime which it knew would hold strong appeal – and would reposition New Labour far away from the soft-on-crime reputation of the old Labour Party. Similarly, New Labour abandoned the idea of scrapping grammar schools (in any case, Tony Blair's son attended one) and once again used market research to identify that class sizes and investment in education were concerns the public felt the Tories weren't addressing sufficiently; out came New Labour commitments on both scores.

Tax, law and order, education, health – wherever New Labour uncovered policies that might be impediments to electoral success, they were abandoned. With less than a month to go before the 1 May polling day, Labour announced that it was now in favour of privatization and would continue selling off public assets if elected. This, after eighteen years of howls of indignation every time the Conservatives went ahead with another privatization, accompanied by rancorous accusations of 'selling off the family silver', stunned the media and public alike. Unlike many other policy changes, this U-turn was not one which Labour had carefully researched and scripted in advance. In fact, to Labour's embarrassment, only six months earlier the shadow transport secretary, Andrew Smith, had told a Labour conference that the party would do everything to block the privatization of the National Air Traffic Control Service. 'Our air is not for sale!' he had declared – a soundbite which no TV news broadcast failed to show the night that Labour became converted to privatization.

There was a very simple reason for New Labour's startling decision to heave its anti-privatization stance overboard: the Conservatives had identified a £12 billion 'black hole' in Labour's tax and spending proposals and the party had to come up, very quickly, with a means of filling the hole. One can't but marvel at the sheer ruthlessness with which Labour was prepared to abandon what had been one of its core policies, even under Blair's leadership, for the sake of averting electoral mishap. As the *Daily Telegraph* commented: 'The effrontery of this reversal makes the term "U-turn" seem somehow inadequate. Mr Blair and his colleagues opposed every privatisation over the past few years.

Apart from some empty generalities, Labour's manifesto contained no hint of this radical policy change.'

In the same week which saw its public conversion to privatization, Labour dramatically dropped yet another policy which appeared as a problem on its radar screen – its deal with trade union leaders. Even though getting rid of Clause IV had stripped away the philosophical influence the trade unions had traditionally exerted on the party, the Tories were able to reveal that Labour had acceded to specific requests from trade union leaders, including the compulsory recognition of unions where the majority of the workforce votes for representation. Confronted with this by the media, Labour's response was swift: to abandon the deal. Trade union leaders were furious, but there was little they could do – Blair was flying high in the polls and wasn't going to risk adhering to anything that would jeopardize his chances.

Underlining this wholesale dumping of problem policies was a clear strategy Mandelson himself spelled out in a piece in the *Evening Standard*: 'For much of the Eighties it was easy to dismiss Labour as irrelevant, as hopeless idealists or worse. Although well-intentioned, many of our policies were outdated and unpopular . . . But as Labour has modernised itself and restored realism and practicality to its ideas for improving the country, the party has become less and less easy to attack. And the Tories have become steadily more desperate as a result.'

made in america: labour's war machine

The final step in the Clintonization of Labour was the recognition that its fight for election must be carried on 365 days a year. For this it needed to assemble a communications war machine the likes of which didn't exist in Britain. An impressive machine did, however, exist in America, and so in 1992 Labour sent over a team to work with the Democrats to find out how political PR was done on the other side of the pond.

Perhaps some of the following messages may ring bells:

- It's time for change.
- Major's failed leadership.
- Tony Blair is the man with a plan to make things better.
- Tony Blair is young and dynamic, a new kind of Labour leader from a new generation.
- Tony Blair promises a new partnership with Britain – the Government will play its part, but in return, families and communities must play their parts too.

Yes, they were all central messages used by New Labour in 1997 – but they were literally the same messages used by Clinton in 1992. Only the names of the parties and leaders were changed before they were unleashed on the British electorate.

During the course of the 1997 campaign in Britain, there were increasingly frequent references to Blair's 'presidential style' of campaigning. Well, that should have been no surprise either. The simple fact is that the Labour delegation that visited America in 1992 produced a document on its return entitled 'The American Presidential Election 1992 – What Can Labour Learn?', which became a blueprint for the Labour campaign in Britain. Every aspect of Clinton's campaign, from the messages used to the techniques employed, was studied and, wherever appropriate, copied to produce the same final result for Labour.

The Labour blueprint makes fascinating reading, setting out, as it does, the key components of the Democrats' success – which was to become Labour's. The document starts off by outlining the dynamics of the Democrat 'War Room': 'The War Room was the nerve centre of the campaign presided over by Carville [the Democrats' communications supremo]. Each department kept at least one of their staff based at a desk there. War Room meetings were held at 7 a.m. and 7 p.m. each day . . . [they] gave Carville an opportunity to rant, berate, congratulate, entertain and motivate staff.'

Labour followed the plan precisely, abandoning the arrangement they'd had in 1992 when the party campaign was spread across four locations. Instead, Labour high command was set up at

Millbank Tower – soon nicknamed Mandelson Tower – close to Parliament and Conservative HQ in Smith Square. In keeping with the Democrat ideal, the war room was open-plan in format, for reasons Mandelson explained: 'The Labour Party machine was shut away in 1992, hidden behind partitions and fragmented. People were competing with one another as much as they were working together. Now we have open-plan offices and tight political management to ensure we act in a cohesive way.' Labour's command centre, which cost an estimated £2 million, occupied 25,000 square feet of floor space, with a staff of 200 or more arranged into different cadres – media monitoring, media handling, and a market research team designed to inform the rapid-rebuttal desk. In addition, Labour had used a donation from multi-millionaire Philip Jeffrey to purchase the Excalibur software for its computer system. Excalibur, an invention of the Pentagon dating from the 1970s, was an instant rebuttal/retrieval system capable of holding vast quantities of statements which could be accessed in a matter of seconds by inputting only a few key words. Every utterance by a Labour MP or campaigner was inputted into the machine – and any variations on what was being said could be picked up almost instantly. It was the ultimate form of message monitoring and made possible the reality of tight message control.

One Labour supporter drafted into the war room describes his impression:

> It was an extremely focused operation. What was amazing about the campaign was that it was all controlled by this incredibly tight machine. Every day there would be a meeting in the war room with Tony Blair, Alastair Campbell, Gordon Brown, Robin Cook, Peter Mandelson and Tim Allen, and they'd hammer out messages for the day. While overall themes had already been decided before the campaign, these were looked at and refined on a daily basis. For example, one day it was decided: 'Today's message is fish.' Soundbites on fish were debated and written up. Statistics to back up the fish message were produced within minutes. Then the soundbites and supporting arguments were faxed or e-mailed to

every member of the shadow Cabinet, key campaigners and candidates nationally. All of them were well aware they couldn't stray
'off message'. Whatever interviews they had lined up that day, they
had to include the fish soundbite.

The concept of 'on message' and 'off message' was, as it sounds,
yet another American import. The underlying rationale was, quite
simply, that if every party source quoted in the media repeated the
same messages consistently, then those messages would start to
stick in voters' minds. The technology to ensure that every
quotable source got the right messages to deliver was relatively
straightforward. A greater obstacle in the past had been persuading everyone in the party to toe the line. But, as one senior
Conservative comments: 'The biggest difference between Labour
and the Tories was that Labour had the enforced discipline of
eighteen years of opposition to focus their minds, and the Tories
had a complete lack of it.' Even those on the Labour left, who had
little truck with its modernizers, knew that they had to repeat that
day's party mantra faithfully if they didn't want to spend another
five years in political oblivion.

No one in Labour was above the 'on message' law. There was an
amusing incident one morning when Robin Cook, shadow foreign
secretary, was doorstepped by a journalist before he'd received his
morning soundbite instruction from Millbank Tower; as a result he
gave journalists the obliquest of answers while summoning his
assistant to ask for the required fax.

The notion of 'rapid response' or 'rapid rebuttal' was also a
prominent dimension of Labour's successful campaign. It was in
Labour's as in the Democrats' war room that the latest attacks on
Labour would appear, either phoned in from the field or picked up
from media monitoring. As commander-in-chief, Mandelson
would give an immediate spin and farm out requests for counter-
attacks, facts or figures. It was adherence to 'rapid response' which
enabled Labour to execute major policy U-turns within hours of
discovering a problem, quashing a troublesome story within a day.
Yes, the privatization and trade union U-turns amounted to

nothing less than the ruthless rejection of policies espoused by Labour for decades. But in the context of the war room, where the only objective is winning, it is easy to see how readily the U-turns could be executed in order to deny the opposition a target to shoot at. The Tories, by contrast, took weeks to counter Labour's '21 Tory Tax Rises' – by which time their response was way too late.

Labour's American blueprint also shows how the party was even able to deny the Tories their few moments of glory:

> The most impressive example of Rapid Response in action was during the Republican Convention. As Bush made his speech, the War Room was packed with researchers recording every claim Bush made, and providing a fact to counteract it. Before Bush had finished speaking, the Democrat team was ready to release a long list of Bush 'lies' followed by the fact to back up the accusation. [Campaign director] Stephanopoulos was ringing or paging the journalists before Bush sat down. Remarkably, as the cheering stopped, some of the TV commentators began by listing the false claims in the speech and outlining the counter-claims from Little Rock.

The efficiency of Labour's war room was such that during the campaign journalists increasingly came to depend on Labour as a source of information – which they always got, of course, with the Labour spin. If a journalist was in any doubt as to what today's story was, a call into Mandelson Tower would soon put that straight. Labour could be depended on to provide accurate facts and figures about who said what to whom. This was again a direct copy of the successful Democrats' practice, where 'a logical message, intellectual vision and efficiency of the campaign staff soon gave Little Rock a reputation for accuracy and reliability. Journalists came to rely on the Clinton campaign for their facts.'

Journalists on tour with Labour were subject to strict discipline. There were three buses used by the campaign – one for the Labour team and two others for journalists. Setting out from central London every morning, journalists were not told where the buses were heading until they were actually on their way – at most, they would have been told if they needed to pack an overnight bag. Halfway to their destination, press briefings were handed out by a team of female press officers, quickly dubbed 'spin nurses' by the hacks. On arrival at the site of Blair's visit, a press barricade was quickly installed, and inside it a three-tier platform enabling photographers to get good shots – 'the animal pen', as it quickly became known. When Blair arrived, he always made sure to walk around the outside of the pen so that there were plenty of photo-opportunities. At the end of a visit, journalists were given two minutes to get back to the bus. There was no time to get interviews with members of the public. If they weren't there, the bus would simply leave without them.

'In the beginning there was lots of resistance,' reports one of the Labour team, 'but by the end they'd given up arguing and relaxed into it. We made sure they were all fed and watered – in fact they went through 2,500 bars of chocolate on our buses. At the end of the day, if they didn't like it, they would have their press pass taken away.'

Labour's copying of Democrat techniques ranged over a long list of areas from negative campaigning, political advertising and rapid response to polling, political messages, endorsements and fund-raising. Ultimately, there can be no denying that Labour ran a brilliant communications campaign which had all the required components for success. They had undertaken mountains of research informing them on every dimension of voters' attitudes and, using this, decided on a clear campaign strategy. Although the overall strategy was fixed, it was flexible enough to enable messages to be modified as required. Messages were controlled at the centre, but disseminated through every individual – and Labour troops were well disciplined to stay 'on message'. A rapid-rebuttal facility worked to great effect, ensuring that Labour didn't open itself up to attack on any front for any sustained period. As *PR Week*'s editor Stephen Farish commented: 'This [election] the spin is also a lot more tightly managed. In this respect, Labour's machine is moving more slickly than its Tory counterpart. Almost too slickly in fact. With such sensitive antennae to every flicker of public, media and opinion poll reaction, it is able to trim policy and soundbite and rebut opponents' accusations as soon as they are made. But the speed of this shimmying for position can sometimes leave politicians – and the voter – in a tangle.'

the party of paradox

While Labour's PR war machine became ever more focused and slick, what of the Tories? In every sense, they were tearing themselves apart. Just as desperately as Labour wanted to win, the Conservatives seemed to have lost their own collective will, publicly haggling over Europe, unable to throw off the cash for questions allegations and dogged by further disclosures of sexual sleaze. And yet the bitter paradox for the Tories was that, in many ways, Britain had never had it so good.

Inflation had averaged just over 3 per cent during the whole of the last parliament – significantly lower than when Margaret Thatcher was Prime Minister. Mortgage rates were at their lowest in thirty years, unemployment had tumbled to below 1.8 million and basic rate income tax had just been reduced from 24p to 23p in the pound. Kenneth Clarke was presiding over a sustained economic recovery described by the IMF as 'enviable'. A Treasury adviser was reported as saying: 'The figures are just amazing, and they are even more stunning because there is no evidence at all that things are getting out of hand. In any other circumstances, a government sitting on this kind of economy would skate home in an election.'

While the Tories' economic figures glistened, however, their opinion poll showing was an altogether different matter: Labour held on to a consistent fifteen- to twenty-point lead throughout the election campaign. Why was the public not willing to give Major's government credit for its super-effective management of the economy? And why did the Tory PR machine fail so spectacularly to persuade voters to focus on the Conservatives' tremendous strengths in that area of government which underpins the success of all other activities?

Some point to Black Wednesday – the day in September 1992 when Britain pulled out of the ERM – as the day that the government's economic performance and its popularity became unhitched. For months the government had been talking up ERM and, in the final days, it had invested heavily to prop up Britain's participation. When it performed its hugely embarrassing U-turn and pulled out, its credibility in matters of economic management became mortally wounded. That, at least, is one point of view.

However, scrutiny of opinion polls since 1990 reveals a more gradual deterioration in support for the Conservatives after 1992 as, on the one hand, the Tories were hit by a leadership challenge and evidence of financial and sexual sleaze, and, on the other, Labour elected Tony Blair as its leader. Major's handling of persistent grumbling in the party about his weak leadership went some way towards proving he could be decisive when it mattered. Calling a snap leadership election in July 1995, he defeated challenger John Redwood by 218 votes to 89. There the matter was supposed to end. But evidence of government weakness persisted, most notably over the BSE scare when, after copious dithering, denials and reassurances, in March 1996 the government was forced to admit a possible link between 'mad cow disease' and the human counterpart, CJD – at which point all beef imports from Britain were banned by the EU, and British consumers deserted beef, the demand for which has never fully recovered.

Meantime, the cash for questions issue, covered from a lobbying perspective in Chapter 13, wrought havoc on the Tories as MP after MP was revealed to have accepted new business commissions from IGA, freebies from many of Britain's biggest businesses and cash from Mohamed Fayed. The impact of a constant succession of headlines charting every twist in the sleaze saga – while all the time Labour bayed for blood – was disastrous for the Tories. Even though, as a proportion of the parliamentary party, only a tiny minority of Conservative MPs were implicated, the self-inflicted negative PR campaign couldn't have been calculated to be more damaging.

Compounding the effects of the financial sleaze were newspaper stories alleging sexual sleaze against a number of Conservative MPs. In March 1992 Alan Amos MP was discovered 'acting indecently' with another man on Hampstead Heath. Then David Mellor's affair with Antonia de Sancha was unravelled – to be succeeded by even more damning evidence that he'd accepted a free holiday from the PLO-connected Mona Bauwens. Steve Norris was implicated in five extra-marital affairs, but managed to stay in office; then Stephen Milligan was found dead on his kitchen table, wearing women's underwear, after having inadvertently strangled himself. And so the roll call goes on ... Gary Waller, Lord Caithness, Alan Clark, Richard Spring, Michael Brown and Jerry Hayes. Again, while the vast majority of the Conservative MPs may have led decent and unremarkable lives, for the party which proclaimed family values and exhorted voters to get 'back to basics', the huge publicity given to the indiscretions of so many high-ranking party members created the most damaging impression: here was a party that had grown complacent in power, its ministers greedy and corrupt hypocrites who said one thing in public and behaved quite differently behind closed doors. The tabloids revelled in portraying the Tories as philanderers and sleaze-merchants; and with each new disclosure the once Tory-supporting press became increasingly disenchanted.

Given the twenty-point opinion poll gap he inherited, reflecting a divided party, perceptions of a weak government and the baggage of financial and sexual sleaze, Charles Lewington, the Tories' chief spin doctor, faced a near-impossible task when he was appointed to head up their election campaign at the beginning of 1996. Lewington, who had grown up in south London before graduating from Bath University, had started his career as a journalist writing for regional papers, including the *Bath Evening Chronicle* and *Western Daily Press*. His first break into the national press was a job on the *Daily Express*, where he covered Margaret Thatcher's removal from office and the Gulf War. It was as political editor of the *Sunday Express* that he covered the 1992 election, little expecting that, next time round, he would be the one in the Tory hot seat.

'It amuses me', says Lewington, 'when we hear about the Labour party machine and the way they created messages every day. We did exactly the same thing – only very few people used them. The Conservatives had been elected four times on the trot without using those sorts of techniques – it takes a losing side to examine its marketing strategy.'

Round the corner from Millbank Tower at Smith Square there were also regular war meetings, involving a high-powered team including John Major, his speech-writer George Bridges, director of campaigning Tony Garrett, party chairman Brian Mawhinney and his deputy Lord Cranborne, communications supremo Charles Lewington, research guru Danny Finkelstein, and those three Tory election campaign veterans – Sir Tim Bell, Lord Chadlington and Maurice Saatchi. From a logistical point of view, the Central Office war machine was in better shape in 1997 than it had been in 1992. Following the hundreds of thousands of pounds spent refurbishing the building prior to the 1992 elections, the Tories had gone on to build a state-of-the-art auditorium fully equipped for press conferences, and fitted with studio lights and wiring for radio and TV, in readiness for 1997.

Twice daily, the Tories went through the same process of scenario planning, message selection, and sending out selected soundbites by fax or e-mail to MPs and spokespeople. Just as Labour had its market researchers running focus groups and targeting wavering voters, so did the Tories, under the direction of Danny Finkelstein. The Tories had also made the substantial investment in Excalibur computer software – though, unlike Labour, they used it more to target the contradictions between what different Labour spokespeople were saying than to control their own people. And, as it happened, voters were more inclined to forgive Labour the most fundamental U-turns than they were to tolerate the constant Tory in-fighting.

The Conservative PR war machine had, in other words, the same component parts as Labour's and it operated in a similar way. But there were several critical points of difference. While Central Office was extremely effective in delivering and responding to news stories, it was in no position to manage overall Conservative communications and was, to the media, a less important news source than Number Ten and the various government departments. The communications effort was therefore fragmented across a number of different players who weren't necessarily following the same agenda. In part this was because they simply couldn't subsume government under the imperatives of the Tory party election campaign. As Dudley Fishburn says: 'If you have an issue coming up and you're in government, you're dealing with the reality and the PR is secondary to reality. In opposition, PR comes first.'

A classic example of the Central Office/Downing Street media split during the 1997 campaign occurred when Tory spin doctors were considering the slogan 'Labour's Sums Don't Add Up'. It was a catchy line and could be applied across a wide variety of issues – the hallmark of any good electioneering slogan. Trying out the concept, a backbench Conservative MP duly asked Major the planted question in the House: 'Is it not the case that Labour's sums don't add up?' To which John Major replied: 'Oh yes they do, and it shows that taxes will soar under a Labour government.' Thus ended the Tory's potential new slogan.

The Conservatives laboured under the additional difficulty that, after years in office, the majority of ministers identified first with their departments and only secondarily with the party. 'They think like civil servants' was the despairing refrain sometimes heard at Central Office. Years of ministerial red boxes and policy debates had rendered senior Conservative politicians unused to thinking in terms of what would be good for party PR – unlike the Labour shadow Cabinet, who would seize on every issue with the objective of extracting maximum PR mileage out of it.

But without any question, the biggest problem besetting the Conservatives' PR effort could be summed up in one word: discipline. No matter how effectively Charles Lewington and his team researched, planned and implemented their campaign, they depended on the combined Conservative chorus to repeat selected messages and stick to the party line – or, if they couldn't do that, then at least to keep their mouths shut. Many could not even bring themselves to do the latter. The leaked results of a TV broadcast analysis conducted by the Conservatives for the month of January 1997, just four months before polling day, showed that on fourteen nights out of thirty-one, the Tories were fighting themselves, disagreeing so vigorously over Europe in general and the single currency in particular that a furious Prime Minister finally blasted 'don't bind my hands' at a major press conference just weeks before polling day – a message targeted at his own backbenchers rather than the voting public.

The question of why there were Tory divisions over Europe was tedious enough at the time of the campaign and is even more tedious to recall now. But underlying the divisions was an issue as relevant now as it ever was – the difficulty of having to send out two potentially conflicting messages about the party's position. 'On the one hand,' says Charles Lewington, 'we were saying "No" to a federal Europe – and watch out, Labour will give it away. On the other, we were saying that scrapping the pound might actually be in our interests, so we must keep our options open. We were sending out two quite contradictory signals about our position.'

Many individual MPs understood the distinction but perversely ignored it – some commenting that there were no circumstances in which economic and monetary union should be contemplated. When various MPs broke ranks, others demanded that they repent or be sacked – and when Major didn't sack them, they criticized him for weak leadership. Senior sources in the party were despairing. Discipline had completely broken down within the parliamentary party and constituency associations themselves were loath to crack the whip. The most humiliating example of the latter phenomenon was the insistence of the Tatton Conservatives on retaining Neil Hamilton as their candidate. Even though the Downey Report had yet to be published, Hamilton had already done more than enough to embarrass the government and had become a constant – and constantly televised – reminder of the financial sleaze the Tories so desperately needed to put behind them. By keeping him on, the Tatton Conservative Association displayed the most crass insensitivity to the greater needs of the party. The net result was to provoke Martin Bell's independent 'anti-sleaze' candidature and create a highly effective sideshow which continued on prime-time television throughout the campaign, constantly reminding voters of Tory sleaze.

It didn't help the Conservative Party that, while its ill-disciplined foot soldiers were running amock, the one dimension to its campaign that could be controlled centrally – its advertising campaign – was bombing out. Few will forget the notorious 'devil's eyes' advertisement of Tony Blair, captioned 'New Labour, New Danger' and used as early as nine months before polling day. Despite Peter Mandelson's protests that the Conservatives had 'plunged to a new low in their propaganda', the advertisement did, in fact, score very well in voter recall polls. The trouble was, no one actually believed that Tony Blair was a devil. 'New Labour, New Danger', the central theme of the Tory advertising campaign, was fundamentally flawed.

Lewington's predecessor as Tory communications director, Hugh Colver, had focused considerable effort on trying to convince the electorate that New Labour was simply Old Labour reincarnated. Charles Lewington, who took over after Colver resigned, declaring his unwillingness to be a party propagandist, adopted a very different position on Labour: 'It would have been a mistake not to acknowledge that we had a new opponent. Our polls showed that by June 1996, 70 per cent of people believed Labour really had changed. So we had to rethink our lines. Danny [Finkelstein] and I had to attack what was new, not what was old.'

Enter Maurice Saatchi, veteran of four successive Tory election victories. He saw things in classic advertising terms. You have a product that's struggling to sell, so what do you do? Repackage it, call it 'new' and promote it heavily. But, as Saatchi pointed out, 'new' has two very different sets of meanings. The 'new' that Labour wanted to promote was fresh, exciting, different. But 'new' could also mean untested, risky, dangerous, inexperienced – and these were the definitions the Conservatives wanted to emphasize. The logic seemed simple and irresistible. 'New Labour, New Danger' not only worked as the basis for the advertising campaign, it made for a catchy mantra which could be repeated by party spokespeople in reference to just about any subject. Whether it was the economy, Europe, law and order, education or any number of other topics, the same phrase could be repeated. In PR terms, it had 'legs'.

And so the Conservative advertising campaign was unrolled on billboards the length and breadth of the nation. Having explained its vital function in the campaign, the communications chiefs of Central Office waited with bated breath for a chorus of ministers, MPs and other party spokespeople to repeat the chosen words. But instead of blowing up a wave of public unease about Labour to an ever-growing chorus from the party faithful, the poster campaign seemed to ruffle few public feathers, and with a handful of notable exceptions, including Brian Mawhinney and Michael Heseltine, the slogan rarely passed Tory lips – at least, not in the prime-time TV environment when it really mattered.

The reason why the 'New Labour, New Danger' campaign fell down so badly seems obvious with the wisdom of hindsight: thanks to the facility with which Labour had unceremoniously dumped its previously unpopular policies without any tangible replacements, there *were* no new dangers. By adopting a policy-free approach, Labour had left the Tories with nothing to attack except their lack of policies. Repeating the time-honoured anti-Labour criticisms – tax rises, job losses, selling out in Europe – was counter-productive because, as every voter knew, those were old Labour dangers. So where were the new ones? If there were any, they weren't big enough or frightening enough to persuade the electorate, particularly the so-called 'floating voters', that they should play safe by sticking to the Tories.

Sources inside Central Office reveal that some of the Tories' most powerful advertising attacks on Labour were vetoed by the party leadership on the basis that a party that has been in power for eighteen years should not embark on a vicious, negative advertising campaign against its opponents. Certainly, the committee approach to advertising adopted by the Conservatives was a recipe for failure: creative advertising ideas can rarely be compromised without losing their appeal. 'Britain Is Booming, Don't Let Labour Blow It' was the Tories' other main advertising platform, and it carried a powerful message; but by the time it appeared on hoardings nationwide, it was too late for the Tories.

It is fascinating to learn the perceptions of the Conservative campaign among those close to the Labour leadership. Roger Liddle, co-author with Peter Mandelson of *The Blair Revolution* and managing director of lobbying firm PRIMA, remarks: 'The Tories' strongest card was the economy. But they chose Europe. This was a gross misjudgement – Europe was counter-productive and emphasized Tory divisions.' But Charles Lewington points out that 'We didn't choose to make Europe an issue. Our campaign was designed to focus on the strength of the economy from start to finish. We had 4,000 sites with the "Britain Is Booming" poster, communicating a clear message. The problem for us was that we were constantly being sidetracked by Europe and by Tatton sleaze, which was an artificially created story.'

Taken together, Liddle's perception and the reality of the Tory PR effort as described by Lewington are emblematic of the entire Conservative campaign: so long as the Tories remained in a rabble of indiscipline, it was impossible for Central Office to control the campaign. It is a stark lesson on the powerlessness of political spin doctors when their parties are too absorbed with internal battles to fight the common enemy. And it stands in marked contrast to the Labour Party, whose impressive 'on-message' discipline was orchestrated by the shrewdest PR operator in the business.

In previous sections of this book, dealing with corporate and celebrity PR, we have asked: 'How strong is the influence of PR in this area?' and 'Is its influence growing?' As our review of the 1997 election campaign suggests, the influence of PR within any political party depends on the willingness of that party to focus on doing what it needs to do to win. When a party lacks focus, PR is impotent to save it. But when it is prepared to heed the campaign rallying call, a political spin doctor can become extremely powerful. Arguably, too powerful.

For when PR imperatives dictate party policy there is a much bigger issue at stake than simply how well a message is being communicated; the whole nature of what the party stands for is essentially challenged. The Clintonization of Labour in 1996–7 saw it dump any policy that was unpopular and deliver any message it thought voters wanted to hear. It had ideals, but few ideas; principles, but no policies. In effect, it became the ultimate invention of PR. One could argue that a party which has such effective means of measuring voter opinion, which is so ready to respond to the tide of public sentiment, is in fact democracy incarnate. The opposing view would be that expressed by Kenneth Clarke when, on learning of Labour's U-turn on privatization, he labelled them 'unprincipled wretches'.

The unfolding story of PR within politics continues to fascinate. Already, the Labour government has shown its will to continue its extremely tight message control with a direct carry-over of its pre-election 'war meetings', now held daily in Downing Street to decide on that day's message. Peter Mandelson chairs these and, as minister without portfolio, he essentially continues in place as the government's most powerful spin doctor. One of Labour's first and most controversial steps was to install additional 'special advisers' in Whitehall departments – political appointees on the public payroll, whose jobs are to ensure that the presentation of government policy follows the disciplined, co-ordinated strategy agreed at the Mandelson meetings. On arriving at the Palace of Westminster in the spring of 1997, newly elected Labour MPs were surprised to find themselves recipients of '2001 election packs', and within weeks Mandelson was talking up preparations for the next general election campaign.

Labour's attempts to continue draconian message management in office are by now so well known that they have become the stuff of comedy. Television comedian Rory Bremner included in a December 1997 show an 'interview' of a Labour MP who sat in a chair, bound and gagged, accompanied by a party whip who 'explained' the gurglings of his colleague. Six months after the election victory it was revealed that only hours after the final election results a Labour spin doctor had compiled a list of potential troublemakers within the parliamentary party. One MP was noted to be 'clinically insane'. As Ken Livingstone, Labour MP for Brent East, commented: 'It's new Labour, new Stasi. The control freak tendency is completely out of control.'

But by the end of 1997 it was evident that the media control strategy that had served Labour so well as a party in opposition was backfiring badly for the party in office. Labour spin doctors' attempts to suppress information made a disaster out of the embarrassments of the Formula 1 tobacco sponsorship issue and the Geoffrey Robinson affair. A million-pound political donation in the case of Formula 1, and complex, off-shore tax-avoidance measures in the case of Robinson, made the Government appear every bit as financially sleazy as the Conservatives in their darkest hour.

Some of Labour's pique that things were not going their way became evident when Labour's communications chief, David Hill, wrote a steaming letter to the BBC complaining about the aggressive interviewing style of John Humphrys when questioning the Social Security Secretary, Harriet Harman, on the fraught subject of cutting benefits to single mothers. Hill threatened to 'suspend co-operation', i.e., prevent ministers from giving interviews to *Today*, as a result of the 'John Humphrys problem'. From a media relations point of view, the idea of not co-operating with one of the most important media channels in the county is, of course, ludicrous, and no doubt there were even more red faces at Millbank Tower when Hill's letter was published in the national press the next day.

What Hill's letter revealed more than anything, however, was that the new Labour Government had still to learn that the 'total control' strategy that had served it well in opposition was simply not a realistic proposition in office. This fact will become increasingly evident in future months as the Government wrestles to introduce much-needed reforms to the welfare state; the disunity shown by the Conservatives over Europe will be as nothing compared to the explosion that will rock the Labour Party if its media minders continue trying to keep the lid on all its parliamentary members' public pronouncements. How the party faces up to a traumatic division, and how presidentially aloof Tony Blair manages to remain throughout, may well determine the battleground of the next general election.

Meanwhile, what about the Tories? Will we see the Clintonization of the Conservatives? Or will the pendulum swing back, and voters become disillusioned with the 'pragmatic' approach to politics in favour of parties with clearly defined policies? With a few notable exceptions, the Conservatives in opposition have been ineffective in making the most of the media relations opportunities presented by Labour blunders. And William Hague has yet to show any voter appeal. He had one potentially invaluable opportunity, on the announcement of Diana's death – but he blew it, his reaction making him seem wooden and out of touch compared to Blair's poignant and politically masterful response, in which he labelled Diana 'the people's princess', thus taking ownership of the extraordinary events that followed.

There is, perhaps, good reason for a party in opposition to keep quiet during the new Government's honeymoon period, and concentrate instead on regrouping its forces – especially after a defeat as resounding as that suffered by the Conservatives in May 1997. But the honeymoon is over. The Tories' challenge is now to reinvent themselves as a party fit to govern. Whatever their policies or even whether they have any – is not, in these Blairite times, really the point. The degree to which they capture the hearts and minds of voters will, rather, depend on their ability to present themselves through the media as a fresh, responsible, coherent alternative to the disunited and untrustworthy party in power. *Plus ça change...*

CONCLUSION
fingerprints in the dust

So, here we are in the midst of a PR explosion. Whether it's big business, show business, political business, or any other dimension of human endeavour you care to mention, you will rarely have to dust the news media for long before coming across the invisible fingerprints of PR. As for what's behind it all, few capture the spirit of the age better than the acerbic American writer and wit, Cynthia Heimel: 'During this vile and grimy decade,' she tells us, 'we have by necessity come to believe that unless you are a celebrity, you don't exist at all. If you are not a celebrity, you are inert filler. If the media aren't flashbulbing your every gesture, it didn't happen. Private epiphanies, soul-wrenching despairs, so what, who cares? You are a tree falling alone in the forest.'

Whether you regard that statement as a bleak commentary on the state of current social mores, or a testimony of monstrous egotism, or both, all the evidence points in the same direction. Individuals, companies and organizations of all kinds have become acutely aware of the need to raise their profile in the news media if they are to exist in the minds of their target audiences. Whether driven by the need to influence share prices, voting patterns or shopping habits, or, as Heimel suggests, by the hunger for more fundamental evidence of corporate or individual self-worth, the news media are clearly the place to be.

At the same time as PR-consciousness is dramatically rising, we are also caught up in an equally spectacular multiplication of available media channels. It took decades for the print media to be joined by radio as an alternative news channel, just years for TV to enter the frame thereafter; now as we approach the new millennium, it is rare that many months go by without the announcement of some new media breakthrough, be it in the domain of cable or satellite TV, digital broadcasting, the Internet or a mind-boggling variety of multi-media applications designed to bring increasing volumes and quality of information to more and more consumers, requiring less effort, at lower costs, and with better and better technology.

Of course, one needs to draw the distinction between what's possible and what's useful. World-shrinking technology is all very well, but language barriers remain; and difficulties experienced by media outlets like *The European* newspaper, which has failed to penetrate the UK market to any great extent, prove that it's more than enough for most of us to keep up with events in our own countries, without wishing to trouble ourselves with the details of what's happening within our national neighbours: 'Think global, act local' remains the mantra of the international spin doctor.

Divining the future is a risky business, as the quotes from Vance Packard's book in the introduction go to show; but we cannot avoid asking: where does PR go from here? Despite the caveats relating to the proliferation of new technology, a huge growth in available news media, coupled with the increasing demand for air time and column inches, means that the future of the public relations industry is assured. The need for professional communicators to advise their clients or employers can only continue to increase. Put another way: we've seen the future – and it spins!

Along with the increase in volume will come an ever-greater variety among those who choose to label themselves 'public relations consultants'. The Internet and related media present challenges quite different from those of press, radio and TV, and PR boutiques focusing on new media can expect to thrive and prosper. Similarly, increased specialization within discrete elements of the PR mix –

sponsorship, corporate hospitality, competitions and the like – is set to ensure that the man on the Clapham omnibus will be even more bewildered about what PR really is: it will mean even more different things to more different people.

And what of that vexing question about whether PR is a force for or against democracy? As I hope the introduction made clear, the vast majority of PR activity has always been at worst innocuous and at best a force for enlightenment. However, there are areas, most particularly in the realms of corporate and financial PR, where the stakes are sufficiently high to induce media manipulation of the most sinister variety. Some form of regulation will prove irresistible, calls for it led by those practitioners who do not wish to be tarred with the same brush as their less scrupulous colleagues. But with or without regulation, among the growing, faceless ranks of the invisible persuaders there will always exist that elite corps of master spin doctors whose influence over the media – and thereby over our perception of reality – is as powerful as it remains utterly unnoticed.

FURTHER READING

The PR Business, Quentin Bell (Kogan Page 1991)
PR luminary Quentin Bell provides a lively initiation into the concepts and techniques used by PR practitioners.

The Prying Game, Christopher Browne (Robson Books 1996)
The grubby underbelly of the media revealed by an investigative journalist, with emphasis on sensational excesses, chequebook journalism, price wars and other techniques of the on-going struggle for higher circulations.

The Good, the Bad and the Unacceptable, Raymond Snoddy (Faber & Faber, 1992)
Authoritative insight into the workings of the press by seasoned media editor.

Full Disclosure, Andrew Neil (Macmillan, 1996)
An engaging account of life at the heart of the Murdoch empire from the perspective of the Sunday Times's former editor.

The Hidden Persuaders, Vance Packard (Penguin, 1981)
The classic study of the American advertising industry by the man revered by sociology and media students since the late 1950s.

Media Virus!, Douglas Rushkoff (Ballantine Books, New York, 1996)
American academic describes how technology and the self-referential media are sucking us all into a media space with which we might not be entirely comfortable.

The Ultimate Spin Doctor, Mark Hollingsworth (Hodder & Stoughton, 1997)
Investigative PR journalist provides a biography of the glamorous Sir Tim Bell which makes for intriguing reading despite the non-co-operation of Britain's most famous PR man.

Risk Issues and Crisis Management, Michael Regester and Judy Larkin (Kogan Page, 1997)
Crisis management guru Michael Regester teams up with his business partner to explain what lessons can be learned from high-profile media disasters of the past, and how to deal with risk issues at an early stage.

Green Backlash, Andrew Rowell (Routledge, 1996)
Environmental consultant provides a compelling account of how environmental causes are being subverted by big business around the globe.

Toxic Sludge is Good for You, John Stauber and Sheldon Rampton (Common Courage Press, 1995)
Two investigative journalists provide a riveting account of how the American PR industry pulls the wool over consumers' eyes – especially when it comes to environmental issues.

Diana, Her New Life, Andrew Morton (Michael O'Mara Books, 1995)
Royal commentator provides more sensation findings about Diana's life at Kensington Palace as a sequel to Diana, Her True Story.

One Man's Word, Ian Greer (André Deutsch, 1997)
Former chairman of what used to be Britain's largest and most successful lobbying company describes how his involvement with Mohamed Fayed led to the collapse of his business.

Sleaze, David Leigh and Ed Vulliamy (Fourth Estate, 1997)
Investigative journalists from the Guardian and Observer teams provide a colourful though ultimately one-sided account of the cash for questions scandal.

Soundbites & Spindoctors, Nicholas Jones (Cassell, 1995)
Respected BBC journalist describes how politicians manipulate the media – and vice versa.

Campaigning, Des Wilson (Hawksmere, 1993)
Veteran campaigner provides an A to Z of public advocacy.

INDEX

319

index